THE COMPLETE BUDGERIGAR

**Other Fine Howell Books for
the Bird Owner's Library**

All About the Parrots, *Arthur Freud*
Bird Owner's Home Health and Care Handbook,
Gary A. Gallerstein, D.V.M.
Birds—Guide to a Mixed Collection, *Irene Christie*
Breeding Cage and Aviary Birds, *Matthew M. Vriends*
The Complete Cockatiel, *Matthew M. Vriends*
Popular Parrots, *Matthew M. Vriends*

The Complete Budgerigar

by

Dr. Matthew M. Vriends

First Edition — Second Printing

1988

HOWELL BOOK HOUSE INC.
230 Park Avenue
New York, N.Y. 10169

Library of Congress Cataloging in Publication Data

Vriends, Matthew M., 1937-
  The complete budgerigar.

  Bibliography: p. 271
  1. Budgerigars. I. Title.
SF473.B8V75   1985   636.6'864   85-8324
ISBN 0-87605-822-5

The color illustrations appearing in this book were furnished by Remi Ceuleers (Belgium). The color photography is by Horst Bielfeld (West Germany).

For my wife Lucy, and daughter Tanya
"Soyons fidèles à nos faiblesses"

The Budgerigar (*Melopsittacus undulatus*) is the sole member of its genus and species. It has been known to aviculture since the early 19th century and has enjoyed the favor of pet lovers and hobbyists since its introduction to England in 1840.

Wissink

Contents

SPECIAL COLOR FEATURE I—First there was the wild colored or
light green Budgie, personable pioneer from the Australian wilderness.
This was the bird that brought the species to the attention of the world.
You'll see him here as well as many of the breathtaking mutations
developed from him. Pages 65 through 72.

Part II —The Theoretical Side

SPECIAL COLOR FEATURE II—Lutinos, Albinos, Harlequins and more added to the fascinating kaleidoscope of Budgie color and pattern as more selective breeding was undertaken. Spectacular mutations such as the "spangle" and crested Budgies are also known and you can see them right in these pages. Pages 201 through 208.

NOTE: This book expresses small linear and liquid measurements in their English and metric forms. For the guidance of readers not yet completely familiar with the metric equivalents of standard English measurements, the following conversion information should prove helpful:

One meter (m) is equal to 1000 millimeters (mm). A centimeter (cm) contains 10 millimeters and is 1/100 of a meter. One inch is equal to about 2.5 cm or 25 mm. Four inches are about equal to 100 mm; 6 inches = 150 mm; 1 foot = 305 mm; 3 feet = 914 mm. The number of millimeters divided by 10 gives the number of centimeters.

To convert degrees Centigrade (or if you prefer Celsius) to degrees Fahrenheit, multiply degrees Centigrade by 1.8, and then add 32 ($°C × 1.8$) + 32 = $°F$. Some good base temperatures to remember are: $0°C = 32°F$; $10°C = 50°F$; $20°C = 68°F$; $30°C = 86°F$; $100°C = 212°F$.

Dr. Matthew M. Vriends

Lucy Vriends-Parent

About The Author

FOR MATTHEW M. VRIENDS, an abiding interest in the animal kingdom is a family affair that spans the generations.

A native of Eindhoven in the southern Netherlands, Dr. Vriends was strongly influenced by his father's example and involvement in the sciences. The elder Vriends was a celebrated writer and respected biology teacher. An uncle also loomed large in the Dutch scientific community, and the Natural History Museum at Asten, which annually welcomes over 200,000 visitors, is named in his honor.

Dr. Vriends vividly remembers the field trips he shared with both father and uncle and the "mini menagerie" maintained in the Vriends family home. The facilities for keeping and observing flora and fauna included a pair of large aviaries housing over 50 tropical bird species. A source of particular pride is the fact that many *first breeding results* came about in the Vriends family aviary.

Dr. Vriends' first published material appeared in magazines while he was still in high school. He wrote and illustrated his first bird book at age 17—an amazing achievement that got young Vriends officially named the youngest biologist with a published work to his credit. This book was also an unqualified publishing success with more than six reprints and sales in excess of 40,000 copies!

During his University career, Matthew Vriends continued to publish literary essays, poetry, short stories, a number of fine bird books and even a novel that helped finance his education.

After graduation he worked as a high school teacher, but eventually left education to devote more time to the serious study of ornithology. His work took him to some of the world's most exotic ports of call in Africa, South America, Indonesia and Australia. And it was in Australia—home of many of the world's most beautiful and unusual bird species—that Matthew Vriends became fascinated with native parrots, parakeets and grassfinches. He remained in Australia from 1964 through 1967 absorbed in study and continuous publication of ornithological subjects.

A number of the books published during these years came to the attention of Dr. Franz Sauer, world-famous ornithologist, who succeeded in persuading Dr. Vriends to come to the University of Florida at Gainesville. Here Vriends worked with world-renown biologists and to broaden his horizons, worked at the veterinary science and medical laboratories. One credit of which the author is particularly proud is having been allowed to work on the influenza virus research being conducted at that time.

Matthew Vriends earned his American doctorate in 1974 with a thesis on the Australian Masked Grassfinch (*Poephila personata*), and returned to Holland following the completion of his studies. Some time later he crossed the ocean again to take a position as the senior ornithology editor with a large American publishing firm until family concerns necessitated yet another return to the Netherlands in 1980. Vriends remained based in Holland until mid-1983 where he worked as an educator with additional interests in publishing and writing. He and his family now make their home on Long Island.

He remains an avid world-traveler, and, with his wife Lucy and daughter Tanya, regularly visits various countries of the world to observe the local wildlife close-up. His extensive travel also includes an annual journey to the United States where he is as well-known and respected by the American avicultural community as by the Dutch.

As his father did, Matthew Vriends maintains a large, varied collection of animals in his home for both enjoyment and study. Fish, hamsters, gerbils, mice, rats, guinea pigs, turtles, dogs and, of course, birds—some 80 different species—constitute the current Vriends family menagerie. Happily, it appears that Tanya Vriends will be the third generation biologist/aviculturist in the family as she joins her parents with great enthusiasm in their interest.

Dr. Vriends generously shares his expertise in various ways. A popular international judge, he frequently officiates at bird shows in many countries. At home he is the host of a weekly radio program and conducts seminars on birds and other animals in conjunction with trade show appearances during his American visits. His greatest fame has come through his writing and the helpful information he has imparted to pet owners and fanciers far and wide.

Currently Dr. Vriends is the author of some 80 books, in three languages, on birds, mammals, bees, turtles and fish, and over 1000 articles that have appeared in American and European magazines.

This remarkably prolific individual also enjoys music, painting, sketching, photography, tennis and gardening during rare moments of leisure when his attention is not directed to the natural sciences.

Dr. Matthew M. Vriends' accomplishments are like those of few others. By his varied activities in his chosen field, he has enlarged the body of knowledge for scientists, naturalists, diverse fancier groups and pet lovers around the world. His international celebrity is earned through more than thirty years of education, achievement and enthusiastic devotion to science and aviculture.

An opaline cobalt (right) with three normal green cage mates.   *van Herk*

Keeping birds means forgetting your wordly concerns by getting absorbed in a pleasant avocation.

Harkema

Preface

BOOKS CAN'T TEACH a person how to become a pet lover. Love of pets is inborn. As children, pet lovers keep beetles in glass jars, bring home tadpoles and lost dogs, or try in vain to raise a baby bird that has fallen out of the nest. Once they become adults, they can't forget the animals they loved in their childhood, and soon there is a canary singing in their living room, or there is an aquarium installed by the window, or an aviary appears in their yard.

A general love of animals can develop into a specific love of Budgerigars through some event or development. Some people are attracted to these birds because of their charm and brilliant coloration. Others hear from friends about Budgies' many other appealing traits.

A Budgie hobbyist usually starts by acquiring a few birds, and then—on the advice of a friend—the hobby expands by an attempt to raise a nest of young. Frequently this is true because the first attempt is so successful. Not that such initial successes come about through dumb luck. The beginning breeder has the enthusiasm to do the key things with the proper care.

When he sees the dividends, he wants to continue. Almost without being aware, he falls under the spell of these decorative, enjoyable birds. He gets drawn into the breeding game by seeing a color that's better. He gets into trading and buying. He adds cages or aviaries. Before he knows it, he is up to his ears in Budgerigars. The fancier who puts effort into his hobby automatically finds a genuine joy stemming from the simple pleasures of life.

Keeping birds means forgetting your worldly concerns by getting absorbed in a pleasant avocation. The bird lover develops a sense of beauty and an appreciation for the pleasures to be found right at home. In most cases, he is scarcely aware of this. He keeps birds because he enjoys it, and doesn't give the matter further thought. One thing is certain: He wouldn't give up his birds for all the money in the world.

This book is written for genuine Budgie lovers. It doesn't matter whether they keep two or 20 pairs—or any birds at all. If the reader is just dreaming about the happy day when he buys his first bird, he will enjoy and learn from this book.

In the first section, the practical side of the Budgerigar fancy is analyzed. The intent is to provide a complete overview. Experienced breeders may find considerable information that is already familiar to them. But they may still enjoy reading it, even if only to be able to say proudly that they have different and better approaches.

The second section covers the theoretical side of breeding. Bird breeders in general often encounter a conflict between theory and practice. One keeps discovering that many hobbyists are not familiar with the laws of heredity or how to apply them. Some people, but not many, can predict the outcome of their breeding procedures with fair certainty through their knowledge of heredity. Experience is a good teacher, but it seldom is sufficient to teach the breeder how to use genetics as a tool. And still, people look with suspicion upon the theoretician who talks about genes and chromosomes, lethal factors, heterozygotes, and similar unfamiliar genetic jargon.

It is hard to blame the practically-oriented breeders. Their interest in everything that concerns their birds is commendable. They don't always understand the language of the theoretician because the learned man doesn't take the trouble to use their way of speaking. An ordinary breeder doesn't want to have to do mental handsprings to understand breeding theory.

This book, therefore, has been written in language the average breeder can easily understand. Some technical language is hard to avoid, but a clear explanation, repeated if necessary, should convert technical language into everyday concepts.

The writer knows the details of heredity, but what isn't necessary for the breeding of Budgerigars will be omitted. Not to say that the details are uninteresting. Those who want to delve more deeply into the subject can find a number of good books on heredity, even if they aren't written only with Budgerigars in mind.

This book never could have been written without the help of experienced breeders who followed the development of the book with interest. Their experience and knowledge as well as their expert advice is woven into the text. To them and to the many other breeders, scientists and other interested persons, the writer directs heartfelt thanks for their practical and theoretical contributions.

MATTHEW M. VRIENDS

Acknowledgments

I AM VERY GRATEFUL to the many aviculturists, curators of zoological societies and Budgerigar enthusiasts who have so generously helped me with this book. Particular thanks is due those who have so kindly allowed me to use many of their notes on breeding and keeping Budgerigars.

My grateful thanks are also due to Mr. Max M. Heppner, M. Sc., of Takoma Park, Maryland for his friendship and his invaluable assistance in the preparation of this book.

Further I wish to thank Mr. R. Ceuleers and Mrs. P. Leijsen, of Herentals, Antwerp, Belgium; Mrs. Ruth Hanessian of "Animal Exchange", Rockville, Maryland; Mr. A. H. van Herk of Hapert, Holland, Mr. S. Harkema of Heiligerlee, Holland, and Mr. D. Wissink of Doetinchem, Holland. This book could not have been produced without the help of these and other wonderful people! Once again, I wish to thank my wife, Mrs. Lucy Vriends-Parent, for her constant encouragement and enthusiasm as well as her spontaneous cooperation in the writing of this book. Without her this work could never have been completed. All the opinions and conclusions expressed in the following pages are my own, however, and any errors must be my own responsibility.

M.M.V.

Part I

The Practical Side

One of a series of plates, published in 1837-38, which John Gould, author of *Birds of Australia and the Adjacent Islands,* used to illustrate the type of work which would go into the folio he planned. This plate shows two male Buderigars and a female, identified as *Nanodes undulatus.* (Vigors and Horsefeld)

1

Introducing the Budgerigar

JOHN GOULD, who, in 1840, brought the first Budgerigars to England, would look with great amazement upon the color variations that these birds have attained today. He would be no less amazed at these developments than the man, who—much earlier—brought the first Canaries from the Canary Islands—if he could only see what had happened to those birds.

There is considerable parallel in the development of captive breeding in these two types of pet birds. The wild, green Budgie has become an animal with many more color variations than one ever could have dared to dream.

While canary breeders attained new colors by crossbreeding, the Budgie's current color variations derive from separating existing colors. The color varieties of yellow, green, and blue are broad enough to safely assume that the end of color breeding has by far not yet been achieved. And in the future, Budgie breeders might expand into crossbreeding, like the Canary breeders who have incorporated red color into their birds through interbreeding with the Hooded Siskin (*Spinus cucullata*). Some day the whole color wheel will be represented and we may be able to admire red, orange, brown, and even black Budgies.

Breeding Canaries can be compared with breeding Budgies only to a certain point. At first blush one could say that the Budgie is at a disadvantage. The song of the Canary wins hands down over the cries or chirps of the Budgie. And the Canary has a considerably longer life expectancy.

On the other hand, the Budgie has an exotic charm that the Canary completely lacks. Color and form of the Budgie differ broadly from what Canaries or domestic birds can offer. Budgies are more decorative, and they have a special attractiveness that makes them most highly-favored in the bird world.

Budgies display an attractive appearance and pleasant behavior. They have a charming chatter, quick wingbeat, gleaming, natural color, freedom of movement, and an everlasting good humor. They have won friends in all countries of the world, and today exceed the Canary in global popularity.

The Budgie's popularity increased markedly following World War I and it found a further resurgence after World War II. This increased interest was undoubtedly due to the new color variations that have been developed and to the good prices that Budgies were bringing on the market.

In the United States, interest in Budgies is quite extensive. There are hundreds of big breeders and the number of small ones can't even be estimated.

Unfortunately many focus too heavily on quantity, so that quality suffers. It is almost certain, however, that breeders of quality will ultimately prevail. As interest in Budgies grows further, the demand for better birds will undoubtedly influence future quality.

Quality in this context means color quality. The health of the birds is above reproach among most breeders. I believe that eventually, domestic breeders will expand the number of shows especially for Budgies, particularly since standards are now firmly established.

Why Budgerigars?

In previously comparing Budgies with Canaries, breeding was not mentioned. Every Canary breeder knows that breeding Canaries takes considerable work and money, certainly in comparison with Budgies. Young Canaries require egg food, and later rearing food and canary seed. All of these are considerably more expensive than the Budgie's staple—millet seed. Breeding Budgies is simpler and cheaper because the young can manage without egg food or other specialty preparations.

Budgies win the heart of breeders because they breed easily and are satisfied with a little. They raise their young with care and adapt to almost any climate. They also become quite friendly with their caretakers in short order.

Anyone can start breeding Budgies with just a small investment. They also are in demand, and any surplus young find a ready market. One also can trade young for other breeding stock and thus build up a first-rate inventory. The breeder can recover his investment in his hobby quite easily and a modest or substantial gain at the end of the season is always possible.

Amateur Versus Professional

This brings us straight to the topic of whether one can hope to get rich by breeding birds. I have yet to meet the man or woman who has been successful in this respect. True, there are breeders who earn a respectable sum from their

Budgerigars and Cockatiels are usually readily compatible in an aviary situation.

birds each year. But I think the true returns from breeding are found in the joy that comes from working with Budgies. This joy derives from discovering new beauties and new developments every day. The true breeder spends every free moment with his birds. He observes them and studies them. He is proud of the results of his breeding and he bemoans the fact that he can't keep all of his birds but must sell some of the young in order not to overextend himself.

The true breeder is a hobbyist and he takes the outcome of his efforts as it falls. If things go well, then his breeding efforts are a source of joy to him. If things go poorly, then he is sad for his birds, and next season he tries with undiminished patience to correct his problems. He learns from his failures and enjoys his successes. Breeding to him is a game of chance that can make him a winner or a loser.

The person who only breeds birds to make money will experience more bad luck and poor results and his joy is limited. If things go well, he only sees dollar signs; if things go wrong, then he blames his birds. He sees his balance sheet turn red from sicknesses and deaths, from trade restrictions, and from a sudden decreased interest in the color varieties that he happens to have on hand. He doesn't see his birds as friends, but only as ciphers, like a jailer, who sees prisoners only as numbers without any personal interest. This type of person generally advertises a close-out sale after a few seasons in which he offers all his birds and equipment for a low price, just to be rid of the trouble. His birds will not have thrived because he skimped on one or more vital aspect(s) of management.

Therefore, I say, stay a hobbyist in the first place. If you love your birds, no money can measure up to the joy that you receive from them directly.

Taxonomy

Budgies belong to the parrot family, which has representatives in all continents except Europe and Antarctica. The family includes parrots, cockatoos, lories, macaws, parakeets and several other genera, but the line of demarcation between them is hard to set. One often speaks of parrots and parrot-like species, which includes all the members of the family—but even these terms clarify very little. Parakeets are supposed to be the smallest of the parrot-like species, and yet there are parakeets that are bigger than some parrots and lories.

This book is limited to a discussion of the Budgerigar, which some count among the parakeets. In Latin, it is called *Melopsittaccus undulatus;* in German, *Wellensittich*; in French, *Perruche Ondulee*. All these terms focus on the wavy line pattern of the feathering. The English speaking countries use the term Budgerigar, which is a corruption of the aboriginal Australian word *betcherrigah,* which is supposed to mean "good food."

Budgerigars have hooked bills like true parrots and parrot-like thick, fleshy tongues. They share with woodpeckers and cuckoos the so-called

In breeding Budgerigars there is always the chance that luck will go against the birdkeeper. The loyal enthusiast carries on in the face of setback as well as success. *Photo by author*

One of the smallest members of the psittacine family, the Budgerigar shares many common parrot traits and is universally loved as a cage bird. *Photo by author*

climbing or "reversed" foot, which has two toes pointing forward and two backwards.

Wild Budgerigars are light green. Their main food is grass seed. They live in the savannahs of Australia where grasslands are interspersed with forests. Here wild birds lead a migratory life because rivers and ponds tend to dry out in their homeland, and they are forced to move in order to find water.

Budgerigars use trees as places to hide and nest and the grasslands are the source of their meals. One can see them move by the hundreds from their nesting places to the grasslands, a veritable cloud of glimmering green birds moving on quickly beating wings and decoratively spread tails.

They nest in tree hollows. Wild birds seem to make these hollows in rotten or soft wood. They don't build much more in the way of nests.

Female Budgerigars lay five or six white eggs. In Nature, it seems that the number of eggs seldom exceeds six, in contrast with domesticated Budgies, which can lay up to ten. It is true, however, that a small number of Budgie experts in Australia claim that wild birds lay up to 12 eggs, but most say six.

Color variations don't seem to occur in the wild. The wild color of Budgerigars can be described as light green with just a small degree of variation from the norm. There are reports, however, of wild albino Budgies.

Today, Australian law prohibits catching and trading in wild Budgerigars, so that it is extremely difficult to acquire a wild pair to refresh existing captive bloodlines.

A Hundred-Year History

The first Budgerigars to reach Europe arrived in England about 1840, although the birds apparently were known earlier. They are supposed to have reached the continent about 10 years later—exact details are not available. The Dutch aviculturist Nuyens, whose book, *The World of Birds* appeared in 1886, states that his brother had brought a pair of Budgies from Australia more than 30 years earlier. That must have been about 1850.

People quickly discovered that Budgies were easy to breed. The first yellow Budgies were bred in Belgium about 1875. Six years later, the first sky blue Budgies made their debut—a development credited to a Dutchman. The first line of albinos that could be maintained by breeders was the result of a chance mating of a pair of sky blue Budgies in 1920. In the succeeding years, the number of color variations gradually expanded, resulting in cobalts, mauves, and dark and olive-green birds.

The first color variants brought a handsome windfall for British breeders. About 1845, an ordinary green Budgie brought fifty pounds sterling, a sum that represented a year's wages for a working man. Yellow, blue, and white Budgies brought double that amount shortly after they were developed.

Between 1925 and 1928, the Japanese suddenly showed a tremendous interest in Budgies. Prices reached a fabulous high; sky blue Budgies brought a

In their native Australian habitat, Budgerigars are commonly found in grassland and scrub regions such as those shown here.

Photos by author

thousand dollars or more. Cobalts, mauves, and albinos brought up to a thousand pounds sterling per couple. The Japanese market dried up as quickly as it came. Many breeders were left holding the bag; they had a large inventory that suddenly was worth much less.

Today, the market is quite stable. Prices rise in the early spring, at breeding time. Good, even excellent prices can be gotten for rarer color variants.

Colony breeding apparently has resulted in a mediocre level of quality, and exceptional birds really stand out. At the same time, colony breeding has brought down the price of ordinary birds considerably, thereby creating a situation that only a reduced and highly selective type of breeding can hope to correct.

The wide variety of color mutations has made the Budgie one of the most interesting and beautiful of the cultivated bird species.   *Harkema*

28

2

Starting in the Breeding Hobby

ONCE A PERSON decides to become a breeder and acquire Budgerigars, he immediately faces the question of which color to select. Many people let themselves be tempted to take a color variation that doesn't appeal to them personally but is currently quite popular and thus brings a good price. In other words, they let the profit motive decide. A decision based solely on potential financial gain would have little likelihood to benefit their hobby.

Which Birds to Buy

A new hobbyist is better served to follow his own personal taste. He selects the color that appeals to him most and tries to achieve something satisfying. Truly beautiful birds, good in conformation and good in coloration, are hard to come by. But when the hobbyist concentrates on breeding only birds of quality, he sets an excellent example for the new and prospective breeders who follow him.

Many new hobbyists don't have a good idea of what is available on the market. People in this position would do well to become informed before acquiring birds. Do not jump headlong into this hobby without first testing the water.

A beginner may only know a few color variants—green, blue, or albino, for example. Only later, he or she may discover that other variants would have been more to his or her liking. But this discovery comes too late if the birds already have been bought. That's why I counsel not to decide too quickly.

Each of the basic three Budgie colors have three nuances: light, medium, and dark. This leads to variants that are light green (normal), dark green, and olive green; light yellow, dark yellow, and olive yellow; and light blue, cobalt, and mauve.

Beyond these variants, there are other possibilities. I particularly like the violet Budgie, a variety of cobalt that has attained an extra color factor for violet.

When the black wavy lines on the wings are lighter, one speaks of graywings. When the lines are brown, we call them cinnamon, dark brown, or bronze.

Breeders also have been able to make the wavy lines disappear entirely in some Budgies. This creates green clearflights and blue whiteflights.

Budgies without color are albinos—white with red eyes. Lutinos are yellow albinos. They are brilliant yellow and also have red eyes. The red eyes can be found in other Budgies as well; those are called fallows. A special wing design distinguishes opalines and rainbows (the opaline form of the yellow-faced clearwings).

One also distinguishes double-colored Budgies. Their upper breast has a different color than their lower breast. And there are pieds (or spotted) types—known as Danish, Dutch, and Australian pieds. Finally, breeders have succeeded in breeding Budgies with a crown; and there are also "curled" Budgies, so called because the feathers are loose and curled on the breast and back—and the small wing feathers as well.

To make things still more complicated, there also are lutinos with black eyes, as well as grays and clearbodies. And somewhere in the world at this very moment, the first black or red Budgie may be hatching!

This list is not of great use to the beginner who can't picture the birds being described. But he can look at the stock of other hobbyists and visit dealers, zoos, and shows to learn which color variation appeals to him most and which birds he will be able to afford. Cost is not to be overlooked!

Considerations When Purchasing

Start with first-rate stock. That is the first and most important rule in breeding Budgies. A person who expects pleasure and favorable results from his hobby has to decide that only the very best is good enough.

Buy thoroughly healthy birds. They should be without major flaws in color and form, lively-looking, and of proper weight. Major flaws include: faulty conformation, hollow or bowed back, wings that are too long and seriously crossed, a head that is too small or poorly formed—with a low back and a high forehead—a deformed beak, or shrunken ceres or wattles.

Feathering should be smooth and shiny. A bird with dull feathers definitely is not in good health.

Coloration must match the descriptions given in the COLOR BREEDING section of this book. Distrust birds that can be caught easily—those generally are not the best of the lot. A healthy Budgie feels heavy to the touch, much heavier than other birds of the same size. When considering a purchase, ask to hold the birds in your hand. Don't accept birds that feel light in comparison with other Budgies.

Never forget the importance of quality, especially when you continue breeding. Most breeders are smart enough to keep the best stock for themselves, but some breeders do keep bad birds for breeding because they try to expand too fast. The results are uniformly bad. Sooner or later they will become convinced that they would have been wiser never to have worked with bad foundation stock; experience is an expensive and embarrassing teacher!

How Many Pairs.

The reader who took in the warnings I just gave won't be surprised when I say, "Better to start with one good pair than with several bad ones."

The beginner—especially the one with big plans—doesn't have an easy time with this advice. He wants to start in with several pairs to fill up his aviary quickly, and he finds himself drawn to cheap stock. But still I repeat, better to start small and good. The numbers will develop naturally, given time.

Furthermore, beginners do themselves a favor not to take too much hay on their fork. A few pairs can be watched from A to Z, and they need to be. The results of early breeding can be controlled easily, and the beginner will acquire a treasure of experience that will stand him in good stead in the ensuing years. Practical experience outweighs the value of a book full of theoretical knowledge.

When you want to buy birds, look for a trustworthy breeder or dealer. A dealer ought to have been breeder himself at some point in his career, so that he will know Budgies by experience. Trust the experienced breeder because he has an interest in providing you good stock. This way you will come back for more. He will give you good advice and possibly he will be able to tell you the color variations from which the birds you are buying have been developed. It is best not to start breeding with birds of complex color heritage; the results for you might be a mishmash. Start with a single color and, if possible, with homozygous stock. Later you can breed with additional colors if you want to.

Be sure to get an agreement that you can exchange the birds you purchased if they won't breed. It is possible to acquire two birds that stubbornly refuse to breed. Usually a newly-formed couple starts within ten days. If after three weeks or so you still don't see the birds getting together, try to exchange one or both of them.

Sexing Budgerigars

When you buy a pair of birds, you naturally want them to be of opposite sexes. Budgies are not distinguishable by sex on the basis of color.

Experienced breeders can tell the sexes apart by the carriage and build, but the novice is better off depending on a clearly distinguishable feature. Fortunately, Budgies have such a feature—the ceres, or wattles, the raised area above the beak in which the nose openings can be found. In males, they are blue; in females, brown.

The nares (nostrils) ought to be well-formed. If they are small and shrunken, then the bird probably is old. Note that old females may have nares that develop some color. So buy birds with properly colored and properly formed nares.

Cages in General

Budgies can adapt to any type of cage. They will breed in a small cage or in a roomy aviary, inside or outdoors. This is yet another advantage to delight any breeder.

Naturally, a proper cage will encourage better breeding results and superior birds. It is wise to select, furnish, and locate a cage properly.

A cage may not be moist or damp, or be put in a moist or damp place. It should be protected from drafts. Outdoors, don't place it on the north side. Don't set it up like a hothouse—with too much glass.

Select a quiet location. Birds can accustom themselves to noise, and a Budgie that is used to noise won't be easily upset. However, breeding results are better if you don't set up the cage in the midst of heavy household traffic.

Use a cage with some depth to it. Birds feel less cramped when people don't face them nose to beak. Cages should have a greater length than height. Some people with limited space think they can make up in height what they don't furnish in floor space. They are wrong. The natural flight pattern of a bird is horizontal—not vertical. Cages should not be too low, of course, but a long cage or aviary always is preferable over a tall model.

Breeding Cages

There is only one way to be sure about the parentage of birds—that is to breed a single pair in a single cage. This has been and remains the best method to achieve good results and control quality.

By contrast, colony breeding sets up a situation where any male can be the father of any young. The breeder can't be sure about the parentage of a single chick in the colony. This assurance is essential if the breeder wants to use genetics in a purposeful way to achieve a certain goal.

A proper breeding cage for a pair of Budgies is 28 inches (70 centimeters) long, 24 inches (60 centimeters) tall and 20 inches (50 centimeters) deep. These dimensions are not absolute. Bigger is better, smaller is possible. After all, there are breeders who breed Budgies in a Canary cage. It's like smoking a pipe. You can make one out of an acorn cup with a straw attached—but a real pipe gives a better smoke!

A handsome group of Budgies enjoying an outdoor flight. *Photo by author*

Mutual feeding is a common behavior pattern among mated pairs of Budgies.   *Photo by author*

33

Attach nest boxes to the outside of the cage. That will preserve the maximum amount of flight space and will permit easy inspection. If you are placing several breeding cages on or next to each other so that there is a common wall between two cages, attach the nest boxes at the rear. That saves room and materials.

The accompanying illustration shows a breeding cage with nest boxes in the side wall. The front is completely removable for easy cleaning. The inner side is whitewashed with natural chalk. Some breeders mix chalk powder with DDT powder, but I caution against this practice in the strongest terms. DDT is poisonous to birds and they could easily take some of it in when they pick at the chalk.

It's best to have an extra breeding cage in reserve. Then, when a cage needs a thorough cleaning, you can put the birds in the extra cage.

It is possible to build the walls of a breeding cage out of plywood or hardboard on a frame of slats. The bottom could be a tray, made of zinc or hardboard. Cover the bottom with a layer of sharp river sand and replace the sand regularly.

If you are breeding albinos, put a bit of bluing in the white chalk on the walls. The birds show up more attractively against the light blue background.

The pictured cage could be used for two pairs if the number of nest boxes is increased.

The front of the breeding cage is covered with wire mesh. One also could use bars. Cage fronts are available commercially, ready to install. Sizes differ. For Budgie cages, I recommend dimensions of 16 to 20 × 24 to 28 inches (40 to 50 × 60 to 70 cm).

Colony Cages

The disadvantages of breeding in colony cages have already been amply covered. It is simply impossible to maintain control over the heritage of the birds. Yet, there are also several distinct advantages in using a colony breeding system for Budgies.

Budgies love company. There is ample evidence that they form pairs sooner and breed more promptly in a colony cage.

If you want to breed several pairs of Budgies in a large colony cage, I suggest you don't use a mishmash of color. If you put green, blue, yellow and white birds in a single cage, you won't know which side is up at the end of the breeding season. If you continue breeding with this jumble of colors, anything may result—only no pretty birds.

So, if you use a colony system, use color variants that will give you decent results. You can put all blue birds—sky blue, cobalt and mauve—in a single cage. You also can combine yellow and green birds or albino and lutino birds. Use the tables in the back part of this book to determine for yourself which birds can be put together. You will have some control over the results and will not be faced with unpleasant surprises.

34

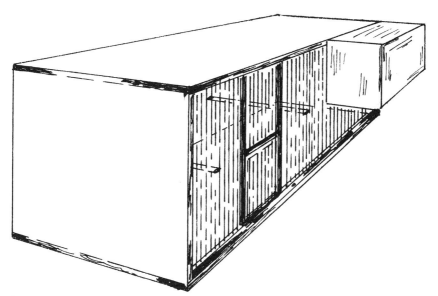

This serviceable breeding cage measures 22 inches long, 10 inches high and 12 inches deep.

Drawing by author

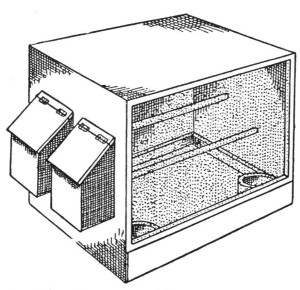

Many different sizes and types of box cages are available, but for breeding purposes, the model shown here is the prime choice of many Budgie fanciers.

Drawing by author

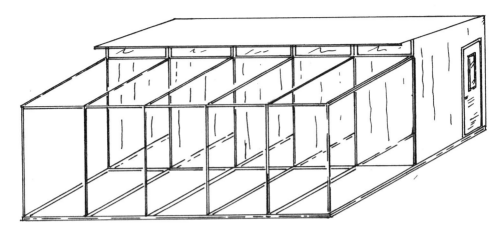

This aviary enables the Budgie breeder to provide spacious quarters for his birds and still safeguard the purity of the various color lines being developed. *Drawing by author*

The design of this aviary allows the Budgie fan to walk right into the enclosure. Any aviary of this type should include a safety door to preclude accidental escapes. *Drawing by author*

Colony breeding cages also offer the advantage of breeding with more females than males. We recommend two males with four females. We even saw a case where two males had been put with six females, and the breeder assured me that he never had trouble with unfertilized eggs.

The accompanying illustration shows an outdoor aviary with two compartments. Because each compartment serves as a flight cage, it must be of a decent size. A person should be able to stand up straight in the front of it. A good dimension would be a front of six feet (180 cm), a back of four to five feet (120 to 150 cm), and a width and depth of five feet (150 cm).

The back, roof, and half of the sides should be made of wood. The roof should be covered with asphalt. I don't recommend a zinc roof because it gets too hot in the summer. And in the winter it provides poor protection against the cold. Corrugated asbestos is better than zinc, but I still prefer wood.

You should be able to close off the front with glass windows in case of cold or inclement weather.

If you are placing several breeding cages in a row, the walls between them can be made of hardboard. Connect them with wire mesh doors.

Equip the main entrance with double doors, so that you can always have one closed to the outside. Without them, you can rest assured that sooner or later a bird will escape. Generally it will be one of your best!

You can achieve the same result by installing a so-called starling net over the entrance. To enter, you crawl under the net before opening the door.

The Aviary

If you don't specialize in Budgies, you can easily add them to a group aviary. Budgies generally are quite tolerant of other birds. If you furnish enough nesting sites, squabbles over them are rare.

Aviaries are actually quite suited for young Budgies. They find abundant light and air. They can move about freely and can develop into healthy adults.

Birds are children of the sun. If you want to keep them in good condition, they must have adequate amounts of sunlight.

A good aviary should have a section that can be closed off, so that birds can find shelter at night and protection from cold or inclement weather. Then there should be a roomy outside cage in which birds can fly about to their hearts' content.

Accustom your birds to spending the night in the night shelter, so that they are never surprised by sudden bad weather.

A night shelter should have a wooden or cement floor. The outside aviary can have a sand-covered floor that is turned over now and then. Be sure to have good drainage, either by installing drainage pipes or by elevating the aviary bottom. It doesn't do for the bottom to remain wet or like a mud waddle after every rainstorm.

An aviary consisting of three parts: a night shelter, a half-open section (with the top covered by a sheet of corrugated fiberglass or similar material) and an open area, called the "flight."

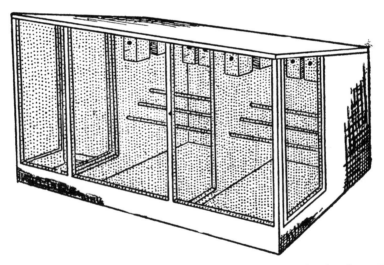

A two-part aviary that is ideal for breeding Budgies or other small psittacines. Note the safety vestibule at the left.

Drawing by author

You may want to put plants in the aviary for greater eye appeal. But remember that Budgies don't have much appreciation for natural beauty. You will soon discover that there are practically no plants on earth that Budgies will leave alone. Put a solid branch in the middle to give them full opportunity for acrobatic demonstrations.

Budgies weather the usual cold winters very well, provided they are used to the cold and you take care to protect them against rain and wind. You can install a glass wall in the winter. In spring, summer, and fall they only need protection against the rain.

If you close off the aviary in winter, be sure to provide for enough fresh air—for example, by installing special ventilation openings. But avoid drafts. More birds die from bad air and drafts than from cold air.

To put together good cages and aviaries takes experience. Before setting up your first one, you go visit an experienced breeder for some helpful advice.

Pay attention to detail. One handy thing is to have a small door through which you can put seed and drinking dishes in the cages without having to open the main door. Install a windbreak on the windy side, such as a privet hedge. Never put cages or aviaries on the north side. Install some protection against too-bright sunshine. Birds should have shade available if they want it.

Cages for Pet Budgies

If desired, Budgies can be housed quite effectively in ordinary living-room bird cages. Budgies are pleasant to have in your own living space, provided you don't object to their screams. I myself find their vocalization quite tolerable. They chatter amicably and are quite loving to one another if kept in pairs. Get the biggest possible cage to give the birds the maximum freedom of movement.

Put a fresh twig from a bush or tree into the cage for the birds to nibble on. That will keep the birds occupied and less inclined to pull out each other's feathers from sheer boredom. Don't use a painted cage, because birds will nibble on the cage no matter what you do, and taking in paint will kill them eventually.

You can use an open cage, if you like—one without bars. This will be discussed in further detail in a later chapter about tame Budgies.

Breeders who know you want a bird for a companion only may not sell you their best stock. The bird will be healthy, of course, but not breeding quality. If you consider breeding at all in the future, discuss your goals clearly, both for your protection and the seller's.

Perches

For any cage, use perches made of hardwood, preferably beech. Soft wood can't withstand the gnawing of the birds for any length of time.

Get perches—round, but flattened slightly on top—having a diameter of about a half inch (13 millimeters). They should not be too slick; otherwise birds would have to expend too much effort to stay put, especially while sleeping.

Install perches so that birds can't foul each other. Protect feed and water dishes from droppings deposited by perching birds and install perches far enough from the wall to keep birds from damaging their tails. And of course don't put perches so high that Budgies would have to sit with their heads bent to clear the ceiling.

Swings don't belong in a breeding cage although they are quite acceptable for companion birds. Birds can't mate well on a movable perch, and swings are a known cause of infertile eggs.

Don't install too many perches. They decrease the flight space unnecessarily. And if you need to catch birds, a forest of perches makes the job much harder.

I recommend removable perches. They are easier to clean, and you can take them out before you try to catch birds—making the job simpler and quicker. The best arrangement is a rack, especially for a large breeding cage. Birds like racks because they love to congregate. And you will like them because when looking over your birds you will find a large part of the family on the rack at most times, simplifying the task of determining how things are going for the birds.

Budgies like to climb. Giving them a "ladder" keeps them from climbing up the wire mesh walls, which is bad for their tail feathers. After all, your pretty birds should maintain long, straight, unsplit tails!

In a large breeding cage or aviary, install one or more solid branches from hardwood trees. In an inside aviary, renew the branches regularly because they soon get quite unattractive from accumulated droppings. This problem is avoided in outside aviaries because rain helps keep the branches clean.

Catching Birds

Birds in an aviary must be caught quickly, but with care. Rough or slow work causes accidents. Preferably, use a net that is roomy and light. Nets measuring 12 inches (30 cm) in diameter and 16 to 20 inches (40 to 50 cm) deep are best. You can make them yourself out of curtain material, or you can use so-called butterfly nets. Don't hold the stick too far down, so you will be better able to see what you are doing.

Before starting to catch birds, remove the perches. Make your first move deliberately—at a moment that you feel practically certain to catch a bird. Catch birds in flight rather than against the wire mesh.

Don't keep at the job a long time. If you have a large number of birds to catch, it is better to catch them in two or three batches, with intervals to avoid tiring the birds. It is not uncommon for a breeder to find one or more dead birds in the aviary the day after he went to catch some of them. The effort and the fear involved killed them.

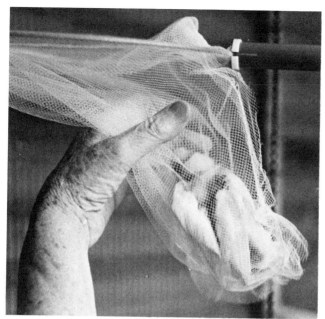

A catching net is an important piece of equipment in any aviary. The mesh should be fine and the wand relatively short.

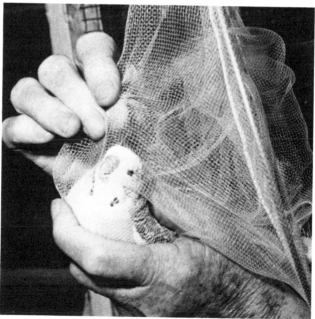

Exercise appropriate caution when catching birds. Rough handling or prolonged capture attempts can sometimes become dangerous, even life-threatening situations.

They Need Fresh Air

Fresh air is as essential for birds as a bit of sunshine. Outdoor aviaries present no fresh air problems, of course—at least not in summer. Indoors, keep doors and windows open in the summer. And even at night and in the winter, ventilate properly, so that the air in the cage stays fresh.

The breeder using an outside aviary has the most serious problem, especially if he is unduly afraid of the cold and seals off the aviary hermetically. As the birds breathe and as the gases from their droppings accumulate, the air quality starts to deteriorate. The objective of the breeder is not to cut off outside air. That's not the way to keep birds warm because even a large number of birds can't elevate the temperature in a roomy aviary with their own body heat.

Believe me, a Budgie that is used to being outside can stand quite a bit of cold. Just protect it from biting winds, wet weather, and drafts. More birds die from stale air than from cold air.

Free Flight for Budgies

Some English breeders successfully let their Budgies fly free in the summer months. They say that they get excellent breeding results with this method. Not too many people want to try this, but the idea definitely merits discussion.

Obviously, this method is not recommended for breeders living in the middle of the city. Your locality should be free of owls, cats and other potential predators.

Free flight, however, remains a possibility for some remote areas. To begin with, keep birds in an outdoor aviary to accustom them to their surroundings—to their seed and water dishes and to their nest boxes hung up on trees inside the aviary. Have nest openings as small as possible to keep out starlings and other intruders.

Don't release the birds until the end of April. As soon as young birds have learned to fly, catch them the first time they visit the feed dishes and place them in a closed aviary. Otherwise the young birds will tend to roam quite far. And at the end of August, catch all the males to keep them from continuing to breed. Let the females raise the last brood. Then catch them also, once you are sure that no young are left in the nest boxes.

Nest Boxes

Budgies are faithful mates. I don't say "monogamous" because if you give a male access to a group of females, he will breed with all of them. But in a group setting, a male will help only his first choice of mate with the raising of her young; the other females are left to do the job alone.

For this reason, avoid breeding a group of female Budgies to a single

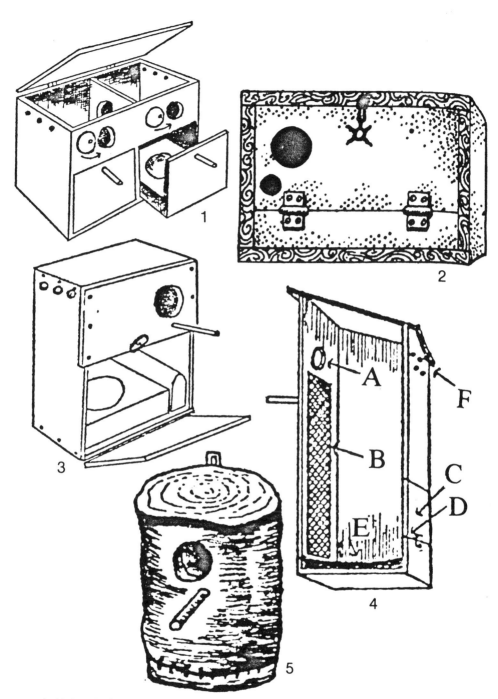

1. A double breeding box of this design is sometimes used for breeding Budgies. 2. A front opening nest-box is useful located high in the aviary where a top opening is either not required or practical. 3. A popular, well-designed box providing easy access for the birds and safety for parents and young. 4. Nest-box cross section: A. Entrance hole. B. Climbing mesh. C. Inspection door. D. Lock. E. Concave base. F. Additional ventilation holes. 5. A Nest-box designed to be closer to natural conditions.

male, even though it is possible for breeders who have more females than males. The extra females who raise their young unassisted have a tough job that makes heavy demands on their strength. To counteract this disadvantage, group breeding should be started early, allowing for rest periods between broods to let the females regain their strength before rebreeding them.

Usually, two nest boxes per pair are required. Experience has shown that Budgies like a choice of nest boxes; it often happens that they have a definite dislike for a certain nest box, for some unfathomable reason. It is possible to help birds over their dislike of a nest box by moving it to another location in the cage or hanging it so that the light does not shine into the nest opening.

In colony cages, you don't have to furnish exactly double as many boxes as you have pairs. Ten pairs of birds can make do with 15 boxes, for example. That offers the birds sufficient selection and they will be able to find an unoccupied dwelling once the young of a brood have been raised and the female is looking for a new place to lay eggs.

You can build your own nest boxes with a little ingenuity and a minimum of expense. Use plywood or boards that are not too thick for the walls and top—but use thick wood for the bottom. Thick nest bottoms (at least one inch [2½ cm]) help keep out the cold—especially important if you plan to start breeding early in the season.

Hollow out a nesting place in the bottom measuring 4-5 inches (12 cm) in diameter, sloping inward so that eggs roll toward the center.

The inside dimensions of the box should be 6 × 6 × 10 inches (15 × 15 × 25 cm). The entrance should be 1½ inches (4 cm) in diameter and should be placed about 2 inches (5 cm) below the top edge. On one side, drill several ventilation holes into one of the corners. Don't make the holes too small, otherwise parasites will find shelter in them.

The top can be connected with hinges. It can be kept loose if you put a few slats under it to hold it in the opening. Some breeders have gone to sloping roofs to keep birds from sitting on them and fouling them with their droppings. For such boxes, put the entrance on the side along the highest part.

Consider putting the entrance in one of the corners of the front or the sides. The major advantage is that you can foster peace in the aviary by alternating the flight openings; that means, putting them in the front in one box, in the left side wall in the next one, and on the right side on the next. That way the birds don't bother each other as much. Some people say that an entry in one of the corners keeps birds from falling into the box, landing on the nest, and breaking the eggs. This turn of events doesn't happen all that often in reality, because the birds will take care not to break their eggs if they fall. The risk of breaking eggs is no greater with a fall from a side entry than a front entry.

A better way of avoiding breakage is to install a riser—perhaps 5 inches wide and 2 inches high (7 cm wide and 5 cm high). The entry should be just above the riser. As a Budgie enters the nest box, it first lands on the riser. It

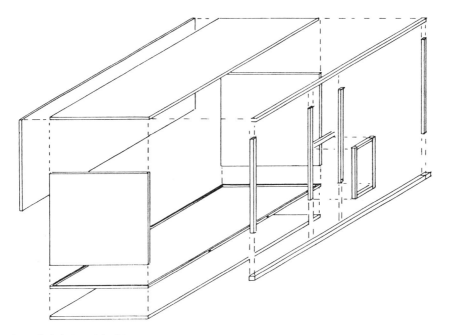

An exploded view of the framework of a well-made breeding cage. Note especially the double floor.

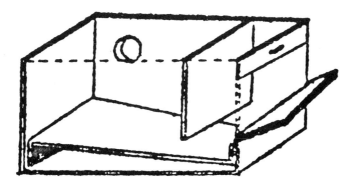

The trap nest-box for smaller species is especially suitable for any Budgies that peck at their eggs. Freshly-laid eggs automatically roll down the inclined floor to a partition covered with sawdust or sand to avoid breakage. They are then removed through a small door and placed in the nests of more trustworthy hens.

then only has to make a short jump before coming to rest on the eggs or the young.

Some people have devised a nest box with a drawer to facilitate checking on eggs and young. This setup allows you to pull the whole nest out of the box—obviously an easy way to look over what is there.

Another variation is the so-called double nest box. It helps solve the problem of cases where Budgies start laying while their previous brood has not yet left the nest. Half- or nearly full-grown nestlings don't make good companions for fragile eggs or hatchlings.

Double boxes have a dividing wall with an opening, just like the entrances in the front of both sections. The openings can be closed with a bit of tin, to close off the unused apartment once a Budgie has selected one of them for its own. When the young are nearly grown, you can open the divider, allowing the female to start a new brood in the second apartment. As soon as the young in the first nest have flown out, you can close the divider again—as well as the entrance to the first apartment—and open the entrance to the second. Budgies quickly adapt to this arrangement.

Breeding logs are now less common than in earlier years—not because they are impractical but because they are more expensive than boxes, particularly those that are homemade from scrap lumber.

Breeding logs are made of birch or fir limbs or trunks that are hollowed out and equipped with an entrance and an outside perch below it, so birds can land before entering. The log stands on end and the top is covered with a piece of wood that can revolve around a nail.

Breeding logs are not roomy, and if there is a large brood inside, the pushing and shoving is considerable. That's why many breeders don't like them. But I am reminded of the coconut shells people used to use—and used successfully—for breeding Budgies under far more crowded conditions.

There are dozens of other designs, but you have enough examples now to make a choice. Results from breeding depend more on proper care than on the design of such things as the entrance to the nest box. Almost every breeder has a favorite model providing successful results.

The Budgerigar itself doesn't seem to care which accommodation it gets. The only real requirement seems to be that there must be a dark space and an entry to get into it that is not too big and not too small. If you add a good, thick bottom, your breeding results should be excellent.

Cleaning Nest Boxes

Clean and disinfect nest boxes before installing them at the beginning of the breeding season. It's a good precaution against parasites and bacteria. Repeat the cleanup, including the disinfectant, several times during the breeding season—at least after every brood. In between, spray an approved

A nest-box with a "pull-out" drawer allows eggs and nestlings to be observed with minimum disturbance.

The design of this nest box provides extra privacy for the parents entering the inner chamber.

disinfectant into the nest box. Be sure to cover the seams and the backside of the nest boxes.

Use of disinfectants or parasiticides requires strict care. You can get a recommendation from your local zoo, an experienced aviculturist or an avian veterinarian. The subject is also thoroughly discussed in *Bird Owner's Home Health and Care Handbook* by *Gary A. Gallerstein, D.V.M.* (Howell Book House).

In setting up nest boxes, cover the floors with a thin layer of sawdust. It will help keep eggs from rolling away. You may note that your birds will remove some of the sawdust—or all of it. Don't worry about this.

There are breeders who don't clean the nests after a brood has matured. They consider the layer of manure that remains to be good insulation. If you are sure that there are no germs in the manure, you might try this. I myself would stick to a thick floor made of wood and covered with sawdust. In humid, summer weather it is hard to keep the nest box floors germ-free and dry if you let manure accumulate.

When to Start Breeding

If you're a beginner at breeding Budgies, I strongly recommend you start breeding in March. There is a special reason for this recommendation. If you have purchased your breeding stock, you have no sure way of knowing when your birds were born. If you wait till March, you avoid any risk that the birds might be too young.

The best age to start a male into breeding is 10 to 11 months. A female should be a little older. If you have definite dates of birth for the couple, you can start breeding before March. But it's best to wait until both birds are at least 10 months old.

You will usually get your best breeding results only during the birds' second breeding season. If you breed birds that are too young, you run the chance of dealing with infertile eggs and an exhausted pair of birds. You will save yourself a lot of trouble by exercising a little patience. The result of this, however, is that late-season birds—let's say birds that became fledglings early in September—can't be used for breeding till the end of the following June.

If you use older birds, start as early as possible. Some breeders start quite early—in December or January. There sometimes are young in their nest boxes while there is a thick cover of snow outside. They reason that although the young may have a bit of a hard time for the first few months, they have the rest of the summer to develop into healthy Budgies. Furthermore, young Budgies can develop quite well despite the cold if they have a proper cage and a warm nest box. You can make up for the lack of sunshine in their environment by furnishing cod liver oil or a quality multiple vitamin-mineral supplement.

Breeders who are satisfied with hatching two broods per year don't have to start so early. It always remains risky to start early wherever it is bitter cold in the spring. If you want three broods in a season, however, there is no alternative to starting early. The last of the young have to be ready to leave the nest at the end of August or early in September. The molting season starts then for the parents, and they ought not to have to worry about tending to young ones at that time.

When climate and available space permit, growing birds will benefit greatly from summering in a flight such as one of these.
Courtesy, Corner's Ltd., Kalamazoo, Michigan

It's a long way from nest box to show cage, but the serious breeder is always looking over current broods to find future stars. The prospect of breeding tomorrow's winner is always exciting and one of the things that keeps breeders active.

3

Breeding Budgerigars

BREEDING BUDGERIGARS, probably the most popular of all pet birds, requires dedication. It is not hard, I know, to get young from a pair of Budgies, but breeding young of good quality is an entirely different matter.

Just look at birds offered for sale shortly after the breeding season. If you know anything about bird quality, you will be appalled at the mediocre to bad birds you encounter. The birds are small and skinny, often far from alert, and, in brief, unsuited for breeding. Nothing of the desired conformation, color, and health is left. This is a worrisome situation.

I have long been astounded at this lack of quality in the great majority of the Budgies available because it really doesn't take much more effort and knowledge to raise truly good birds. With this chapter, I want to help you get first-rate hatchlings that grow into birds of which you can be proud. That should be your objective as a true bird lover. If you succeed, you will be a force for the good of this species, which needs rapid improvement in quality.

The Breeding Season

The breeding season for Budgies is not the same for all breeders; it depends largely on facilities. Indoor breeders, for example, can start breeding in mid-December—using spare rooms, an attic, garage, or a specially constructed indoor space. On the other hand, breeders who exclusively use an outside aviary can't start before March or April, depending on the weather. Still, both indoor and outdoor breeders should stop breeding by the end of August or the first week in September at the latest.

If the birds themselves still show tendencies to want to go another round, don't be tempted to go along. They need at least a three-month rest. Separate the sexes and house them apart in spacious quarters. It is best if the former partners can't see or hear one another while they are separated. That's hard if you have just a few pens in the garden. Still, you can minimize contact by placing mats or other sight barriers between them. After a while, the birds hardly respond to each other's call because of distracting outside noises.

At this time, it pays to have a good system of identification and record-keeping. Color-coded rings can help you separate males from females and aid you in restoring former mates for the next breeding season. Knowing who is who in the aviary is an important step toward responsible breeding. Good records are also useful at the time you sell a bird you've bred. The new owner then can continue breeding in a responsible manner.

Even if you have removed the mates from a group of females, they still may go through the motions of breeding. So be sure to remove all nest boxes and breeding facilities and take away any eggs they still may be laying. Give these birds that don't want to quit some flax climbing ropes, extra branches for gnawing and climbing, calcium blocks to peck at, or anything else that diverts their attention and natural drive.

I recommend three months of rest from the tiring activity of the breeding season for both sexes. Don't take them out to shows till they have recovered. Major shows are usually scheduled in October, November, and early December, with regional or local shows falling even earlier. Your best birds— those you plan to show—need to be selected in advance and trained for several weeks so they will quietly allow judges to see all their beauty.

If you want to leave yourself time for shows, simple arithmetic tells you that there can be no more than about seven months of breeding. I recommend limiting the breeding season to two rounds, at any rate. This way you take no chance on overstraining the female, which pays dividends by keeping active and able to raise healthy young.

Many fanciers prefer three breeding rounds per season, but two rounds per year is better for many reasons. That's ample time to expand your stock of good birds, provided you go at it responsibly and unhurriedly. Make quality your goal—not quantity. You can produce just about as many first-rate birds as birds of lower quality.

Correct Breeding Age

Don't start birds into breeding at too young an age. Too many fanciers start breeding birds that hardly are eight or nine months old, but there are great disadvantages in this. Biologically, females are not full-grown at this age, and their bodies are not able to produce eggs without risk. Birds that start laying too young are too nervous and unsure, something often misinterpreted as youthful enthusiasm. They leave the nest for the slightest cause, lay infertile eggs, don't brood some eggs, and, in short, aren't really up for the job.

Make an exception to this rule only if necessary to rapidly establish a special mutation or to propagate it rapidly. Then let your nine-month-old females start breeding if they are closely supervised and limited in the number of eggs they are permitted to lay. Give these eggs to foster parents to raise, to save the young mothers from the tiring effort involved in brooding and raising their own young. But don't misinterpret this exception as license to convert young females into egg-laying machines!

Ordinarily a breeding pair of Budgerigars should be at least 12 months old. The male may be only 10 months, but definitely not younger. I emphasize this point because many bird fanciers are overeager and rush into breeding as soon as they think their birds are grown.

In fact, however, birds like Budgies that reach adulthood at about one year of age don't reach their optimal breeding condition until their second and third year. Only then is the bird's body truly full grown and fully developed, and the bird has learned the tricks of brooding and raising young.

If you keep good records, you can check these facts, established by research, with your own birds. You will notice that results with birds in their second and third years are substantially better than those with birds in their first year. After the third breeding season, the performance of the female especially tends to decline, while the male's strength clearly abates after his fifth or sixth year. Young from later breeding seasons clearly are of lower quality, and champion breeders prefer working only with breeding pairs two or three years old.

Housing and Furnishings

Proper housing is of prime importance, next to proper feeding and lighting. If you want to concentrate on raising just a few really top-quality birds, house them as couples in separate breeding cages or mini-aviaries. If you wish, you can put unrelated species of other birds in with them—perhaps one of the smaller Australian grass-parakeets or their relatives.

Separate housing is the only way to properly plan, control, and keep accurate records on your birds. Keep an eye on each individual chick and note any observation on a separate index card or other record keeping system.

The alternative to breeding individual pairs is communal or "colony" breeding. If a colony consists of several pairs of healthy birds with the same color mutation, colony breeding is not such a disadvantage. It is harder to provide proper care to all the young, but breeding is done more easily and quickly. Even birds that have been domesticated as long as Budgerigars retain the habits of their wild relations in Australia, which breed in colonies.

Well constructed breeding cages for Budgies are available commercially. I prefer models with dimensions of at least 24 inches long (60 cm), 24 inches deep (60 cm), and 20 inches high (50 cm). You can build the basic cage yourself and buy trellised fronts on the market to fit the 24 × 20 inch (60 × 50 cm) dimensions of the home-built cage. You also can buy fronts 12 inches (30 cm) high with lengths of 24, 32, 40 and 48 inches (60, 80, 100 and 120 cm). I prefer the 32 inch length.

Cages require preparation. Even if bought new, they should be washed and disinfected thoroughly. Previously used cages also are cleaned, submerged in water with disinfectant, and thoroughly dried out before use. If paint is needed, be sure to use lead-free paint.

Get good nest boxes. Best for Budgies are the closed variety with an entrance hole about 1½ inches (4 cm) in diameter. The minimum inside dimensions are a 6 × 6 inch (15 × 15 cm) floor with a height of 10 inches (25 cm).

Cages differ as to access for the breeder. I like the type with a sliding bottom. There also are models with a door on the side or back—or a roof that swings open.

The floor of the nest box is completely filled with a nest base that has a gradually sloping bowl shape inside it with a diameter of about 5 inches (12 cm). In this nest bowl, put a handful of sawdust. Some birds will push this out of the box gradually, while others seem to appreciate it. Wild Budgies also like having rotted wood and similar natural material in their nest holes in most cases.

You can attach the nest box to the inside or outside of the cage. I prefer the outside. Attach it thoroughly; you don't want it to fall down by accident. The vibrations of a truck thundering down your street can spell disaster.

Get everything else ready before the breeding season. Complete your records. Check the lighting, heating, and thermostat. Buy your supplies.

Hang cuttlebone against the front of the cage near a roost. Stores also carry excellent calcium and iodine blocks for hookbills. Prepare a bin for grit and another for water. Also get a couple of stalks of spray millet to hang in the immediate vicinity of the nest opening.

The advantage of the millet stalks is that they draw the newly introduced female to the nest box, so that she can become acquainted with it promptly. This is important because she gets introduced to the cage first.

Buy a starting supply of food. Be sure you have large enough seed bins, because birds should never be out of food. They should have enough each day to last till you come home. Remember that you also will soon have young to feed and they will need considerably more food than adults. The youngsters will eat practically half their body weight in food during the work day— sometimes even more. In 24 hours, consumption can even exceed body weight. One female captive Budgie can make more than 800 trips to and from the feedbin in a given day.

Do replace food daily, however, to keep it fresh. And get the parents used early-on to hatchling food, so that they will give it to their young as soon as they are hatched. Also be sure to make fresh drinking water available daily.

The results of your breeding efforts will be strongly affected by how well you prepare for the season. When your supplies are plentiful and your equipment and facilities are clean and in order, you stand a much better chance of producing vigorous birds that will enhance your reputation as a breeder of quality.

Breeding Condition

Normally, Budgerigars get into breeding condition in November or December, the females somewhat earlier than the males. Naturally, both sexes should be in breeding condition at the same time, or else they won't mate. Note that the mating urge slowly wanes between the end of December and the end of January.

Continue to keep the sexes separated during this first phase of the mating urge. Give all your birds a varied, balanced menu, including animal fats. Again, give the birds uncontaminated twigs from fruit trees, willow, or the like for diversion.

You can practically depend on the first breeding phase to end by late February, and in early to mid-March the second breeding phase will commence. By the end of March both sexes are usually in top breeding form. These dates, of course, are approximations, and experience will teach you when your own birds pass through the first breeding phase.

The determining factor for the onset of the mating urge is day length, the number of hours of daylight per day. This is equally true for wild and domesticated birds. Wild birds are also influenced by the presence of ripening grass, weeds, and grain and the availability of water. But these supplies don't materially influence the mating urge in captive birds, because the breeder constantly furnishes these necessities.

Artificial light affects the birds in the same way as natural light, and this factor causes grief for breeders who aren't careful with their lighting. If you want to trigger the mating urge, expose the birds to 13 hours of light and 11 hours of darkness. This means keeping lights on at night from dusk to 8 PM, and again in the morning from 7 AM till sunrise.

Breeders run into problems with day length when they get careless with their lighting schedule and leave lights on an hour or so longer one night and shorter the next. This much irregularity is enough to upset the triggering mechanism in the birds.

The message in all this is that you have to be consistent in timing the lights. You can find timers that do the job automatically, some with dimmers, some with fancy electronics that allow you to make timing variations from three seconds to 30 minutes.

I prefer exposing the birds to as much natural light as possible. I don't leave the lights on beyond 8 PM in winter. I don't furnish any lights in the morning, to force the birds to take advantage of the natural morning light, which increases as the days go by. I do switch on a 15 watt night light for the birds, so they can get up and eat in the early morning if they want to.

A male in good breeding condition has a beautiful blue cere. He is in constant motion and takes in everything in his surroundings. He reacts to everything that interests him by pulling his feathers together tightly and carrying his wings high. And just about everything interests him!

56

Even when no outdoor facilities are available to the aviculturist, his birds can still enjoy spacious, well-lit quarters as shown here. *Courtesy, Corner's Ltd., Kalamazoo, Michigan*

Cultivated birds are as much affected by day length as are their wild counterparts. Some aviculturists use electric timers to make sure indoor birds have sufficient amounts of light and darkness. *Photo by author*

A female ready to breed has a deep brown cere. She also is highly active and especially in the morning, she constantly calls to her mate. Now and then she will approach him closely.

Forming Breeding Pairs

In forming or reforming breeding pairs put the female in the cage first and let her explore it alone for about 24 hours. Start at about 11 AM, so the female will have time to get used to her new quarters. Usually she is taken from a larger enclosure to the breeding cage. My Budgies spend the winter in roomy flights, where their body systems can come into good condition. I prefer that over restricted caging in winter.

A newly-caged female sits uncomfortably in her unfamiliar surroundings at first, which is not surprising, considering the change. She jumps nervously from roost to roost or hangs uneasily against the bars of the front of the cage. This behavior is most pronounced in females being mated for the first time.

I prefer to give the female immediate access to the nest box, but there is a difference of opinion on this. I think, however, that it is advantageous for females to experience the nest box as part of their new cage. You can decide which method works best for you through your own experience.

After 24 hours—again about 11 AM—the male can be put into the cage. You will notice that he becomes accustomed to his new surroundings almost immediately. Often he reacts positively to the first approach by the female within the hour, but that can vary. It can take up to several days before mating begins.

Mating

At first there is no actual body contact. Both sexes, especially the female, gnaw at twigs almost constantly. They also gnaw at wire mesh and woodwork. In short, they always have something in their bills or fuss at something with their bills. All this should take place more or less in mid-March if you want to raise young from the first round of breeding to show in October or November of that same year.

Mating starts with a little dance, consisting of a series of small steps along the roost, accompanied by both birds scraping their bills along the roost rod. Soon they rub their bills together and you can expect copulation soon. During the mating dance, and especially during the bill rubbing, the pupils of the eyes of the couple widen greatly.

But don't get close enough to check this for yourself. If you want to watch the mating scene, do it at a distance. I have found that successful copulation tends to take place in the early morning, between 6 and 8 AM approximately. It is an advantage to witness the act to be sure that the desired mating has occurred—it can save you time and prevents uncertainty.

At a certain point, the upright position of the female changes into an

58

almost horizontal position—parallel to the roost. Then she lifts her tail into the air. This is a sign for the male that she is ready to mate. He then climbs on her back, holding his head close to hers. He seems to wrap his tail around her rear section.

To maintain their precarious balance, both birds flap wildly with their wings, especially the male. He holds his cloaca against hers and with several rocking motions he inseminates her.

Sperm is packed, as it were, in a semi-liquid which allows the sperm to move easily. The female organs also contain a liquid which is increased in quantity rapidly during mating and copulation. The sperm are thus able to swim up the oviduct to the ovum. Usually only one sperm pushes its way through the ovum's wall, although it occasionally happens that sperm fertilize more than one ovum with a first copulation. The ovum then forms a cyst, an impermeable wall that withstands the pressure of additional sperm trying to enter.

Rejection

Sometimes the paired birds seem totally disinterested in each other. In that case, give the birds at least a week to get used to the situation. It may be that the birds just need extra time and opportunity to get used to their new surroundings. Females can be particularly fussy. Just moving a female from one aviary to another can make her feel ill at ease enough to act suspicious toward a mate with which she had previously been paired successfully. Similarly, females may be unaccustomed to a new owner, his work methods and habits.

If the birds still don't seem to want to get together, try to discover the reason for the rejection, usually by the female. It could be that you inadvertently put their cage in a cold, wet place. It could also be that you're working with birds that are too young and you'll simply have to wait until they grow up.

With newly-acquired birds, the change in ownership could be involved. They may have previously been bred under poor circumstances and now are frightened of the situation. Or, it could be that they have intestinal problems caused by malnutrition.

Another reason could be a difference in day length. Not every fancier sets his timers the same, and it could be a previous owner gave eight hours of "night" while you are providing 12. You can tell if females fall out of breeding condition if their ceres lose their brown color.

Finally, the female may have previously selected a mate if she had been kept in a flight cage with males. So she can hardly feel attracted to another, suddenly-introduced male not of her choosing. She may absolutely refuse to accept him.

There is a fairly simple method to determine if two birds really aren't compatible. Remove the male for a day or so and reintroduce him around 7 to 8 AM. If they don't get together then, find another partner for the female.

Egg Laying

If all goes well, the female starts investigating the nest box and spends an increasing amount of time there. Sometimes she may spend the better part of a week in and around the nest box before she starts laying. At night, however, she is likely to sleep outside the box, though very near it.

Sometimes a female spends all night hanging from the bars of the wire mesh or the cage. It's a mistake to force her to "sleep right" on a roost or something apparently more suitable. The result of moving her would be to create a nervous and out-of-sorts bird, meaning a delay in further breeding activity.

After mating, the female no longer pays much attention to the male. She spends her time principally with inspecting the nest and its immediate surroundings. She keeps going in and out of the nest box and gnaws at the roof or entry of the box. To help dispel this nervous gnawing, provide several twigs from fruit trees, willow, or other soft wood. Put these in the nest, next to the bowl. She will continue to enjoy working on these once she is brooding eggs. It efficiently helps relieve her boredom.

Seven days after copulation, the first egg is due, although it can take up to 19 days to arrive. Leave the female undisturbed at this time. She is very sensitive to disturbances.

Stop cleaning the cage for a while. Young females can get so upset from people coming to clean their cages that they lay their next eggs on the floor of the breeding cage or stop laying altogether after producing one or two eggs.

Don't worry if the female pulls out several breast and stomach feathers. She is just preparing to brood her eggs better by baring her brood spots— places on her body where the surface temperature is higher than elsewhere because of an increased blood supply.

It happens that young females lay eggs on the cage floor without apparent reason. They can be put into the nest box carefully if they aren't cracked or broken. The female may or may not accept such eggs for brooding—it's an open question. Most females, however, catch on quickly as to how things are supposed to go and deposit their eggs properly in the nest box.

Budgies usually lay their eggs in the afternoon. After the female has laid the first egg or two, she tends to spend a lot of time in the nest box and she even spends the night there. Her cloaca relaxes and she is able to relieve herself again. When she leaves the nest from time to time, it usually is to defacate. The droppings are large and soft, compared to their normal character.

Each additional egg produced is preceded by a new copulation, although it is quite normal that after the first copulation several additional ones take place the same day and the following days.

Although the female does most of the brooding, the male does help incubate the eggs. He often keeps the hen company on the nest and remains vigilant for the approach of any potential danger.   *Wissink*

Budgie eggs should only be handled when absolutely necessary and then only as little as possible. Even the most meticulous handling of eggs can lead to embryo death.   *Photo by author*

While laying eggs, the female may throw all the sawdust out of the nest box. I believe it is safer from the standpoint of preventing egg breakage to put the sawdust back—but do it very quickly at a time when the female is off her nest. If the female again exerts herself to remove the sawdust, then let it be as she prefers.

The female will produce a new egg every other day. She may start brooding the moment she has laid her first egg, and if so, the first egg will hatch two days before the second egg and so on. If she doesn't keep brooding the first egg consistently, however, there can be a day's delay in the hatch. It is even possible that the first two eggs will hatch the same day. Ordinarily, however, if five eggs hatch, one can assume that the oldest member of the clutch was hatched eight days before the youngest.

The first clutch consists of five or six eggs on the average. The second clutch can go up to 10 or 18. Especially in such large clutches, the infertile eggs should be removed. If you can't tell, or if there still are a large number of eggs left, distribute the extras among other breeding pairs of Budgies. Don't forget to keep good records on the switch!

Brooding and Hatching

The incubation period lasts from 17 to 21 days, depending on the temperature in the room and the relative humidity. In a warm room, with temperatures between 65 and 72 degrees F (18 and 22 degrees C), the embryos develop faster, but the brooding period is never shorter than 17 days.

Normally one egg produces a single young, although twins do occur in exceptional cases. These twins have a much lower chance of survival.

Brooding is almost totally the task of the female. At times, however, the male keeps his brooding mate company at the nest. They sit side by side on the eggs, the male with his head toward one side, the female with her head to the other side. But the most important task of the male is to take care of peace and security.

It is important for the breeder to know whether the eggs that are being produced are truly fertile. After three or four days you can usually tell the difference. If you hold a fertile egg against a strong light on a transparent plastic spoon, you will see dark red stripes on the upper yolk, a sign of new life. If the embryo is not visible after five days, you can be sure that the egg is infertile. But don't overdo the checking—once or twice is enough! You don't want to upset the birds.

Eggs usually hatch in early morning. The hatching bird has an "egg tooth" on the upper mandible of the bill, which it uses to scratch its way out of the shell. Once it has wormed its way out, the little one will start softly begging for food, which the mother bird has made ready in her crop—the so-called "crop milk."

Sometimes the male assists her, but ordinarily there is a definite separation of duties. The male fetches food and offers it to his mate, and she, in turn, feeds the young.

The young are hatched naked and pink-skinned. During the first days of life their protruding eyes are still closed.

Hatching doesn't always go without involvement by the breeder. Infertile eggs have to be removed, because hatchlings would otherwise break them and make a mess in the nest.

You also need to decide once again if some females have too many hatchlings to feed. Distribute any extras in large broods to couples with a smaller number of hatchlings to raise. Select foster parents that have young of about the same age. Don't give either eggs or young over to the care of foster parents that didn't produce eggs or young of their own. They peck the eggs apart and kill the young. Don't delay in moving hatchlings around, as foster parents are more likely to accept young a few days old than halfgrown hatchlings 2½ to 3 weeks of age.

To promote acceptance of foster youngsters, especially older ones, rub their backs and wings with some droppings taken from the nest of the foster parents. They will then not give off their "own" odor, but rather the familiar smell of the foster parents. Use a small spatula to gather the needed droppings.

Mark eggs or young to be moved to foster parents with an odorless felt-tip pen and record the marking in your records. On live birds, put the marks on their backs. To avoid the possibility of mistakes altogether, give foster parents youngsters to adopt that have a totally different coloration. Don't depend only on feather color, but also use eye color. Lutino and cinnamon Budgies, for example, have red eyes and can thus be moved to foster parents with normal eye color.

Leg Banding

You can use leg bands on birds at least eight days old. Breed associations have leg bands available, and ordinarily, a diameter of 4 mm., inside measure, will do for Budgies.

Putting legbands on Budgies and other psittacines isn't difficult. They have four toes, two pointed forward and two pointed to the rear, forming a type of X. To start, wash your hands in warm water. Hold the young bird in your left palm if you're right-handed. (Left-handed persons do the reverse.) Squeeze the three longest toes together between the thumb and index finger of your left hand so that they lie in a line with the ball of the foot. Take the band in your right hand, also between thumb and index finger, and shove it over the toes and the ball of the foot. The hindmost toe now is caught between the band and the leg. Take a sharpened matchstick and shove it under the toe to liberate it. It's best to visit an experienced bird breeder and watch the way he or she does it. If you have an agile and steady hand, the job is easy.

Growing Birds

Young Budgerigars get the first feathers on their backs and have their whole bodies covered with down when they're about nine or 10 days old. Now is the time to check if they're getting enough food. This requires close supervision, which some people find a little tedious. Look to see if the little crops are well-filled, if the young birds are growing well and if they react sharply and alertly to your presence.

If they don't have enough food in their crops, you can feed them extra yourself. Use a feeding syringe, of which several models are availabe commercially. Or you can remove some underfed young for care by foster parents.

It often happens that females suddenly start laying new eggs while they still have young about 35 days old in the nest. See to it that you remove these eggs from the nest as quickly as possible if you want to save them. Otherwise the very active hatchlings will surely damage them.

Keep the eggs in a cool place, packed in a box with sterile cotton. Don't use dry sand for packing because it could harbor harmful bacteria. You can keep eggs up to nine days without risk, provided you turn them extremely carefully. Warm your fingertips before touching the eggs.

Alternatively, you could give prematurely-laid eggs to foster parents.

The female may have such a strong drive to start brooding new eggs that she throws her old brood out of the nest. You'll notice that she is seldom seen in the aviary but spends long periods on the nest. And, of course, you'll notice the evicted hatchlings on the floor, loudly begging for food and trying to climb back into the nest with flapping wings and clawing feet. That's particularly true for older hatchlings.

You don't want all that commotion and the possible harm that could result. Take the young away from their mother and put them in a roomy cage with their father. He will take care of raising them further, with help as needed from you, the breeder. They can be housed without their father if they have started to peck and have clearly defined tails. House them indoors, if at all possible, because they really aren't prepared as yet to cope with night temperatures. Keep a close watch on these youngsters and feed them by hand if necessary to keep them fit. It would be a pity to lose them at this stage.

Under normal circumstances, young Budgies can eat on their own about a week after they become fledglings. At that point, separate them by sex and house them in a spacious run where they can develop further.

Egg Binding

An important problem connected with egg production is *egg binding*. When housing and feeding are appropriate, egg binding shouldn't occur very often.

Egg binding is a condition in which the egg literally gets stuck or "bound"

Above: A normal light green cock of good type. *Right:* A normal gray green cock showing exceptionally good throat spots, displayed on a wide mask.

Above: A normal skyblue cock showing a very high forehead or cap. *Left:* An opaline dark blue cock displaying excellent overall type, color and mask.

Right: A normal mauve cock, showing typical blue spots on flanks and upper tail coverts. Its head, however, is too small for a successful exhibition bird's. *Below:* A yellow-face opaline violet cock. Color could be sharper in this bird, but the yellow areas in head, mask and tail are acceptable to most written standards.

Left: Normal cinnamon skyblue cock with a faulty backskull and irregular throat spots. *Center:* An opaline gray cock. *Right:* An opaline gray green cock of poor type.

68

Top: Normal light gray yellow cock. This large bird would be better with a broader head. *Bottom:* An opaline cinnamon gray green hen showing a narrow head and irregular throat spots.

Left: An opaline white dark blue cock showing excellent sharp back color and markings. This bird would be a good breeding partner for an opaline clearwing. *Below:* An assymetrical, bi-colored or half-sider opaline light green skyblue cock. Such birds appear spontaneously. They are "freaks" and cannot be reproduced by any controlled means. The striking color comes from a certain form of chromosome breakdown within cell division during reproduction so cannot be inherited.

Top: An opaline white violet hen showing poor, but clear, wing markings. *Bottom:* A normal white gray cock showing excellent color and markings. This bird shows a very light cheek patch but could have a better-proportioned head.

Left: A yellow-face white gray hen showing typical, light cheek spots. Below: An excellent clearwing dark blue cock that would be improved with lighter markings.

during the process of being laid. It strikes young birds in particular, but any bird can be affected when stressed by producing too many broods per season. That's why I repeatedly advise against trying to produce an extra brood after birds have raised their quota of young. Birds need a rest, even though it is possible to keep Budgies laying and brooding winter and summer.

Egg binding also can be caused by housing birds in flight cages that are too small, or by exposing them to repeated temperature changes.

You can recognize a bird suffering from egg binding by the way she usually sits on the floor like a little ball of feathers, shivering away. She lets herself be caught easily. Her vent is swollen and her eyes have large pupils.

A second type of egg binding occurs with a normal egg when the laying muscles don't function well for some reason. That reason is a shortage of vitamins. Vitamins influence not only the deposition of calcium for the shell but also muscle movement in the oviduct. So a vitamin deficiency clearly is behind both kinds of egg binding.

Budgies, like all birds, have definite vitamin requirements. Because they are more exposed to sunlight in the summer, birds get more vitamins naturally—a probable reason for seeing less of the problem during the summer months. But breeders who furnish a vitamin-rich diet don't have to fear egg binding in any season. Greens and cod liver oil are the solution.

Budgies, however, don't take as well to greens as other birds, so many breeders depend mainly on cod liver oil or a multiple vitamin-mineral supplement. They feed millet seeds soaked in cod liver oil or vitamins all year long. The need for vitamins will be discussed in more detail in a later section.

Egg binding, to be sure, is not solely a question of vitamin shortage. Certain birds have more of a natural inclination toward the problem than others. You can recognize these susceptible birds by a "hollow" belly—one that doesn't run toward the breast with a proper curve. Others produce superlarge eggs, which obviously are more difficult to lay. Both conditions can be prevented by proper vitamin-mineral supplementation.

To remedy either type of egg binding, utilize warmth. Even just putting a heater near the birds can provide the desired result. The bird also can be wrapped in a towel and laid on a warm fireplace mantle for a short time. Or, one can hold the cloaca of the bird above (not in!) a pan of boiling water. Don't use steam from a kettle; that would fatally burn the bird. Warmth will soon free the egg and preserve it for brooding if you wish.

When egg binding occurs, you can also relieve the immediate problem— the stuck egg—by helping it slip out. Smear some salad oil under the tail. Or else hold the bottom end (and *only* the bottom end) of the bird in a bath of alternately cold and warm water. Be sure the egg shell doesn't crack inside the bird, because that usually causes a fatal infection.

Birds that suffered through egg binding shouldn't be bred again for four or five months. Then watch them carefully to prevent a recurrence.

There are various commercial products on the market that can help prevent egg binding. Cod liver oil or other vitamin-mineral supplements can be mixed into some seed. Follow label directions to prevent overdosing the birds on vitamins.

Other Potential Difficulties

Budgerigars being prepared for brooding must never be exposed to temperatures below 47 degrees F (8 degrees C). You should take no chances on this score, meaning that you can't start breeding early in the year unless you breed indoors.

Good care and good supervision yield good results, generally, but things still can go wrong. Eggs can be infertile, for a number of reasons. First, birds may not be in condition. Second, poorly shaped roosts may interfere with proper copulation. Round roosts are totally unsuited, unless flattened on top. Square ones are good. Swinging or loose roosts, like round roosts, are unacceptable for breeding birds.

Third, be aware that there are females that jump into the nest box the moment they are placed into the cage, never to reappear, not even if a male is placed in the cage with her. Further, check if the feathers of both partners are soft in makeup around the anus.

It's also important to remember that birds need proper artificial lighting and a constant supply of food and water to come into breeding condition. But, despite all else, birds need to have ample periods of rest. That's why lights should be out by 8 PM. If lights stay on longer, the birds not only get tired but also quite nervous. It's best to dim light gradually, which is simple to do with the right type of dimmer switch and timer.

Note, finally, that there is a type of genetic defect that keeps affected birds from coming into breeding condition. Proper records can help trace such a problem. And successful matings leading to well-fertilized eggs can also be interfered with by a lack of vitamin E, more comprehensive dietary insufficiencies, nervousness, or under-age birds. I also think it's important that the birds should always be able to hear each other's chatter. I have noticed that in quiet breeding quarters, where one hardly hears a sound, the rate of success in breeding is far from ideal.

I want to add some further remarks about eggs. Budgie eggs, according to measurements made in H. L. White's collection, range in size from 18.3 to 19.8 mm. by 13.7 to 14.7 mm., with an average size of 18.6 by 14.2 mm.

Always handle eggs with the greatest of care. The yolk and the developing embryo that is attached to it are held to the egg white by only two ligaments. A quick worker can easily turn an egg between his fingers without causing visible damage. But inside, all sorts of trouble can occur. One or both ligaments could tear, so that once the egg is returned to the nest, the yolk gradually sinks through the egg white, settles to the bottom of the egg and attaches to the inside of the shell.

A typical group of well-kept Budgies.

A clutch of day-old hatchlings and, as yet, unhatched eggs.   *van Herk*

75

When the brooding bird turns this egg—as she will, several times per day—the misplaced yolk first gets too much and then too little warmth. As a result, the embryo stops developing and dies. The lesson in all of this is to be extremely careful when handling eggs.

When you check on eggs, it's best to handle them with a plastic spoon. If you prefer using your hands, first warm your fingers. Cold fingers can kill embryos in their first stages of development, as strange as this may seem.

Remember that the egg you pick up should be returned to the exact same spot where it came from in the nest. If you aren't careful about this, the bird will return the egg for you. This exposes the egg to more unnecessary movement, to the possible detriment of the embryo.

Embryo Mortality

Check for possible dead embryos. Embryos can die at any stage, from early development until minutes before hatch. Still, the most common period for embryos to die is during their first week of development.

Between the 1st and 16th day of brooding, the most frequent cause of embryo mortality is a female that leaves the eggs too long because something has disturbed her. Such disturbances include sudden noises, the sudden flash of an automobile headlight, and the appearance of mice, rats, cats, and other animals. Another cause may be a sick female, or one that has gone out of breeding condition—perhaps because the diet isn't quite right.

A proper diet includes food from animal sources, like egg food and universal food—commercial brands are fine. Don't just furnish these at the point where females begin brooding, but rather, start offering them several weeks earlier. Provide a choice of several brands to start with, so she can indicate her preference.

Embryos also can die if the egg shell gets smeared with dung. In my experience, a day or two after an egg gets dirty, the embryo dies. Smeared feces harden and form a seal, which clogs the pores in the shell—making exchange of gases impossible. Bacterial contamination compounds the problem, especially if the smears are caused by a female with diarrhea.

Other reasons for the deaths could be weak embryos produced by underage parents; poor housing, no protection from cold and drafts; wet food (including green food), among others.

Remember that embryo death is Nature's way of selecting out unfit birds. If you want to avoid embryo deaths, work only with superior parents. That way, you substitute your own selection for Nature's way—saving yourself unwanted losses.

Assisting the Hatch

Hatch is a critical period in a bird's life. Strong embryos from healthy

A skyblue hen in excellent breeding condition.   *Harkema*

parents usually hatch with little or no trouble. Embryos that are weak die, usually from lack of oxygen.

You can prevent the most common cause of mortality at hatching by making sure that the shell membrane stays supple. Chicks hampered by a shell membrane that's dry and tough have problems even if they hatch out. You want chicks that are vital and active after hatching, not chicks exhausted by the process.

Tough membranes that hamper or prevent hatch are caused by dry air in the birds' quarters. Central heating, especially, provides "dry heat." You can keep the membranes from drying out by putting several containers of water on the radiators or by setting up some commercially-made humidifiers. The best policy is to use both—you need to keep the humidity up!

It does happen that young can't hatch without our assistance. But don't be hasty. If you act too early, the embryo could die.

You timed your intervention right if an active chick emerges that has a pink-to-red colored body. You were too early if the new hatchling looks pale and white and a bit of the yolk is still attached to its belly. Unfortunately such a chick is doomed. And if you suspect the embryo is weak, don't bother to help it hatch. A bird too weak to hatch normally may live a day or two, but then will die anyway.

Let us suppose that you have an egg from which you suspect the chick can't liberate itself on its own. The 18 days of brooding have passed and the egg should be ready to open. You are expecting to hatch a totally healthy young—but nothing happens.

In such a case, I follow the approach of Budgie expert Gerald S. Binks, described in his fascinating book, *Best in Show* (Elbury Press/Pelham, London, 1977). He has prepared a table to guide your decision whether to assist or stand by:

Sound	Appearance	Action
Quiet tapping	1/16 in. crack	Too soon - replace
Quiet tapping	Group of fine cracks	Too soon - replace
Quiet tapping	Cracks plus brown line	Too soon - replace
Weak squeaks	Cracks plus tiny hole	Too soon - replace
Medium squeaks	Cracks and early discoloration	Too soon - replace
Loud squeaks	Crack line round circumference—creamy patches, moist membrane	Normal hatching —replace

Loud squeaks	Crack line round circumference—creamy patches, dried membrane	Assist
Loud squeaks	Large hole—drying membrane	Assist

Binks suggests laying the egg in question on a prewarmed, thick bath towel, with the part of the egg shell that has been cracked the most facing you. Cut a circle around the crack with a sharpened wooden matchstick. Be sure to cut through the membrane under the shell. You will see a little blood in the process, but if your timing was right and everything else went as planned, you should have assisted in bringing a healthy chick into the world.

If the chick you helped hatch is the first one to hatch, Binks suggests that you should be absolutely certain to put the broken shell back into the nest bowl. If you return a first hatchling to its mother without the shell, chances are great that she won't understand what has happened. She will experience the youngster as something foreign—a disturbance in the usual process—and she will kill the little one with a few chops from her beak.

Additional Cautions

There also are infections in the oviduct that interfere with peristalsis, the natural contractions that expel the egg. The remedy is to segregate the affected bird and to warm it up, as warmth can restart peristalsis.

Another threat to eggs is long toe nails on brooding birds, especially the females that do most of this task. Budgies can develop long, dagger-sharp nails that can pierce the egg shell and—if any eggs hatch—can hurt the hatchlings. If you notice any damaged eggs, remove them. There's only a slim chance they'd develop properly.

Cutting toe nails requires skill. Hold the bird up against the light and you'll see a red stripe through the nail, formed by blood capillaries. Cut up to the stripe, but have a fast-acting coagulant handy in case you accidentally cut into the live part of the nail anyway. See to it that the cut nail doesn't have a sharp point remaining.

Keep nails short by natural action. Put some rough stones in your aviary or cage, or some rough-surfaced plants, like reeds or rushes.

Another problem to avoid are eggs with weak shells or no shells at all. Breeding birds need calcium in their diet to form strong shells. Yes, some females lay shell-less eggs only, despite being properly nourished. Obviously, these birds should be retired from breeding. If you notice any shell-less eggs, remove them. They have no chance of developing and would break, smudging the normal eggs. As stated, smudged eggs with clogged pores also fail to develop.

Oversize eggs are undesirable, too. They usually contain two yolks. Don't keep birds that persist in laying two-yolk eggs. Remove any such eggs you find unless you like to experiment to see what happens. The chances that you'll raise twins are minimal, but you could succeed! If you attempt it, keep good records.

A related problem to the double-yolk egg is the singleton chick. Some females lay only one egg per clutch, brood after brood. Such birds exist in greater numbers than one would suppose. Often there is no apparent cause. The birds come from a good line, are fed excellently, and can even score high at shows. Keep good records. If you are dealing with a heritable trait, don't breed from these birds.

If you do have to deal with a single egg in a nest, or if mishaps reduce the clutch to one egg or one hatchling, it makes no sense at all to have the mother go through brooding and/or feeding. It is extremely draining for parents to brood and feed their young. Research confirms that most of the demands and stresses on birds occur during the breeding season. I recommend taking the only chick and giving it for adoption to another nest with young of as nearly the same age as possible. Alternatively, you can raise the chick by hand.

One of the worst occurrences in breeding is to encounter an egg-eating bird. It often is hard to identify the culprit, certainly so if you breed in colonies or keep several breeding pairs in an aviary or cage.

A quick method I've found useful, especially when you have sudden evidence of egg pecking in the middle of the season, is to replace the eggs with fakes. You'll see which bird is responsible, and it gets a good lesson! The real eggs that are intact are given to other birds to brood. Once again, keep good records.

If egg pecking happens in a one-pair cage, it is best to remove the male first. If he proves to be the culprit, you have no choice but to remove him after you have observed several matings and before you expect the first egg. You will have to do this after each breeding round if you continue to breed from him.

Suspect birds are not necessarily out of the running for the next round of breeding. Make sure the diet is adequate and provide extra vitamins, cuttlebone, and green food. Then put the affected cage as far away from others as possible for the next round.

If a female persists in pecking at eggs, you have two choices. First, don't let her breed any more for the season. Or, second, use a nest box designed to "harvest" eggs. These boxes are oblong with a double bottom. The top floor is slanted, so that the freshly laid egg rolls away into a tray, lined with a thick layer of sand for protection. If you build the sloping floor yourself, it's all right to use plywood, because it doesn't stay in use long. Birds will stop pecking at eggs if they don't have any eggs around for a while and if you make sure their nutrition and housing are in order.

A breeder can only be sure of the genetic make-up of his birds by following a strict program of pair breeding. *Photo by author*

Colony breeding facilities usually mean that the genetic background of your birds is unknown. Eventually, what colony-bred birds will produce becomes anyone's guess! *Harkema*

These normal green cocks indicate a uniformity in their breeding that suggests their breeder is achieving the results desired.
van Herk

Problems can result in any breeding activity regardless of the amount of precaution taken. A positive approach and sufficient preparedness for unwelcome developments are the best means a breeder has of dealing with any unforeseen developments with his birds.
Wissink

The same solution—a nest box with a double bottom—applies to another problem, namely birds that take their newly-laid eggs out of the nest. They sometimes move the eggs in the oddest ways—none of which do the eggs any good. So remove eggs from birds that need to be broken of this bad habit as well.

Other causes for problems in egg production are birds that are too fat to produce eggs without difficulty and danger. Or there can be cysts or tumors in the ovaries and/or the oviduct, which can cause the oviduct to rupture. Badly infected birds like these are really not much further use for breeding. The same is true for males which get infections in their reproductive organs.

The following remarks apply not only to Budgies, but also to other birds, including hookbills.

• Sometimes there are females, especially inexperienced ones, who overdo their job of brooding and sit on their eggs too long. One cause can be a temperature difference between the warm nest and the cool air outside. Obviously, people who want to start breeding outdoors too early face this problem frequently.

The result generally is dead or injured young, since they are smothered by the female immediately after hatching. They are too small and weak to draw her attention.

This analysis leads us to a solution. Take a young chick, about a week old, from another nest and put it with such a persistently brooding female. Smear the adoptee with droppings from the adoptive nest to get it accepted. Because of the bigger size of this foster chick, the female is forced to sit higher. The smaller, natural young can now move around, and soon are begging for food. This simple method usually works well—it has for me, and it is recommended by Binks and many others.

• Sometimes chicks have abnormally swollen crops, which prove to be filled with air, not food, upon closer inspection. This problem highlights the advantage of checking nests as soon as young are hatched—latest after a whole brood is hatched.

The solution seems cruel, but it is effective and painless. Sterilize a sewing needle in an open flame and pierce the crop with it, preferably at the place where the pressure is greatest. This allows the air to escape. The crop returns to its normal size and the chick is relieved of its discomfort. If you don't relieve the bird, it wouldn't accept food and would starve to death. Keep checking on the affected bird because the problem may recur and will then require a second operation.

• Sometimes a female doesn't start providing food right after the first chick is hatched. This usually is not the fault of the female, but of the young, which is too weak to raise its head, open its beak, and beg for food. The female won't start feeding unless properly stimulated: no begging, no food! The crying sometimes needs to be stronger than even a group of young can utter.

In such cases, again, an older "adoptee" can solve the problem with its loud begging cries. You need to leave it with the new hatchlings only until the female starts feeding actively.

You can intervene directly with a little extra trouble. Remove one youngster from the nest and feed it a teaspoonful of baby food heated to body temperature and enriched with grape sugar. You can obtain special plastic feeding syringes, which are frequently used by Canary breeders.

Now you have the task of getting the little beak to open. Lay the little one on its back between folds of a smooth, warm towel. It will immediately try to right itself. If that doesn't work—and it won't because the folds of the towel restrain the bird—it begins to complain as loudly as it can yell. Then, put the feeding syringe into its throat and gently let some drops of feed fall into the crop. Don't administer the feed too forcefully to avoid getting it into the windpipe and lungs. (A mistake here would be fatal.)

After the crop is filled, clean the bird's head and beak with a flannel rag, so that no food is left to become caked on the bird. Then, return the little one to its nest, where it will continue to complain loudly. This reaction will motivate the parents to start providing food on their own. It usually works with just one intervention by the breeder on a single young.

Of course, there are cases where a female won't start feeding, no matter what. Then adopt out all the young.

• Sometimes the parents stop feeding their young suddenly, after an unproblematic start. The causes can be many—among them cold temperatures, illness, or serious disturbances. The only response is to end all breeding with the affected parents and distribute the young among other nests in the aviary. Remember to coat the young with dung from the intended foster nest—but don't overdo it. It is probably wise to give them a few hand feedings as described in the previous paragraph. You can take on the entire job yourself, although it's preferable to use foster parents.

Feeding birds by hand ought to work well if the young are at least 10 to 12 days old. Be aware, however, that hand-raised Budgies become extremely attached to humans and very tame. Once they have their feathers and are independent, they can be taught all kinds of tricks. You can teach them to say a few words, and there are tapes and records on the market to help accomplish this. On the other hand, hand-raised birds are usually not suited for breeding, although there are rare exceptions.

• Sometimes one of the parents wildly attacks a young Budgerigar when it is leaving the nest. The bird generally dies. Binks, in his book *Best in Show,* discusses this phenomenon.

The cause is not clear. In some cases I have examined the slain bird and have found that it was weak in constitution.

The phenomenon may be related to that of wild Cuba finches, which sometimes expel all female or all male young from the nest. This points to a natural population control measure, because research has shown that this happens in a year where there is a corresponding surplus of either male or female birds. I personally have seen wild Budgerigars kill their young and believe this could be another form of natural population control.

• Sometimes a parent bird dies during the breeding season. If the male dies, problems are relatively few, because a female usually can brood and raise a clutch of eggs and hatchlings on her own. If it is an exceptionally large clutch, you can distribute a few eggs to other nests. (Again, keep good records.) If the female proves unequal to the task, distribute the whole brood to other nests.

Lacking enough nests, ask for help from other breeders. You can see how important it is to belong to a bird club for this purpose alone.

If the female dies, the situation changes. If she dies on the nest, it may be hard to spot. If you've been checking regularly, however, you'll find out soon enough.

You don't have to worry about the eggs being spoiled. Eggs often can take a lot more neglect that is commonly supposed, despite the remarks made earlier. A clutch that has not been brooded for several hours definitely can be saved. Put the eggs in a basket lined with cotton and put it under a lamp for several hours. Turn the eggs every hour. Use a 40 watt lamp and check with your flat hand under the bulb—it needs to be comfortably warm.

Meanwhile, look for a way to harbor the eggs with other brooding pairs. Don't be surprised if these eggs eventually hatch a little later than the clutch with which they were put. There can be a two-day difference.

If the female dies while raising young, you can't expect the male to take over the job unless the young are almost ready to leave the nest. I have known of several instances where the male has done an efficient job, but I still would keep an eye on such a brood to prevent accidents. If the young are older—at a stage where they are feathering out—you also can hand-raise them if you have the time. Use a feeding syringe, as described earlier, to furnish nourishments. In all other cases, distribute the young to other nests.

The breeder who has raised birds for some time knows exactly when something is going wrong with his stock. The birds eat little or nothing, sit with feathers erect, and don't interact with each other. The breeder can also diagnose trouble from the looks of the nosecaps (ceres or wattles). Female Budgies that aren't properly housed and fed or bred too intensively have pale, almost white nose caps. Stressed males have dark brown to black ones. The experienced breeder knows when and how to react to trouble. If he has badly stressed birds, he will not continue to breed from them.

Foster Parents

Some Budgie breeders use foster parents to raise young from their most valuable stock. These breeders believe that raising the young taxes the strength of the parents, much more so than laying eggs and brooding the hatchlings. The breeders, therefore, let their valuable stock lay eggs and perhaps brood them, but the rest of the job of raising the young is transfered to other, less valuable birds.

In this way, the more valuable stock can be bred again after a month or so of rest, and the breeder can count on three broods per year from his stock without stressing his top birds.

One way to go about this is to substitute the "foster" eggs for those naturally produced by the foster parents. Another way is to distribute the eggs or young of the valuable birds among several other nests.

Raising the Young

Breeders can and should learn quickly to check the condition of their young birds. After a few days, the young should have a bright color and feel substantial in the hand. A bird that feels lighter than the rest is bound to be in less than perfect health.

You can check how the birds are eating by noting the condition of the crop. Before feathers appear, you can see right into the crop through the skin, and I would say the least attractive crop is best! A bulging crop means that the young are well-fed and—in most cases—that they are healthy. If you come across a crop that isn't as full as it should be, take one or two birds out of that nest and place them into another where they will get better care.

The skin of the bald young, which some people don't find very attractive, should be shiny as satin. After the feathers appear, the quills should feel sturdy as soon as they are a centimeter long. Also note that a healthy young bird has quills on its topside, just above the tail, and these also should be strong and resilient.

As soon as feathers appear, one can see which color the bird is going to be. But an experienced breeder will be able to predict the color much sooner. The color of the naked skin gives him the clues. And eye color also makes a difference. If the eyes are red, then you can be sure the bird is an albino, a lutino, or a fallow.

As soon as the young are independent, they should be separated. Be sure, however, that the young truly can take care of themselves and no longer are being fed by the parents. Give them a roomy aviary, where they can climb and fly about to their hearts' content as they develop further into the totally healthy birds you want.

Mating the New Generation

As soon as you have a good idea how the young birds are developing, you can start thinking about how you want to mate them. Making up breeding pairs from your young stock is an important matter, of course, and it must not be done thoughtlessly.

If you had a good season, you must decide, first of all, which birds you want to sell and which you want to keep. It would be foolish not to keep your

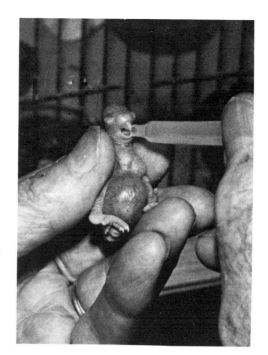

There is a number of ways to handfeed baby Budgies. The choice of accepted methods should depend on what you are comfortable with. Note the expanding crop on this dropper-fed baby.

At five days, these chicks show the beginnings of what will become beautiful plumage.   *Harkema*

87

best birds for further breeding. Look for the best ones among the first broods hatched. These were raised at a time that the parents still were in top condition, and they had the longest and most favorable time to develop.

During the winter, look over your birds carefully to find a partner for each male. If you intend to breed in colonies, you also should decide which couples ought to be placed together.

In selecting mates, consider the preference of the birds, if you can. You will notice that young birds form couples spontaneously—meaning that every male will select his own mate. If possible, leave these spontaneously formed couples together; they will give you the best breeding results.

Often you can't just let Nature take its course because you have special goals in your breeding program. An albino bird may select a green partner, and you may want to mate two albinos. You then, of course, have no choice but to separate the couple and to more or less force a new combination on each. Be sure, however, that you keep the laws of genetics in mind; these will be discussed in greater detail in the second half of this book.

If you rematch couples, give them extra time to get used to each other before putting them into the breeding cage. You want to foster the greatest harmony possible before your birds start reproducing.

Once your selections have been made, band both birds with the same color. That way, you will be able to reconstitute the desired pairs properly and without trouble the following spring.

Make sure you establish a good reputation based on the birds you sell. As I said earlier, you can sell birds with minor deviations as pets if they are otherwise healthy—but you shouldn't sell them to anyone who has any thoughts about breeding Budgies. Don't slide into deceptions, especially not if any of your birds have serious defects or are in poor health. To avoid temptation, humanely destroy young birds that you wouldn't buy for your own use under any circumstance. You not only save your own reputation, you also encourage newcomers to the hobby who don't have enough experience to know faulty birds from quality. One day, they will be wiser and will remember who cheated and who helped them.

Good birds that remain after you have made selections for your own future breeding can be sold to other breeders or to dealers. Wait for the proper moment. Consider whether any higher price you might get for your birds in the spring would be offset by the food they eat during the winter. If so, sell in fall. If not, sell in spring. Remember, prices often also depend on the export market.

To a degree, Budgerigars are subject to fads. A certain color variation can fall into disfavor for a while; prices drop because there is no demand for the birds. At the same time, the star of another color variation may be on the rise. If you want to stay on top of this change in fads, you must be on your toes. You may switch over to a new color and have a bunch of birds to sell just after the demand for that color has peaked. The smart breeder who wants to make some money from his hobby lowers his risks to the minimum literally by not putting all of his eggs in one basket. And he tries to be ahead of the market. If you don't see a chance to latch onto something popular or to develop it yourself, you still can stay ahead of the market price by raising the quality of your birds to the top. Fortunately, there are always breeders who value quality enough to pay a premium to get it.

The gray cock on the left and the normal graywing skyblue cock on the right are high quality examples of modern exhibition Budgerigars. In conformation, condition and deportment, they leave little to be desired for the fancier or judge seeking a worthy prize winner.   *Harkema*

Pair breeding identifies which birds produced which young and meticulous record keeping gives the breeder the advantage of knowing what his birds can produce with reasonable certainty. The chart shown tacked outside the nest above becomes a "road map" to the future paths the breeder must take for future generations.

Photo by author

4
Selective Breeding

SOME BREEDERS, motivated to get the most young from their breeding stock, breed indiscriminately. You can often find practically any kind of color variation in their breeding colonies. There is no selection. Not a single bird is homozygous for key traits, and there are any number of in-between colors.

This kind of breeder may show you a "cobalt" in his stock, but chances are it won't be a pure cobalt. It may have some white feathers, or the cobalt may shade into light blue or mauve. All the breeder goes by is outward appearance. He has no idea whatever about the hidden traits of the bird. He won't be able to say with any certainty how any young that he will get out of this bird will look at maturity.

Specialized Breeding

The way to avoid this chaos in a colony breeding system is to *specialize.* Put only birds with the same color factors in a colony, if possible. Specialize in just the white and blue color variations, for example, so that your breeders would be white, light blue, cobalt, or mauve—possibly including graywings.

You may get more satisfaction from specializing more narrowly in a color variant that especially appeals to you—say, cinnamon green. If so, study the laws of genetics to know how to put together the population of the breeding cage. If you select your breeders from just one variation, you will become intimately familiar with a special bloodline and learn all the tricks of color breeding for the chosen variant. In the end, you will have the best results from your breeding—results truly beautiful to behold.

91

You may arrive at the same decision—to specialize in a certain variant—out of pure economic motivation. You may select the bird that is in fashion and brings the highest price on the market. In that case also, your road to success is to breed from birds of which you not only know the external appearance but also the hidden traits. Only then will you be able with reasonable accuracy to achieve the breeding results that you have set for yourself.

Breeding Records

Records are essential in order to accurately know the obvious and hidden traits of your birds. You need to know the parents of every young bird. And there is only one way to get this knowledge—by breeding in cages with just one pair per cage. You can approach this certainty in colony breeding situations if you use only purebred males of a certain type in the colony. If you are breeding lutinos and you have six purebred lutino males in the colony, then you don't need to worry at all about the heritage of your future young.

Good records are not kept widely enough. There are all too few birds of a line that are bred consistently enough to know precisely which hidden traits the birds are carrying.

As a result, few birds are truly pure in color. You can notice this best on the breast and wings. Seldom will you see green Budgies that have an evenly colored green breast. You will generally find some dark or light feathers among the rest. And the markings on the wings are seldom perfect—not to speak of the overall appearance and conformation. So, good records are of signal importance in helping you breed superior birds.

Proper record keeping starts with the original breeding pair. Identify the birds with plastic color bands next to their permanent aluminum legbands. That way you will be able to tell at a glance which birds make up a pair when you isolate them for breeding.

When the young come, give them a band of the same color as the parents. Then, when all the young are placed together in an aviary, you will be able to identify their parents without problems. You can secure a private number from your bird club and order bands with your individual number, club and year issue number. You enter the appropriate information in your record book, along with other relevant data on the parents and offspring.

If you have to start a record book without knowing the parentage of the original birds, start with the externally visible features. The hidden traits will become apparent in future generations. Then you can work backward to establish the color factors and other traits of the original pair. Having established the geneology of all your birds after a few seasons, you will be able to constitute future matings to avoid unpleasant surprises. At the same time, you will have an overview of everything affecting the background of your birds and you will be able to trace the lineage of every young bird hatched.

Below is an extract from a good geneology.

In addition to the record book (or instead of it), you can establish a card index on your birds. Make up a card on each bird and keep it in a metal box. Arrange the cards in numerical order by band numbers, or by family lineage. A typical card might carry the following information:

Band number:	416
Color band:	red
Coloration:	white-cobalt
Hatched:	June 30, 1983
Sex:	male
Band no. (father)	146
Band no. (mother)	212
Color (father)	mauve/white
Color (mother)	skyblue/white
Remarks:	Bird sold to Jim Johnson for $20.

You can, of course, expand the information put on the card to fit your needs. For example, you could include deviations, health status, feathering, etc.

A bird with a proper family tree is not a drug on the market that brings only a few dollars. When you sell a bird with good records behind it, it will outsell similar birds without records. A serious breeder values a well-kept individual record for saving him time and trouble because he doesn't have to puzzle out hidden color factors. In England, real premiums are being paid for quality birds of good background. A standard green with good records brings between 15 and 30 pounds sterling—or a good 300 percent increase above normal prices. The buyer pays the premium for the assurance of getting first-rate stock. So you can see that the extra time needed to breed in a cage and keep good records pays off in the end.

Banding for a Breeding Program

Once young birds are a week old, band them with closed aluminum leg bands. They must be installed early because they have to be slid onto the leg. They remain there for life.

Installing the metal bands is described on page 63.

Plastic or metal color bands can be added later. They don't have to be slid onto the leg, but are clamped around it. They can be changed if you want to mate a bird with a new partner.

Common Breeding Misconceptions

Some beginners harbor some rather odd misconceptions about breeding Budgies. Often, they believe that all one must do is to get a cage and some nest boxes, put a couple of pairs of Budgerigars inside and young birds will come rolling out like cars on an assembly line. Sure, they know that you have to give the birds seed and water and a bit of clean sand now and then, but after all, any assembly line needs some input. They buy five pairs and count on 20 eggs per season, each. So they figure to have 100 young to sell at the end of the season.

Experienced breeders sadly shake their heads at this line of reasoning. Any breeder certainly has days when he wishes things would be this simple. And, true, there can be a season when everything goes right and reality closely approaches the dream.

But even the best breeder has a bad season. Bad luck can catch up with anyone.

Basically, however, breeding good birds is a question of patient care, including love of the birds and the work involved in keeping them. It means devoting one's spare time to real work. I can't emphasize strongly enough that without real dedication to the hobby, birds will be neglected and with the first stroke of bad luck, the would-be hobbyist will seek other diversions.

What can you reasonably expect? Look for the first egg seven to 10 days after putting the pair in the breeding cage. You should get an average of five eggs from the first hatch and seven to 10 from the second.

However, a good breeder doesn't set his expectations too high. He is proud of a high average hatching record, and he is able to accept a season full of bad luck because he knows he doesn't have full control of all the variables. No one has that!

Let me sum up some of these variables. A pair can "go on strike" and show no interest in producing eggs. Eggs can be infertile. Young can die at hatch or shortly after. Birds can get sick or die. Parents can eat their own eggs. And the list can go on.

Bad luck, of course, is not altogether out of the breeder's control. But to keep the upper hand, he has to devote constant attention and care and never let up on his love for his hobby.

To be totally honest, the devoted hobbyist doesn't even want things to go totally smoothly. He doesn't want to operate a bird factory. There is no fun and no challenge in that.

Medication

In general, it's better not to doctor Budgies too much. A bird that exhibits serious disease symptoms, deviations, or malformations ought to be humanely destroyed. That saves needless grief and trouble, not only for the breeder himself but also for others who might buy a bad bird.

When serious problems arise and especially when you fear an outbreak of communicable disease, consult a veterinarian immediately. You don't want to risk danger to all of your stock. Your veterinarian can put you in touch with specialists if the need arises.

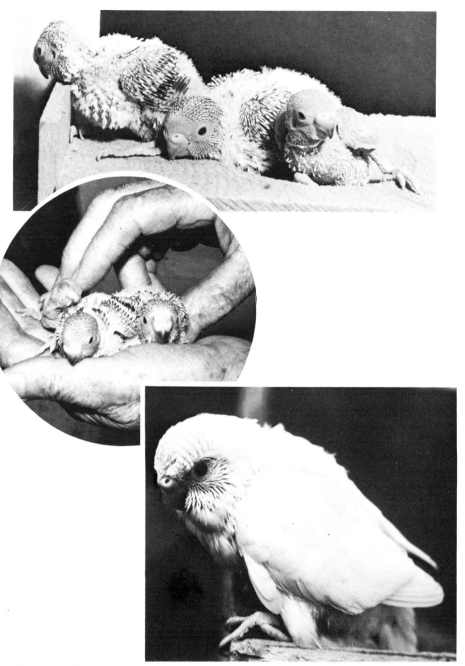

Like most small birds, Budgies grow very rapidly. The three nestlings in the photo above are two weeks old and well along in feather development. The two larger birds at left are also two weeks old and provide a striking contrast to the hatchling shown with them. The youngster below is 28 days old and growing nicely. *Photos by author*

Breeding Condition

Budgies are in top breeding condition during their second and third years. Outwardly and internally, they are completely developed at that age. Avoid mating two young birds or two old birds together. Instead, give an older male or female a young mate.

Beginning breeders must be aware that Budgies mature gradually. They often worry when they note that the young they raised are lighter in color than their parents and that they are less developed. The worry is unnecessary. As the birds mature further, new breeders discover that the colors darken and become stronger. This, however, is not necessarily true for light-colored birds, where wavy markings on the back and wings are not desirable. One may find that these become more pronounced as the birds grow older. And yellow Budgies may gradually develop a green haze over their feathering.

Vigilance is Important

Checking the nest boxes every two or three days from the moment you expect the first egg must become second nature. Do it yourself; you need the personal insight into how things are going and the birds need to learn to recognize their keeper. In that way, they will become used to that fellow who peers into their home and handles them from time to time.

Look for and remove broken eggs, infertile eggs, and dead young. Removing infertile eggs is not that urgent, however. But don't assume you need to leave them as support for newly hatched birds—a practice frequently used by Canary breeders. Budgie nests are roomier and the young may lie some distance from each other and remaining unhatched eggs. Furthermore, a brood of Budgie young almost always includes an "older brother or sister" that will protect the younger hatchlings.

Check the crop of all young for indications of how well they are being fed by their parents. A young bird that feels relatively light-bodied and seems to get insufficient food should be transferred to another nest box where the parents are more ambitious.

You can avoid a host of troubles, especially in summer, by keeping nest boxes scrupulously clean. The moist droppings that build up in the nests are a good breeding place for summertime bugs, mites, and lice. The bottom of the nest absolutely may not become a wet, sticky mess. Now and then, spray with a safe insecticide. Take care to include the back wall and especially the seams in the spraying operation.

Once a group of young has left the nest, disinfect the nest boxes in boiling water, treat them with Lysol, and preferably coat them inside and out with natural chalk. You also can use creosote for sanitizing.

Budgies can be extremely messy. Not only can they cover the nests with droppings, they also can cause a mess in feeding the young. This is due to the peculiar way Budgies feed their young. They feed the young from their crop after having let the food mix with digestive juices. Then, they pump the food back from their own beak into the waiting beaks of the young. It can happen that a parent bird hasn't mastered the feeding technique properly or can't feed properly because of a small deviation of the beak. Or a parent bird may be overly ambitious in feeding a young one.

The resulting mess defies the imagination. The young can be dirtied from head to toe. The head and beak, especially, can be caked with goo, so that the young look like monsters. The disadvantage is more than cosmetic. The caked mess hampers beak growth in that the upper mandible is stunted while the lower one keeps growing. As a result, the young don't get enough food and fail to grow properly. Even if they mature, they keep having difficulties eating. The lower mandible grows into a dish shape and the upper one slips inside it when the bird tries to eat.

You can try to remedy the problem by moving young from messy feeders to other nests. If that's impossible or impractical, clean off the messy heads twice a day. If the lower mandible grows excessively, you can trim it, and thus give the upper one the opportunity to develop properly.

Breeding stock should be selected for vigor as well as for pleasing color and conformation.

van Herk

Whether you keep one or two Budgies as pets or maintain extensive aviaries, always keep a sharp lookout for any sign of disease or disorder. Treating a problem early often determines the fate of affected birds.   *Top photo courtesy Aquariums Inc., Chatsworth, California.*
Bottom photo A. van Herk

5

Diseases, Disorders and Parasites

Feather Picking

Feather picking, which causes so much grief for Canary breeders, also occurs in Budgerigars. Picking is a misleading term. What happens is that feathers are chewed off at the "roots," and sometimes they are even swallowed. Old birds do it to the young ones—or sometimes to one another. Especially the head feathers are targeted.

The cause appears to lie in a vitamin deficiency, particularly vitamin F. However, it takes more than a vitamin supplement (including vitamin F) to solve the problem. It may be that breeders tend to give the supplement to the victims rather than the perpetrator of the deed, who—after all—indicates by his bad habit that he has a need for these vitamins. But then, it obviously takes more than vitamins to cure a bad habit.

Basically, feather picking is a sign of boredom, especially so for psittacines. If you give birds something to gnaw on—like a fresh willow or birch branch every day, feather picking quickly ceases. Also, you can give them something to climb on for diversion. And by providing rearing food, you can stimulate new feather growth in the birds that lost feathers.

If parents pull the feathers of their young, there is an obvious solution: distribute the young among other nests. If that isn't possible, put the young in a separate nest box hung next to the original one. That will generally motivate the female, usually the culprit of the pair, to begin a new brood. Dad, who usually doesn't take part in the picking, will continue caring for the previous brood.

For older birds, try a broth of groats as a substitute for the regular drinking water.

Splayed Legs

Splayed legs, a condition you see from time to time, refers to legs that are set far apart, so that the bird can't pull them under its body. The cause can be a neonatal weakness of the bones, but if you have been furnishing cod liver oil or a good multiple vitamin-mineral supplement during the breeding period, weak bones (called rickets) are an unlikely explanation.

There may be a simpler cause—a new, smooth nest bottom. Young birds may not be able to get good footing on the smooth surface. They may lie splay-legged in the nest for a long time, causing their legs to grow outward. Another cause may be a late-hatched bird that gets the worst of it from the other hatchlings.

While the splay-legged bird still lies in the nest, you can correct the problem by tying its legs together with a thin piece of string. Run the string from the right leg underneath the wings and across the back to the left leg. Be careful not to tie this string so tight that it interferes with the bird's blood circulation. By the time the bird leaves the nest, the problem should be corrected.

French Molt

This discussion of French molt is one of the most detailed in this book, and appropriately so. French molt is, undoubtedly, the worst illness that a Budgie breeder can experience among his birds. It can ruin the joy of an entire season or even destroy the incentive to keep Budgies forever.

Even a beginning breeder can recognize a victim of French molt. Early signs of trouble are dropped pin feathers. Then you'll notice birds that can't fly at the time they ought to be ready to leave the nest, even though there seems to be no reason why they aren't able to fly. Tail and wing pin feathers are partially missing at that time and pin feathers continue to drop.

Dropped pin feathers look weak and curled. If you take one in your hand, you notice that it lacks resilience and feels weak. The last centimeter of the quill is filled with a red liquid. This appearance of "bloody pins" in young birds is a sure sign that French molt is a problem.

Birds with French molt move by climbing around the cage. It takes months before the birds have enough pin feathers to fly. Those born late in the season have poor prospects because they don't have a chance to recover before the onset of winter.

Beginners, especially, should never buy birds that have had French molt. There always is a good chance that they will produce more birds with the same problem. Your best protection is to always buy from a reliable dealer or breeder. Watch to see that you get birds that look strong and well developed, have good feathering, and are a normal weight. Birds with French molt almost always weigh less than completely healthy birds.

There are a number of theories attempting to explain the cause of French molt. Most of the explanations agree that it isn't really a true "illness." And many of them hold that a basic cause is inbreeding that has gone too far.

People who fear inbreeding point to the fact that new Budgie blood has not been imported for some time, so that all captive birds have become more or less related. This, they say, has caused a weakening, which can lead to French molt under certain circumstances. Therefore, people should keep "freshening up" the blood of their Budgies by buying or otherwise acquiring unrelated birds. The theory holds that there are many outwardly normal birds who carry the tendency toward French molt. When these birds are mated, the tendency is intensified and outward signs of problems appear. More technically, French molt is triggered by a recessive gene that must be received from both parents.

Another theory holds that the illness is caused by weak parents. In other words, it would be nothing more than a weakness inherited by the young, manifested by the symptom of French molt.

Dr. Mannaerts, a breeder from Bladel in the Netherlands, believes firmly that you can avoid the problem altogether by not breeding with any birds that have small gray or black cross-stripes in the pin feathers. You can easily note these stripes—especially on the light colored pin feathers—by spreading the tail and wings. The stripes, supposedly, indicate carriers of the problem.

In a recent interview, Mannaerts pointed to his record of complete freedom from French molt in his aviaries, while another, neighboring breeder had dozens of cases. This breeder had not "freshened up" his bloodlines in an earlier season and had not paid any attention to the tell-tale stripes. Be that as it may, Mannaers has been breeding Budgies for years and has a reputation among breeders for the high-quality birds he produces.

In a way, Mannaerts's theory also includes the notion that inbreeding promotes the development of French molt—even if it isn't a direct result of this practice. He believes that you can avoid the problem by not breeding from birds that don't have it.

The late Mr. H. Van Dijk of Eindhoven in the Netherlands believes that French molt is caused by parasites—specifically the larvae of a type of moth. These moths deposit their eggs in the droppings found in the nest and in the seams and walls of the nest box. The resulting larvae feed on the horn of the feathers and thereby interfere with their growth. This moth can in fact be found in some nest boxes. It looks like the ordinary clothes moth, but the wings have brownish spots instead of being silver-grey.

Van Dijk also was well-regarded in the Budgie fancy. He had been breeding for 30 years, had bought, sold, bred and traded tens of thousands of them, and was the founder of a bird park. He claims never to have had a problem with French molt in his aviaries. His theory rejects the inbreeding hypothesis totally without implying that inbreeding isn't a problem. Van Dijk saw inbreeding as a problem that has nothing to do with French molt. Still, his theory does not do away with the notion that a bird which is weak by nurture or by nature would show the effects of French molt to a greater degree than a completely healthy bird.

Van Dijk's theory is supported by the fact that birds with the illness can develop into normal birds after the pin feathers of the tail and wings have grown back. The theory also implies that the continuous molt that occurs in older birds is caused by breeding or housing them in infected nest boxes.

The upshot of this theory is that absolute cleanliness in the nest boxes can completely prevent the occurrence of French molt. Nest boxes would have to be serviced daily and cleaned after each brood by boiling them in water and disinfecting them with insecticides.

Dr. M.D.S. Armour, an English Budgie expert, doesn't recognize French molt as a true illness or disease. In his book, *Exhibition Budgerigars,* he rejects inbreeding as a cause, but expresses the belief that the problem is caused by a type of mite. This mite is said to resemble the grain mite. It gnaws a path to the roots of the pin feathers and causes an infection that inhibits their growth. The infection irritates the skin, causing the bird to bite and pull at the feathers, thereby aggravating the condition.

Dr. Armour is certain that the mite saps the feathers' ability to grow. He points to the dark mass that can be found at the bottom of the shaft of feathers that have fallen out.

Many breeders accept Dr. Armour's theory because it accounts for a number of symptoms associated with French molt. The dirty, red fluid in the shaft could be caused by blood associated with the infection and the dirt could be the excrement of the mite. Because the mite infection could occur at any time, it is consistent with finding cases of French molt in the second and third brood as easily as in the first. It also explains why certain birds are affected to a worse degree than others. And it accounts for cases of continuous molt in older birds, which, naturally, can also be infected by the mite. Therefore, if one could prevent mite infestation, problems with French molt could possibly be avoided.

As a cure, Dr. Armour recommends chloroxylenolum, an antiseptic that is safe for use with pets. He recommends removing all infested feathers and then dipping birds in a bath of warm water to which a tablespoon of chloroxylenolum has been added. Repeat the treatment every three or four days, and infested birds will recover completely, Dr. Armour says. The repeat treatment in a chloroxylenolum solution serves to kill mite eggs and larvae. The birds aren't damaged by the treatment, even if they get some of the solution in their mouths and eyes.

Put treated birds in a cage without sand on the floor for several hours. After they have dried, they will look fresh and fit.

Apart from French molt described herein, molting is a normal physiological process. This photo shows the molting pattern for primary flight feathers.

van Herk

Molting pattern for tail feathers.

van Herk

Dr. Armour also says not to use birds with bloody pin feathers for breeding until they have been treated and have recovered fully. If you breed from affected birds, you will almost certainly find that one or both parents had the tell-tale bloody pin feathers. According to Dr. Armour, you will never raise birds with French molt if you treat all breeding stock with chloroxylenolum before breeding.

French molt sneaks up on your flock without warning and must be prevented at any cost. This is a clear case of where an ounce of prevention is better than a pound of cure. The preventive recommended by Dr. Armour is disinfecting the cages with sulphur-fume or spraying them with chloroxylenolum twice per week.

Not everyone considers chloroxylenolum a complete solution, although most English breeders report good results. For example, C. Enehjelm, the director of the Helsinki Zoo, has his reservations—which I pass on without comment.

American scientists believe that French molt is a dietary deficiency caused by improper feeding. They also believe that the trouble also has a hereditary form.

Dr. Steiner of the University of Zurich (Switzerland) agrees with the hereditary explanation and calls the problem a type of genetic degeneration. The worst cases of French molt—birds that never learn to fly—are called DD cases by Dr. Steiner. Dr. Steiner gives a genetic designation (or genotype) of Dd to birds that were affected in their youth but later learned to fly. He calls normal birds "dd" types.

Using this model, Dr. Steiner has shown that the putative factors for French molt follow Mendelian law. (This law is explained in the chapters on genetics.) Accordingly, Dd birds are heterozygous for the disease. This means that they don't have the disease themselves but are carriers of it.

Dr. Steiner holds that French molt cannot be caused by a dietary deficiency. His feeding experiments showed that Dd-type birds continued to exhibit symptoms of French molt after being placed on a diet rich in vitamins and other dietary supplements.

Now that you've read a wide range of theories about French molt, I'll present the one that makes most sense to me. It is put forward by the American Budgie expert, Cessa Feyerabend, who believes that nutritional deficiency in the young Budgie plays a major role in the development of French molt. The theory is supported by the newest research findings, which indicate that nutritional deficiency most certainly is involved.

Feyerabend's theory supposes that this trouble starts when the feeding behavior of parent birds or the so-called "Budgie milk" they provide is not adequate over a period of time. This milk, made up of half-digested food, is rich in fats and proteins. If certain proteins or protein precursors (called amino acids) are missing, then the young are supposed to exhibit French molt symptoms. Even if the deficiency is corrected later on, the symptoms are supposed to remain.

For proof, Feyerabend points to the fact that some birds in a brood may have French molt, while others are free of it. She attributes this situation to the large difference in age that sometimes occurs within a brood. And she postulates that the sick birds were deprived of Budgie milk of a certain composition at a time when they needed it critically. Instead, they received milk of a composition suited to the needs of their brothers and sisters.

Budgie milk of the wrong composition could be present as the result of negligence, inbreeding, or excessive breeding. A second cause could be a supply of the wrong kind of seed or too-old seed. Thirdly, vitamin deficiency could be involved. Experiments have shown that vitamins from the B and G groups are essential for feather growth. Fourth, extremely warm weather during the feeding period could be a possible cause if the parents then don't feed the young properly.

To avoid providing the wrong seed, Feyerabend advises against using red millet and old seed that may have lost some of its critical feeding value. Instead, Feyerabend recommends white millet mixed with cod liver oil and powdered beer yeast. She uses a tablespoon of the yeast in five pounds of millet.

I add the following advice: 1. Buy and breed only totally healthy birds; 2. Thoroughly clean and disinfect nest boxes so that parasites don't get a chance to develop; 3. Always furnish a properly constituted diet that provides the proper vitamins. A supplement that includes a protein rich in Vitamin A is also strongly recommended.

Parasite Control

A number of parasites can infest nest boxes. I have already mentioned mites and moth larvae; now let's consider fly larvae.

Fly larvae are most common in summer, when they develop easily in the wet droppings in nest boxes, where the flies lay their eggs. The larvae don't seem to bother the birds directly, but it doesn't require much imagination to realize that they don't do the birds any good. An infested box soon gets to be a messy place. So, in summer, take special care to see that the wet droppings are removed as speedily as possible. Scrape them off the floor and disinfect. Spread a fresh, thin layer of sawdust before replacing the eggs or young in the nest.

The so-called "red louse" or "bird louse" is harder to eliminate. It really is a type of mite that some believe to be related to the supposed causative agent of French molt. It isn't really red either—more nearly gray. But once it has sucked its fill of blood, its body swells and the ingested blood shines red through the thin skin.

During the day, the louse remains in the cracks of nest boxes. At night, it stages raids on the young and even the older birds sleeping on their perches. These raids are most damaging, largely from loss of blood. Affected birds lose their zest for life and look so depressed that you can tell at a glance what the trouble is.

This parasite, also, can be fought by cleaning and disinfecting nest boxes and using antiseptics and insecticides. Nest boxes should be cleaned in boiling water, disinfected, and whitewashed with natural chalk or treated with creosote. Prevention is better than cure. Taking preventive measures keeps the louse from gaining a foothold.

Psittacosis and Ornithosis

The two most dangerous illnesses of Budgies—especially from the viewpoint of transmissibility to humans—are psittacosis and ornithosis. The two diseases are closely related to each other, with psittacosis the more dangerous for handlers.

Budgies are basically healthy birds with good natural resistance. Given good care, the birds generally don't suffer much from disease. But psittacosis, when it occurs, is a serious problem that should not be taken lightly.

Psittacosis is a communicable disease of birds. It is not limited to Budgerigars, but also occurs in domestic birds and tropical birds, including birds of the finch family, pigeons, ducks, turkeys and certain sea birds.

Birds with psittacosis may exhibit typical symptoms or be silent carriers that look healthy while shedding germs and infecting other birds. The method of transmission is through the droppings or nasal secretions. Humans can be carriers, too.

Humans infected with psittacosis have symptoms reminiscent of pneumonia or typhus, with high fever and frequently spots on the abdomen. Not all cases reach this dangerous stage; often, symptoms are mild and disappear quickly. The disease almost always is picked up from birds; there are practically no known cases of transmission between humans.

Few people die from psittacosis, and fear of bird diseases should not keep people from the hobby. The best lesson to draw from the human risk is to promote cleanliness. It seems reasonable that people generally get infected by breathing in dust containing dried droppings. So clean the cage bottom regularly and cover it with clean sand to minimize this problem.

The birds themselves exhibit serious symptoms in the respiratory organs. Nasal secretions are common. So is a type of diarrhea that is green, slimy, and sticky—generally causing the feathers around the cloaca to stick together.

The remedy of choice since 1959 has been aureomycin. American research proved this antibiotic effective for treating psittacosis at that time. Aureomycin can be purchased premixed into seed, or it can be bought in powder form for use in the drinking water. The yellow powder is available at drug stores; quantities no larger than the head of a matchstick should be

106

Warmth and isolation are vital requirements for the recovery of sick birds. Thermostatically-controlled hospital cages are widely used by aviculturists and veterinarians when illness strikes.

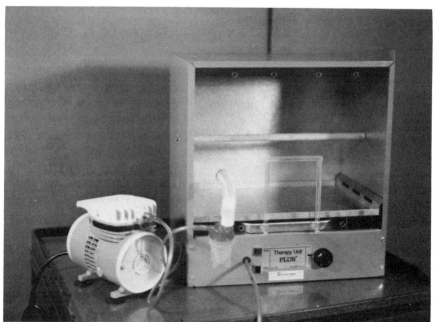

This hospital cage provides total control of the environment within the unit.

Courtesy, Corner's Ltd., Kalamazoo, Michigan

mixed into about a pint of water. Furnish medicated water for several weeks when psittacosis is suspected. Within that time, infected birds should have recovered and carriers should no longer pose a danger. More recently a newer antibiotic, chlortetracycline, has proven even more effective than aureomycin. Ask your veterinarian for instructions for use.

Any bird exhibiting symptoms of psittacosis should immediately be placed in isolation. Don't try to save it, even if it is from your most valuable stock. The dangers inherent in keeping the sick bird around far outweigh the value that any one bird represents.

Don't assume that every bird with a runny nose and diarrhea has psittacosis. A number of other illnesses could cause the same symptoms. Enteritis is a prime example.

Enteritis

Although the symptoms of enteritis may resemble psittacosis, enteritis doesn't present a danger to humans. The one intestinal infection of Budgerigars that can be transmitted to humans is the type caused by paratyphus bacilli. Laboratory work is needed to make a differential diagnosis.

Standard enteritis is an intestinal infection, and affected birds exhibit a sticky, green diarrhea. Birds with serious cases are deathly ill. Enteritis is highly contagious and in a single aviary you can have dozens of cases at the same time or close together. There are known instances where a breeder lost his entire stock inside several weeks.

Early symptoms are dull looking feathers that tend to be loose. The sick bird flips its tail from time to time, sleeps a lot with half-closed eyes, and is listless and depressed. It breathes laboriously and seems to lose all fear of man.

The diarrhea is a later symptom. When it occurs, the bird spends a lot of time on the cage bottom. Producing droppings appears to be difficult and accompanied by hefty movements of the tail. The cloaca seems to evert, and the feathers around it show the same stickiness as with psittacosis. Sometimes the droppings contain blood. If that happens, it is a sure sign that an intestinal illness is involved. If diarrhea is accompanied with nasal secretions, then the problem is more likely to be psittacosis.

With enteritis—and certainly in serious cases—it is recommended to humanely destroy affected birds and burn the carcasses. In any case, the ill bird should be quarantined. I recommend isolating any sick bird; in a hospital cage, you will be able to study the symptoms calmly, and you will eliminate the chance of infecting other birds.

If enteritis is suspected, thoroughly disinfect the cage of the suspect bird. Use Lysol or chloroxylenolum. Bathe the bird itself in chloroxylenolum as well. Be extremely careful not to let intestinal diseases spread.

108

In most instances Budgies are normally healthy with reasonable care well into old age. Being aware of potential illness and injury problems prepares the Budgie fancier to adequately handle any emergency.

Harkema

109

Colds

If Budgerigars catch colds diarrhea may be a symptom—an added difficulty for the breeder who tries to diagnose his birds' illnesses. The diarrhea may truly mimic the symptoms of enteritis even with an "ordinary" cold. A bird with a cold may also sit puffed up on the cage floor like a bird with enteritis—its feathers loose and dull.

Two remedies can help Budgerigars—and other birds—with colds. One is a good antibiotic (tetracycline); the second is heat.

Tetracycline (or tyclocine) is available from any drugstore. It is a yellow powder that should be mixed with the seed and fed to the bird.

Use tetracycline according to the directions on groats or oatmeal if birds are used to these foods. Don't start sick birds on new foods, however. You don't want to upset their system further with indigestion.

Respiratory difficulties can come about through all kinds of problems: drafts, low temperatures, exposure to various bacteria, fungi, and viruses, vitamin A deficiency, and stress. In all cases consult an avian veterinarian.

Heat can have wondrous results for birds with colds. Put the ailing bird in a hospital cage and place it in a dark, warm spot; about 61-76 degrees F. If necessary, cover the cage with a cloth. Birds can stand a considerable amount of heat, so don't be too afraid to get the patient too hot. Sprinkle some seed in the cage and put a dish of fresh water in it. Tonics can also help.

Colds often are caused by drafts. Especially when you keep birds indoors, be careful to avoid drafts, for example when opening or closing doors and windows. Also avoid sudden temperature changes, as when you move a bird from a heated room to an outside aviary, or vice versa.

Be especially aware of this after a bird recovers. If it recuperated in a warm cage, don't immediately put it back into an outside aviary. There is every chance of the bird suffering a relapse worse than the original cold. So accustom the recovered bird slowly to the temperature change. First move the hospital cage a distance from the heat source. Then put it into an unheated room before finally moving the recovered bird back outside.

Cannibalism

Budgerigars, by and large, are good-natured birds that don't bother others of their kind and only rarely get into rather mild fights. It does happen on rare occasions that a bird is overcome by truly murderous inclinations. This happens more rarely with males than with females.

The victims of this ire are the bird's own young, young from other nests, and often the male. The behavior occurs suddenly and apparently without any motivation. The cause is unknown.

When too many birds share the same space, illness and injury have a "foot in the door." Always avoid overcrowding and provide new facilities for increased populations or find new homes for extra birds.

Photo by author

Fledglings about to leave the nest, such as these, are occasionally attacked and killed by an older bird. When such a killer is discovered in any population it should be humanely destroyed at once. *Wissink*

The solution to such a murderous turn of events is to humanely destroy the perpetrator. Do it promptly—before the bird can inflict extensive damage in your aviary.

Vertigo

Vertigo—or dizziness—is a disturbance of the equilibrium that can occur in all psittacines. Sick birds seem to lose all ability to judge distances. In the earliest stage, they keep missing their target as they try to jump from one perch to another. They also have difficulty in maintaining their balance. In a later stage they stop trying to perch and stay on the cage floor, often bending their head backwards in a cramped position. The bird eats less and less and finally dies.

In the early stage, supplementing the birds' ration with calcium and vitamin C seems to help. In later stages, there's nothing much you can do to help.

As far as one knows, vertigo is not contagious. The problem often occurs in recently imported birds. In these cases, it probably can be attributed to improper care given en route and the sudden change in feed. Another cause appears to be excessive inbreeding.

Seizures

Budgerigars can suffer from sudden seizures. The bird falls from its perch to the bottom of the cage, where it makes twitching movements and usually dies after a short time. In zoos and bird parks the illness sometimes affects birds that have received the most meticulous care.

The cause of these seizures is unclear. Females are afflicted more often than males and it is more common among birds weakened by excessive inbreeding.

Some people attribute the problem to a fear of heights that afflict birds suddenly exposed to a big, roomy aviary after having been accustomed to the protection of a dense forest or a small cage. Others believe that summer heat is the cause. More likely, however, a sexual disturbance is involved. It has been found that seizures almost always strike birds deprived of a mate during their normal breeding season. The problem does not occur in colony breeding cages and aviaries.

Blindness

Blindness also appears to be the result of excessive inbreeding. The first symptoms of the onset of blindness is a tendency for the bird to turn its head because it can't see well (or at all) with the eye on the side where you happen to approach it. It tries to see with the good eye. But even this "good" eye suffers from increasingly poor sight, and in its efforts to see anyway, the bird keeps turning its head. Soon it is unable to find the perches and stumbles helplessly along the cage floor.

It is possible to maintain such a bird in a small cage because it will learn to find the seed dish without sight. But it is wiser and more humane to destroy the bird. A bird that pines away on a perch instead of flying about happily is a heart-rending sight for any bird fancier.

Tumors and Lameness

Tumors are a serious problem for which no effective cure has been found although birds that are supplemented with vitamins almost never develop such problems. When tumors appear on the breast of the Budgerigar, they probably are caused by keeping them a long time in a cage that is too small. They have too little exercise and their wing muscles degenerate. Tumors on the head look more like cancer tumors.

If tumors occur, lance them with a needle sterilized by boiling or heating them redhot under a flame. Squeeze out any dirt inside the swelling. Then sterilize the wound with mercurochrome. The bird survives this type of operation remarkably well. But the affected Budgerigar will tend to develop another tumor in a new location. Sometimes, it may also develop a fatty degeneration. Humanely dispose of such a bird because nothing will help it. The cause is a disturbance in glandular function. Ask your veterinarian for advice!

Wartlike excema on the head near the eyes and under the beak—the well-known scaly face, can be cured by applying penicillin as a salve. Isolate the affected bird till the cure is complete.

Swellings on the feet often are caused by mosquitos that suck the birds' blood while they sleep. These swellings are easily cured by making a few very small cuts using a properly disinfected razor blade. Treat the wounds with mercurochrome—not tincture of iodine because that stings too much! Then wrap the treated leg with a small adhesive bandage. You don't have to worry about removing the bandage later. The bird will remove it, or else it will just rub off naturally. This treatment prevents infection when the bird scratches around the cage floor with the sore leg. If you have any hesitations about doing this, it would be better to consult an experienced avian veterinarian.

I recommend mercurochrome to prevent infection in all types of wounds, whether caused by accidental injury or by a fight.

A bird that no longer can use its legs properly suffers from lameness. The cause is thought to be a sexual disturbance. The lameness worsens with time till finally the bird can no longer perch and starts lying on the floor, unable to so much as move its legs. For the rest, such a bird is completely healthy and even will continue to eat normally. Since lameness is incurable, it's kindest to humanely dispose of afflicted birds.

This ingenious unit is a feeder on one side and a nest box on the other.

van Herk

The feeding unit shown above is pictured here in actual use. Note that in this cage of young Budgies, both food and water utensils are safe from being fouled by droppings.

114

6

Food and Feeding

THE NATURAL DIET of Budgerigars on their home range in Australia consists principally of grass and weed seed. In captivity, the birds will continue to enjoy this type of food, of course. But the modern, cultivated Budgie has become accustomed to a menu consisting mainly of millet seed and white canary seed. They thrive on this and hardly need anything further in their diet.

The usual mix for Budgerigar seed is two-thirds millet and one-third canary seed, to which a bit of oatmeal and linseed is added. About a half cup of each additive is added to each pound of seed mix. Some breeders furnish millet and very little else as an economy. If the proper supplements are used, such a diet should be satisfactory.

Energy Requirements

Budgerigars have a great need for proteins, which must constitute 12 to 15 percent of their diet, according to research findings. That's why feeding just millet seed will not fulfill their requirements. Supplements therefore need to be rich in proteins.

Birds burn up more food in winter in order to maintain their body temperature. Therefore, they need to eat more—or to take in a food that's richer in fats and carbohydrates. That is why feeding more linseed during the winter months is a wise adjustment in the diet.

A properly constituted diet for Budgerigars needs to contain a proper balance of carbohydrates, proteins, fats, salt, and vitamins. White canary seed contains a somewhat larger percentage of fats and protein than millet seed. Millet seed contains more carbohydrates. The percentages are:

Seed	Carbohydrates	Fats	Proteins	Salt and Minerals
Canary seed	56.0	6.1	15.1	2.1
Millet	59.8	3.7	11.1	3.1
Linseed	22.3	34.2	21.5	5.6
Oats	59.7	4.9	10.4	2.8

It is, of course, impossible to constitute the Budgerigars diet to absolutely include all constituents in the proper proportions. But studying the table of constituents above teaches us that linseed contains a lot of minerals and fats. That makes it an extraordinarily good supplement during the winter, the molting season and the breeding season. Another good supplement for the breeding season is spray millet, which can be hung in the cage.

Other good supplements for Budgies are oatmeal, ground oats, small groats, as well as different types of seed intended for song birds. Budgerigars sometime have a dislike for one or more of these seeds and leave a certain type of seed uneaten. In that case, it is better not to furnish the rejected seed.

Make certain to provide sprouted seeds. Most Budgies love to eat sprouted grass seed, barley, clover seed, canary seed and rape seed. You can sprout the seed in separate ceramic dishes. Fill the dishes with sand and top that off with the seed. You can feed the contents of such a dish in a week's time. Refill the dish with seed so that you will have a constant supply.

Weed seeds are also highly recommended as supplements. Gather the weed seed in late summer and fall from empty lots, fallow fields, and roadside strips. Weeds grow there in abundance and gathering them is no problem.

Feeding Systems

Mix your own seeds and you can vary the menu according to the circumstances of the moment, and allow for the preferences and condition of your birds. That is a better system than furnishing the basic ration in one dish and various supplements in other dishes. Such double feeding takes unnecessary time and money. Especially if you have several breeding cages and aviaries, you would be wise to feed your birds as simply as possible.

A variety of containers can be used to furnish food. Place the containers so that fouling of the contents with bird droppings is minimized—particularly if you use open-top containers. For example, never place food under roosts.

Check on the available food daily. Shake the dish first to bring the hulls of the consumed seed to the surface and blow the hulls out of the dish. Then refill the dish if necessary.

Use a properly designed feeder for Budgies—like the one shown in the drawing. Budgies by nature can ruin a considerable amount of seed if they start messing around in open containers. You can build a proper container yourself with minimum carpentry skills. You can vary the interior design according to the number of birds to be served. Birds are literally forced to eat neatly and to waste little or no seed with such a feeder. Most of the hulls fall into the tray at the bottom and therefore don't fall onto the cage floor. You can make the feeder big enough to contain several pounds of seed, providing enough rations for an extended time. Finally, the seed in the feeder can't be fouled with droppings.

Water Requirements and Utensils

Budgerigars don't drink much water. Some breeders go so far as to say the birds can go without drinking water for weeks or months, but that certainly is not true.

The birds definitely need to be supplied with fresh water every day. You can make a water dish out of an empty glass jar. Invert it, and set it on a simple frame of wood or stones in a galvanized or glass tray. After filling the jar, put the wood frame on the lip, invert the tray on top of that, and then invert the whole thing. Alternatively, you can buy commercial waterers that are handy and sanitary.

Grit

Grit is part of the required menu of Budgies. It helps them grind up their food and aids in digestion. The main ingredients of grit are calcium and charcoal. The bird uses the calcium not only to help form egg shells during the breeding season but also to build its own bones.

There are several types of commercial grit on the market. The formulated products are preferable because in addition to calcium, they contain charcoal, iron, iodine, and magnesium. You can also furnish ground oyster shell, boiled, fresh, finely ground egg shell, mineralized lime or cuttlebone which contains valuable minerals. But I recommend the commercially mixed grit. Some breeders also furnish ground sea shells.

Greens

As mentioned earlier, sprouted seeds are relished by Budgies and provide valuable nutritional components. Other green food also is very useful. It supplies vitamins as well as salt—essential for Budgerigars. Carrots, spinach, endive, Brussels sprouts, and curly kale are all highly recommended for feeding Budgies.

Budgies must learn to eat greens. Start them by adding finely cut greens into the seed ration. Once they get the taste of it, they will also eat greens hung in the cage.

Don't overdo it. Too much and stale greens are harmful.

Vitamins

All bird food must contain vitamins. Sunlight and greens are the main sources during the summer. In the winter, greens, cod liver oil or a quality vitamin-mineral supplement supply birds' vitamin needs.

The term "vitamin" derives from the Latin *vita,* meaning life. Vitamins are essential parts of the human and animal diet; deficiencies of one or more can cause illness and even death. For example, scurvy in humans is caused by eating a diet deficient in vitamin C. This illness used to plague crusaders, whalers, mariners and anyone else who took long sea journeys. Science has identified a great number of vitamins—the best known are vitamins A, B, C and D. (B and D are composed of various substances; complex.)

Vitamin A is required for growth and disease resistance.

Vitamin B promotes health and steadies the nerves.

Vitamin C is essential for good appetite and strength. It is contained in fresh vegetables and fruits. Deficiencies of vitamin C cause skin diseases.

Vitamin D promotes good bone formation, among other things. Deficiencies cause rachitis. Birds can only utilize vitamin D_3.

Vitamin E promotes fertility.

There are many other vitamins in addition to these five. They are often classed into various types. For example, there are some 14-plus different types of vitamin B, each of which have their own use in vitamin nutrition. Going into detail would take us too far afield, however.

Sources of vitamins for birds are sunlight, cod liver oil, a good quality multiple vitamin-mineral supplement, powdered beer malt, and greens like sprouted seed, vegetables, and fruits. I can't emphasize the great utility of cod liver oil. It is especially important to provide during the colder months. In summer other vitamin sources become more available. Still, many breeders routinely provide cod liver oil throughout the entire year. I have already remarked that birds that get cod liver oil seldom or never encounter egg binding, because their general condition tends to be first rate.

Mixing cod liver oil into the seed, at the rate of one half teaspoon per pound is recommended. You can mix it in easily by stirring.

Feed the mix immediately or store it for several days. Storing it allows the oil to penetrate the seed more completely. Once the cod liver oil dries, it loses its odor. Store the mix in a cool, dark place. In addition to cod liver oil, also furnish a tablespoonful of beer malt powder per five pounds of seed.

During the breeding and molting seasons, cod liver oil is particularly recommended. It also should be furnished during the cold of winter. Be careful with the cod liver oil, however, when parents are feeding young. The fat in the oil could upset the young birds, raising the possibility of diarrhea. If you want to furnish vitamins at that time regardless, use one of the commercial vitamin preparations—just one or two drops mixed in a pound of food.

Keeping It Simple

A beginner in the "science of Budgerigars" might conclude from the sections on feeding that composing a menu is a complicated and difficult task. That would be quite a mistaken conclusion. Budgies do well with a simple diet composed of a mix of millet, canary seed and some linseed—supplemented with grit and now and then some greens and cod liver oil.

The other-named seeds should be considered extras; you can feed them if you want, and they will provide some advantages. But for the proper thriving of Budgerigars, they are not essential.

The basic menu can be fed all year. You don't have to worry about providing anything special, even during the breeding season. It will suffice for both young and old birds.

BUDGIE-KEEPING ESSENTIALS: Top row (from left)—standard seed mixture which includes millet, canary seed and oats, egg food, a hygrometer to measure moisture in the aviary. Center—Cuttle bone furnishes essential minerals and also provides necessary diversions. Bottom row (from left)—egg shells for calcium and other minerals, grit, a thermometer. *van Herk*

Just for the fun of it, it's nice to pick out a young bird from those you've bred to be a pleasant pet in your home. *Wissink*

7

Training Budgies

I STILL REMEMBER how as a child I stood transfixed before a Budgerigar sitting on a swing in front of a fortune teller's tent. At a signal from its master, the bird pulled a letter from a nearby bin and handed it to the young man or woman who had paid to know the present, the past, or the future as described in the letter. Today you still can see Budgerigars at carnivals, doing unbelievable stunts. They climb on ladders, engage in every kind of sport on command, ride in cars, perform somersaults—in short, they perform as accomplished acrobats. These examples show that Budgerigars are "intelligent" birds, which possibly still have unexplored talents that may not have received enough attention.

If you raise Budgies in an outside aviary, you probably will want to have a charming pet bird in your living room as well. With just a little effort, you can make a Budgie into a delightful companion. This chapter does not suggest you make your birds into carnival performers, but this book could not be considered complete without some comment on this side of the Budgie hobby.

Finger Taming and Talking

Did you know that Budgies can learn to speak? They are not serious competition for African Greys and other renowned talking birds, but one can teach Budgies to say a few words.

Experience has shown that male Budgerigars usually are the best talkers, although many females speak quite well. The best results are attained by starting lessons early. For that purpose, select a bird several days before it leaves the nest. Put it in a roomy cage in the living room. Put some millet on

121

These Budgies are in training for competition. Like birds that are trained to be pleasant, finger-tame pets, a confident attitude around people is essential.   *Photo by author*

the floor of the cage since the youngster still has to learn to eat on its own. Make sure that it does so during the first few days; if not, feed it by hand. Make up wads of soaked seed and put them in the bird's mouth.

Then, finger-tame the bird. That can be done quite quickly if you handle the bird calmly, talk to it quietly, and avoid unexpected or sudden movements. At that stage, the bird can't fly yet, or can't fly well. You can take advantage of this. First, teach the bird to sit on a thin stick or on your finger. Push your finger or the stick softly against the bird's breast in a way that gives it the choice of either sitting on your finger or falling off its perch. Naturally, the Budgie will choose the first alternative.

Once a Budgie is finger-tamed, the rest goes easy. In a relatively short time, you will have a mini-parrot, which will let you stroke its crop with every bit as much pleasure as its big brothers exhibit.

The talking lessons, meanwhile, will have been going on full speed. Clearly recite several words or brief phrases. Preferably, have a woman do it, because a woman's voice tends to be clearer than a man's. Of course, patience is the first requirement of such talking lessons.

Visitors will love your house pets. Their appeal can help make the keeping of Budgies even more popular than it already is. That's to your advantage. The demand for new Budgies, naturally, depends on their popularity.

Be sure to keep a Budgie in training out of hearing range of others. Don't place a bird of the opposite sex in the cage; that would give the bird other ideas that constitute unbeatable competition for talking lessons.

Designate a specific person to give the talking lessons. Start off with just short words, like "daddy, polly, hi, bye-bye," etc. If you were fortunate to select a bird with more than average talent, then you can expand its repertoire as far as it will go. If you find a bird of lesser talent, then select another one and try again. Not all Budgerigars are talkers.

A Climbing Structure

With just a little imagination and skill you can construct an attractive climbing structure. You can build ladders, a bell, a swing, and whatever else you can design. A cage might even be unnecessary if your Budgie has access to such a structure because the Budgie will stick to its territory. It may make some side tours through the house, but it will always return to the structure.

Part II

The Theoretical Side

Both colony breeding and pair breeding have positive and negative aspects. The prospective Budgie breeder should consider both in view of his objectives to determine which would best suit him. *Photo by author*

Developing the best quality in a line of Budgerigars requires constant observation and evaluation of both the breeding stock and their pedigrees.

8

Genetics and the Budgie Breeder

REMEMBER the hobbyist that started breeding with just a pair of birds—the one featured in the first chapters of this book? He has since developed into a full-blown breeder.

The "Street-Wise" Breeder

He has built cages and aviaries. He has tried out five different types of nest boxes. Finally he has developed a sixth type of his own, and claims to have achieved wondrous results. He has developed his own feeding scheme. He laughs at the problem of French molt, about which he has developed his own theory that lets him avoid all problems. He has a record system that's fine-tuned to his needs. He swears without blinking or blushing that he has the best birds in the whole country. Last year he cleared at least $3,000 from his hobby. He can spend hours telling you about his birds. At meetings of his bird club he monopolizes the podium. People say about him that he can look at the perches and divine when the first egg will hatch. He is the type that knows all there is to know about Budgies. All—really all?

Well, no. He doesn't want to be bothered with a lot of theories concerning heredity. That is good for ivory-tower types. He knows how to breed Budgies by the hundreds—the rest leaves him cold.

This type is like the farmer with a broody hen who sends his daughter to fetch him 13 fresh eggs. Where she gets them is immaterial. An egg is an egg and a chicken is a chicken. The color doesn't interest him—just as long as he gets his chicks.

This farmer of course will get his chicks, and I'm willing to concede that for a farmer it may not matter whether they will grow into white, brown, or black chickens. It does very clearly matter to him whether these chickens will lay 140 versus 240 eggs per year. Had the farmer been smart, he would have been more choosy about where he got his breeding eggs. He should have seen to it that he started with chickens from a good egg-laying strain.

A Budgie breeder doesn't have to overly concern himself with the question of egg production. If his birds are healthy, the necessary eggs will come. But for him the color is of prime importance—no question about it.

The "street-wise" breeder we presented above can't convince us that deep in his heart he considers himself a completely accomplished breeder. A good part of the Budgerigar hobby remains a closed book to him—the very part that knowledgeable people consider the most interesting and challenging. And because the "street-wise" breeder is interested in a bit of extra change, we want to stress that this part of the hobby can help him achieve his biggest profit.

This breeder has let himself be scared away by a few scientific words that weren't included in his first-grade reader. He has let himself be convinced by other breeders that genetics of birds is terribly complicated. He acts as if nothing fazes him, and he speaks bravely about albino blood and lutino blood—and about Danish fancies and opalines. But when he breeds, he keeps getting surprises. He has white Budgies that produce blue young, and blue birds that bring forth green ones. His cinnamons yield plain Budgies, and his fallows have young with black eyes. He was one of the first to have Danish fancy birds, but that is now some years back and he still hasn't been able to raise a set of young that also was Danish fancy. He thinks the whole thing rather miraculous.

The Wonders of Genetics

The science of genetics, indeed, deals in wondrous happenings—and that's most certainly true with Budgerigars. It's nothing short of miraculous that the original green Budgie gave rise to more than 50 different color variants.

The miracle is on a different level than the way the "street-wise" breeder I mentioned sees it. The miracle is not random. It is neatly predictable with just a few exceptions wrought by Mother Nature. The facts add up well, and they are simple enough for a person with ordinary intelligence to grasp and use. After a short time, they seem easy to work with.

True, a bit of patience and perseverance is needed. Take out a sheet of paper and note unfamiliar scientific words you'll need to understand. Write down the meanings and study the implications. Soon theories will lead to

Unless the genetic formula for an individual bird is known, whether it's pure or hybrid for a given color is always subject to speculation in the absence of a breeding test. *Wissink*

practical benefits in your hobby.

You can take your new knowledge quite far and achieve your "miracles" rather quickly with minimal expense. Genetics provides you with the peace of mind that nothing will happen to throw a monkey wrench into your breeding plans. It also provides you with insurance that you won't chase after unattainable goals. And you'll know what you need to achieve the goals that you can attain.

For example, if you want to breed a violet variant, you will know that you don't have to buy more than a single violet bird. When a new variant comes into vogue, you will be able to meet the demand while the price is high. And you can graduate to the highest level of Budgie breeding—the development of an entirely new color variant. No one can say that the breeding programs that led to 50 new color variants have to stop there. You can be the person of the future who will add something new and desirable to the Budgerigar fancy.

Building Blocks of the Body

Every form of higher life derives from the merger of an egg cell contributed by the mother and a sperm cell from the father. This merger forms a new cell called a *zygote*. After a period of development, this zygote forms a new living being. To put this into avian terms, when a female and a male Budgie mate, the egg cell of the female is fertilized by the sperm of the male. These two cells meld into one, out of which the Budgie embryo grows. If the egg housing the embryo is properly brooded, it develops into a young Budgie.

The body of man, beast, bird, or plant is made up of millions of cells, all of which are derived from the one starter cell by means of *cell division*. At a certain moment, a wall is formed within the starter cell and soon the cell splits in two. In this way, one cell gives rise to two; two cells develop into four; four cells become eight—and so on, till after seven more divisions we have 1,024 cells. Cell division can be quite rapid once it gets underway.

Cell division, then, is the method by which an egg develops. The zygote (or starter cell) forms the egg yolk, which comes into the world surrounded by a layer of egg white and another protective layer of egg shell. And there it lies in the nest of your Budgies, ready to be brooded until 20 days later a young is hatched. Cell division keeps progressing after hatch until a full-grown Budgerigar has been formed.

To understand the process, let's return our attention to the original egg cell and sperm cell, which also are called *gametes* or reproductive cells. The reproductive cells contain everything that contributes to the development of a new bird. Once the gametes meld, they give rise to a new body, to feathers and legs, to wings and eyes—and to color traits and behavior.

Chromosomes

The whole miracle of reproduction occurs inside the melded new zygote.

130

The carriers of life operate in that small space to organize the construction of the new bird to be. These carriers of life are called *chromosomes.*

As I just mentioned, the zygote successively forms into two, four, eight, sixteen cells and so on. If this process were to go too far, we would get a Budgie of gigantic dimensions. There has to be a mechanism that regulates growth, that says at a given moment: "Stop! Development is complete. We now must start into maintenance."

This mechanism is provided by the chromosomes. You can see them under high magnification in a microscope as small clumps inside the cell. Inside the chromosomes are housed still smaller bodies, called *genes.* These genes determine the genetic traits of the developing Budgie. They determine the color and every other detail about the new Budgie. For the breeder, they do the most important of jobs.

Each body cell contains a certain number of chromosomes—always in even numbers. When a cell divides, the chromosomes also divide. Therefore the new cell contains the same number of chromosomes as the original cell. If the original cell starts with eight chromosomes, then cell division results in two cells, each also containing eight chromosomes. Normal cells always have the same number of chromosomes. No matter how many times they divide, each daughter cell maintains the eight chromosomes.

The Exception: Reproductive Cells

Reproductive cells represent an exception to the basic rule of cell division. The egg cell and the sperm cell described above contain just half the usual number of chromosomes. For example, body cells of Budgerigars normally contain 14 chromosomes. But the egg cell of the female contains only seven; so does the sperm cell of the male. Once these two reproductive cells meld into the zygote, the femals contributes seven chromosomes and the male contributes another seven. Together, they once again provide 14 chromosomes. As the zygote with its 14 chromosomes starts dividing, normal cell division occurs once again. And again, every daughter cell gets 14 chromosomes, derived from the original zygote.

Why does this happen? Nature never does anything without a reason. If the egg cell and the sperm cell would contain the normal number of Budgie chromosomes (14), then after mating we would get a melded cell with 14 plus 14 chromosomes—a total of 28. If that cell were to divide in the normal manner, we would get cells that all contain 28 chromosomes, giving rise to a Budgie with body cells of 28 chromosomes. But a Budgie by nature has just 14 chromosomes per cell. So we would get a bird that would not have the proper number of chromosomes to be a Budgie!

Such reflections are, however, academic. By the dictates of heredity the egg cell and the sperm cell must have one-half the number of chromosomes of ordinary cells—half from the male parent and half from the female parent.

A very fine exhibition quality gray cock. This bird has an especially good head. *Harkema*

Any breeder would be proud to bring two specimens as exceptional as these to the show bench.
Photo by author

Because chromosomes are the carriers of the various hereditary traits transmitted by the genes, the bird inherits traits from both parents according to their own genetic make-up.

No Watercolor Set

If the parent birds are white and green, the young inherit both white and green color genes. So they should look more or less half green and half white, or some color in between. But Nature doesn't work like a watercolor set that makes up light green by mixing white and green together. There are more elements that influence heredity.

You see, there are visible and invisible genetic factors called *recessive* and *dominant*. If you dislike strange words, you can call them *shy factors* and *aggressive factors*. For the heredity of Budgies, these are of prime importance. In most cases, one color factor appears to dominate the other.

For example, a green Budgie can be "white" at the same time, even though it doesn't look white. Its whiteness is overpowered by its greenness, or in other words, green coloration dominates over white, so that people speak of "dominant green." The bird being described is obviously green, but has received the white gene also from one of its parents even though it isn't visible. The white color therefore is called *recessive*—or *shy* if you like.

To repeat—the zygote receives the genes of both the male *and* the female. It thus contains a gene for white, and therefore the developing young will carry this gene in all its cells. But you can't tell that from the young bird's appearance.

Homozygous Versus Heterozygous

A bird that carries a second, hidden color trait in addition to its apparent color is called a *heterozygote*. That's a difficult term. A good translation of that word would be: *inheriting impurely*. A bird without hidden color traits is called a *homozygote,* which could be translated as *inheriting purely*.

If you have understood the previous discussions clearly, you now know that a *heterozygous* bird and a *homozygous* bird can look exactly alike. A homozygous (or purely inheriting) green bird is completely green in its makeup, while a heterozygous green bird can look just as green, but carries a hidden, invisible trait for another color.

Two homozygous green Budgerigars will always produce homozygous green young, for the simple reason that no Budgie, in fact no organism, can give its young a trait that it doesn't carry itself.

Let's look at a practical example.

John Williams, the barber, wants to start breeding Budgies. One of his clients told him that Budgies are truly pleasant birds that are easy to breed. He has a preference for green Budgies and therefore he goes to a dealer where he blithely purchases two green Budgies.

133

Everything goes according to plan. A few weeks later, the couple produces eggs. Another 20 days later, Williams tells his clients at the shop that he has new young Budgies.

"Which color," a client asks?

"Green, of course," Williams replies. "Naturally you can't see that yet," he adds. "They still don't have their feathers. But the male and the female are green, so the young will be green as well."

A few weeks later, however, our friend the barber discovers that those crazy Budgies of his are not turning out to be green. At least, not all of them. Believe it or not, he has two *blue* ones in the brood.

Williams doesn't really mind. He can learn to like blue Budgies just the same. And maybe he thinks he has bred something quite unusual.

But really, it is the most usual thing in the world. If Williams had wanted to be sure to breed only green Budgies, he would have had to ask the dealer for genetically pure green birds. If he had known the scientific term, he would have asked for "homozygous green Budgerigars."

Instead he got hold of possibly two heterozygous Budgies—or one heterozygote and one homozygote. Both looked green. But one of them, or both, had a hidden trait for blue.

It might not have been an easy task for Williams to purchase a pair of homozygous green birds, even if he had known about the concept and the difficult word involved. Far too many breeders work with colony breeding cages, so that they are unsure about the heritage of their birds. Only breeders who breed one pair per cage can be sure after a few seasons what type of birds they are dealing with. Only then would they be able to sell breeding birds that are genetically pure for a specific color. And only then would their hobby be on a certain course.

When geneticists speak of dark green, olive yellow, cobalt, etc., they always refer to the pure color—the color of homozygous birds. If a bird is heterozygous, they indicate this by recording the invisible color after the visible one. A green bird that also carries a white factor is called green/white. When read out loud, this is sounded as "green split for white," and the bird could be called "white blooded." Similarly, a graywing cobalt/white would be a "white blooded graywing cobalt" or a "graywing cobalt split for white." The latter designation is simple and clear, and will be used for the balance of this book.

By now you understand that someone who buys a pair of Budgies without a forethought never can be sure how the young will turn out. You can't just go by looks, because you might be encountering heterozygous or homozygous birds, or one of each. In the great majority of cases, the haphazard buyer will get heterozygotes—impurely inheriting birds—because most breeders understand too little about the theory of color inheritance. They breed shotgun style under the motto, "Whatever will be, will be."

Serious breeders attain a good understanding of the colors lurking in their stock after a few matings. If you know what is hidden inside your birds, then you can accurately and easily predict the result of any crossing. The way to do this is covered in later chapters.

Careful management of the breeding population eventually leads to known formulas of what the birds can produce. A breeder who knows both the genotype and phenotype of his birds can reasonably predict the outcomes of his matings with a fair amount of accuracy.

From the original green form of the wild Budgie, cultivated birds now appear in an incredible rainbow of beautiful colors and combinations of colors. This has all come about through the operations of genetics and the skill of breeders who properly understand how the science works. *van Herk*

9

Crossbreeding and The Mechanics of Color

The FOB Theory

The FOB theory for Budgerigars was devised by two geneticists—scientists who specialize in heredity—based on the theories of the discoverer of genetics, Gregor Mendel. Their names were Dr. Duncker and Dr. Cremer. They distinguished three main colors or critical factors for Budgerigars: The yellow factor, designated by "F"; the blue factor, designated by "O"; and the dark factor, called "B." The corresponding recessive (or "shy") factors were indicated by "f," "o," and "b."

Later a fourth factor was identified, namely the one for graywings. The graywing factor is recessive for the O factor, but dominant for the o factor. To clarify the differences, one now uses the designation "On" for the plain dominant dark factor; "Ow" for the recessive dark factor; and "Og" for the graywing factor.

By this scheme, a light green, homozygous, purely inheriting Budgerigar gets the F factor from both parents, and is designated as FF. Both parents also contributed the factor On, which makes it On On. And it has the b factor from both parents, making it bb.

The complete designation for light green homozygous (purely inheriting) Budgerigars therefore is:

FF On On bb

After repeated crossings, geneticists determined the following:

Birds designated F are green and yellow
Birds designated On are green or blue
Birds designated ff are mostly bluish
Birds designated Ow Ow are yellow or white
Birds designated bb are light in color
Birds designated Bb are in between light and dark
Birds designated BB are dark
Birds designated Og are graywings.

With this list in hand you can make up a designation for any Budgerigar, indicating both the visible and the invisible (recessive) coloration. The designations for the best known mutations are as follows:

1.	Light green	FF On On bb
	Dark green	FF On On Bb
	Olive Green	FF On On BB
2.	Light green/blue	Ff On On bb
	Dark green/blue	Ff On On Bb
	Olive green/blue	Ff On On BB
3.	Light green/white	Ff On Ow bb
	Dark green/white	Ff On Ow Bb
	Olive green/white	Ff On Ow BB
4.	Graywing light green	FF Og Og bb
	Graywing dark green	FF Og Og Bb
	Graywing olive green	FF Og Og BB
5.	Light green/graywing	FF On Og bb
	Dark green/graywing	FF On Og Bb
	Olive green/graywing	FF On Og BB
6.	Light green/blue graywing	Ff On Og bb
	Dark green/blue graywing	Ff On Og Bb
	Olive green/blue graywing	Ff On Og BB
7.	Graywing light green/blue	Ff Og Og bb
	Graywing dark green/blue	Ff Og Og Bb
	Graywing olive green/blue	Ff Og Og BB
8.	Graywing light green/white	Ff Og Ow bb
	Graywing dark green/white	Ff Og Ow Bb
	Graywing olive green/white	Ff Og Ow BB
9.	Skyblue	ff On On bb
	Cobalt	ff On On Bb
	Mauve	ff On On BB

10.	Skyblue/white	ff On Ow bb
	Cobalt/white	ff On Ow Bb
	Mauve/white	ff On Ow BB
11.	Graywing skyblue	ff Og Og bb
	Graywing cobalt	ff Og Og Bb
	Graywing mauve	ff Og Og BB
12.	Skyblue/graywing	ff On Og bb
	Cobalt/graywing	ff On Og Bb
	Mauve/graywing	ff On Og BB
13.	Graywing skyblue/white	ff Og Ow bb
	Graywing cobalt/white	ff Og Ow Bb
	Graywing mauve/white	ff Og Ow BB
14.	White skyblue	ff Ow Ow bb
	White cobalt	ff Ow Ow Bb
	White mauve	ff Ow Ow BB
15.	Light yellow	FF Ow Ow bb
	Dark yellow	FF Ow Ow Bb
	Olive yellow	FF Ow Ow BB
16.	Light yellow/white	Ff Ow Ow bb
	Dark yellow/white	Ff Ow Ow Bb
	Olive yellow/white	Ff Ow Ow BB
17.	Graywing light yellow/white	FF Og Ow bb
	Graywing dark yellow/white	FF Og Ow Bb
	Graywing olive yellow/white	FF Og Ow BB

Conclusion to Be Drawn

These lists have a special purpose. Let's have a look at what they tell us.

Take, for example, the second item under category 5: Dark green/graywing. As I mentioned earlier, this refers to a dark green Budgerigar with a hidden graywing trait. The bird, therefore, looks green and can't be distinguished visually from a plain green Budgie. Speaking professionally, the bird is a dark green with a graywing gene, or dark green split for graywing. The designation is FF On Og Bb.

The list also shows that a bird with F in its designation is green or yellow. A bird with On is green or blue. The Budgie in our example, therefore, has two reasons to be green, namely the F and the On factors. In the designation, we further encounter Og, which identifies it as a graywing according to the list. This is not visible, but the designation clearly indicates that the bird carries graywing blood. The last letters in the designation indicate that the bird is neither light nor dark, which in this case means neither light green nor olive green, but dark green.

Consider another example: Item three under category 13, graywing mauve/white. Technically it is a graywing mauve split for white. This bird therefore has the outward appearance of a mauve Budgie with gray wings, but it carries the hidden trait for white. Its designation is ff Og Ow BB.

By referring to the list, you can draw the following conclusions:

The Budgie is ff, thus bluish.

The Budgie is Og, thus a graywing.

The Budgie is Ow (no conclusion possible).

The Budgie is BB, thus dark.

From all this you can see that the designation can tell you the color of the bird.

If you take a random designation, say ff Ow Ow bb, and refer to the list, you can deduce the following:

The Budgie is ff, thus bluish.

The Budgie is Ow Ow, thus yellow or white.

The Budgie is bb, thus light in color.

And the list shows that this bird is white skyblue.

Say that you consider buying a Budgie about which it isn't known whether it is homozygous or heterozygous, but you can see that the bird is light yellow. By referring to the list, you find that the bird could have the following designations: Ff Ow Ow bb or FF Ow Ow bb. In the first case, the Budgie is homozygous—pure light yellow. In the second case, the bird is heterozygous—light yellow split for white.

Visually, the genetic color picture cannot be determined. But if the bird is crossed with another Budgie, you can tell by the young if the bird you're considering is homozygous or heterozygous. One crossing usually can help you determine what the exact designation of the bird is. If you know the proper designation of your stock, then it is easy to predict in advance the result of any crossing. All you need is to write the designation of the birds you want to cross as an arithmetic problem and compare the result to the numbered list.

Crossbreeding

Now let's look at some examples to show what will hapen when two homozygotes—two purely inheriting birds— are mated. Take white skyblue × white skyblue.

For a simple look at the results, write the designation of the birds at the top and the left hand side of a plain diagram. In the small boxes, on top and to the side, write half of the designation of both birds, since the young inherits half of its chromosomes from its mother and half from its father. Add the "half designations" two by two, put the result in the big boxes, and you will get all possible designations that can result from this crossing.

The diagram looks like this:

White skyblue   ff Ow Ow bb

	f Ow b	f Ow b
f Ow b	ff Ow Ow bb White skyblue	ff Ow Ow bb White skyblue
f Ow b	ff Ow Ow bb White skyblue	ff Ow Ow bb White skyblue

White skyblue
ff Ow Ow bb

In the four big boxes you keep seeing the same designation of ff Ow Ow bb. That shows you that the young all have the same designation as each other and the same designation as the parents. From this calculation, we can conclude that all birds issuing from this cross will be white skyblue.

However, as soon as one of the factors is different, the situation changes. Say that we pair a white skyblue Budgie with a white mauve Budgie. The resulting diagram would look like this:

White skyblue   ff Ow Ow bb

	f Ow b	f Ow b
f Ow B	ff Ow Ow Bb White cobalt	ff Ow Ow Bb White cobalt
f Ow B	ff Ow Ow Bb White cobalt	ff Ow Ow Bb White cobalt

White mauve
ff Ow Ow BB

In the four big boxes you keep finding the designation ff Ow Ow Bb for the results of this cross. Referring to category 14 in the list, you find that this means white cobalt. The calculation shows us that all the young from the white skyblue × white mauve cross will have the coloration of white cobalt.

Another cross, mauve/white × olive yellow, yields the following diagram:

	Mauve/white	ff On Ow BB
	f On B	f Ow B
Olive yellow **FF Ow Ow BB** F Ow B	Ff On Ow BB Olive green/white	Ff Ow Ow BB Olive yellow/white
F Ow B	Ff On Ow BB Olive green/white	Ff Ow Ow BB Olive yellow/white

It's easy to see that the young from this cross will be half olive green/white and half olive yellow/white. At the risk of excessive repetition, let me add that all the young are "split for white," meaning heterozygous, or inheriting impurely. They look like homozygous olive green and olive yellow Budgies, but they all carry the white trait. By devising the proper cross, the next generation can be made to exhibit this hidden trait like a rabbit coming out of a hat.

Let's try another example. If we cross mauve/white with graywing cobalt, we get:

	Mauve/white	ff On Ow BB
	f On B	f Ow B
Graywing cobalt **ff Og Og Bb** f Og B	ff On Og BB Mauve/graywing	ff Og Ow BB Mauve/white
f Og b	ff On Og Bb Cobalt/graywing	ff Og Ow Bb Graywing cobalt/white

The result of this cross, which again is shown in the large boxes, is as follows:

One quarter mauve/graywing, one quarter graywing mauve/white, one quarter cobalt/graywing, and one quarter graywing cobalt/white.

Half of these birds will have a trait for graywing, although this trait isn't visible to the eye. The other half has the hidden trait for white. All birds out of this cross, therefore, have a hidden trait for a color different from the one they show; and all these birds, therefore, inherit impurely—they all are heterozygotes. To the eye, these birds look as follows: One quarter mauve, one quarter cobalt, one quarter graywing mauve and one quarter graywing cobalt.

This analysis is credited to the German geneticist Dr. H. Duncker. He continued further by writing a book about color inheritance of Budgerigars.

142

This book contains detailed tables based on the results of 1830 various crosses. If you use this book, you can easily see the results of any cross you want, just by referring to the tables.

The Law of Averages

In analyzing the last table, I spoke of "halves" and "quarters" in predicting the coloration resulting from a certain cross. Don't assume however, that in a brood of eight, precisely two will belong to each of the four designations I listed. Nature doesn't work that way. The outcome follows the law of averages. The designations will come out in the predicted ratio if the number of cases involved is large enough, say 100 birds.

In any one nest, things can be different. It is possible, in the extreme, that you will get only olive green birds in a brood where you expect to find both olive greens and olive yellows. In the next brood, things could work out differently, and you might find more olive yellow birds than you expect.

Those who have had a hen brood a clutch of eggs know that you might have the good luck of hatching out mostly females and just a few males. Yet in theory, you know there ought to be equal numbers of hens and roosters. A large scale breeder will tell you that this is true if you use large numbers.

(The sex ratio in Budgies also is about even. The young are theoretically half female and half male. But you still might hatch out a brood with only females or only males.)

To become familiar with the mathematics of crossbreeding, make up some theoretical combinations of your own and see what the results would be. Take two types of Budgies at random from the numbered lists and see what they would bring forth.

You are convinced by now, I hope, that you can use this system to predict what you can expect from crossing your own stock. Of course, you need to know what hidden color traits might be tucked away inside the cells of your own. The easiest way to find out is to buy birds whose heritage is known to the seller. All you need to do then is to look up the proper designations and make your diagram. If you can't buy what you need, you will have to determine the correct designation of your birds with one or more test matings. Then you will have to keep careful records on your stock. Accurate bookkeeping is essential for a breeder who wants to know what he is going to be breeding.

Limitless Possibilities

As soon as you delve into the genetics of Budgerigars, you will come to learn that there are limitless possibilities. One keeps facing surprising discoveries. "Theoretical breeding" is a pleasant sport to occupy your time with. The Budgie breeder can sit by the fireplace on a cold winter day, and relax while pondering the possibilities that his birds present. He can search for the right combinations and then make up the right couples to attain a definite goal during the next breeding season. He can think about the difference between a cobalt/graywing and a graywing cobalt/white. And he can work backwards to find which parent he would have to have for breeding, let's say, a graywing light green. He discovers that olive green/blues only can produce cobalts and mauves. Birds that are green/white, can bring forth blue, yellow, and white Budgies, provided they are mated properly.

Dr. Duncker found more of these good bits of information. A "split for blue" designation doesn't say anything about the type of blue factor the bird has. If you want to be sure about it, then you have to designate the blue factor more precisely with cobalt, etc. In practice, that can be difficult because the proper designation of a visible blue already is quite hard.

Another point, which ought to be clear to any breeder, is that there can be a wide difference in the color of two skyblues or two mauves. One skyblue can be a bit darker than another, but not really quite dark enough to be called a cobalt. With other colors, similar situations can arise. A look at any cage with ten light greens will easily convince you of that point.

Practice Versus Theory

I have discussed the advantage of breeding from one pair of birds per cage. There is no way to know the father of a bird bred in a colony. But I don't want to reject colony breeding since I know that practical limitations often impose themselves on theoretical preferences. But a single colony breeding cage is suitable only for a limited combination of birds. You could, however, breed cobalts or pure olive greens or pure lutinos. If you remove all young with deviant coloration, you will eventually have a pure race from which you can keep selecting the best individuals.

In addition, you could put all birds from the white series together in an aviary—for example, light green/white, dark green/white, skyblue/white, etc. You can be certain that every bird hatched in this aviary will be born with a visible or invisible white factor in its makeup. All birds from the blue series can be put together in a cage with yellow Budgies. You can be sure that every bird that looks green carries the factor for white.

All the white series with so called blue, mauve and cobalt "haze" can be put together in a single breeding cage. (In reality, there are no white birds. White Budgies all have a more or less vague ground color, which lies like a haze over the white. Truly pure white Budgies are albinos.)

Your calculations will show you which birds can be put together in a cage to achieve the results you desire. If you specialize, say in lutinos, blue whitewings, or light blues, then things will go quite easily for you. All you have to concentrate on is one key element: rigorous selection.

I want to mention, before leaving the subject, that next to the FOB theory of Dr. Duncker, there are others. For example, Dr. H. Steiner of Zurich speaks of a "regulating factor," which he names "R." Those able to read

There is a fascination in working to achieve a goal set for oneself. In breeding Budgies, achieving the colors you admire from the birds you have can be both rewarding and satisfying.   *Photo by author*

Well-established colors are the result of selections from color mutations. Judicious matching is necessary to achieve the desired success.

German should see his book, *Vererbungsstudien am Wellensittich*. Crew, of Edinburgh, in his book, *Genetics of the Budgerigar*, does not connect the so-called genetic analysis with the biochemical analysis.

All in all, however, the results of Dr. Duncker's FOB theory of crossbreeding are recognized as correct by all geneticists, including the two just named. After all, the theory has been proven correct time and again in practice. However, if you wish to delve further into the truly exceptionally interesting study of the genetics of the Budgerigar, I gladly recommend these two books to you.

Breed for a Different Color Variation

If you want to get into a new color variation, the easiest way, of course, is to buy a couple of birds of that color—pure breeding birds, that is, homozygotes. Then you know that all young from the mating will be of the desired color; the pure and simple reason is that the young get this desired color both from their father and from their mother.

Unfortunately, this easiest of methods also is the most expensive, particularly if you want to go into something that was just recently developed. You can get the same results with a much smaller cash outlay by buying just one bird of the desired variety. In a few matings, you can build a whole race of the new variant.

Say you have skyblues and you want to build a race of graywings. Go out and buy a single graywing blue—a pure one, of course. Starting with the mating skyblue × graywing blue, you will get all skyblue-looking young. But you can be sure that every bird out of this crossing is "split for graywing"—that is, it carries graywing genes. Next, cross one of these young back to the original graywing, that is graywing blue × blue/graywing. That will yield half blue graywings and half "split for graywings." You have reached your goal with just two crosses, in this case!

You could save still more money by buying two "split for graywings," that is, two birds with graywing genes. Start by pairing two skyblue/graywings. The first generation of young would yield 25 percent graywing blues. These birds can be identified immediately as graywings.

You even could make do by buying just one "split for graywing," but it will take more time to reach your goal and you'll encounter more difficulties along the way. Start by crossing skyblue × skyblue/graywing; there won't be any visible difference between these parents. You will get young that are partially skyblue and partially skyblue/graywing. There also won't be any visible difference between these young. Mate them among themselves and you will eventually achieve a mating between two "split for graywings." Before your own eyes, two Budgies that are blue in appearance "suddenly" will produce graywing young.

This discussion will clarify for you how two green birds (or birds of any other similar appearance) can produce a completely new color. You can get white birds suddenly in a breeding cage where you wouldn't expect any. The explanation is similar. Both parents would be "split for white" in this case, even if this never came to light in earlier matings.

Inbreeding

Inbreeding, a word that sounds like a curse to many Budgie breeders, is one we have encountered earlier in this book. French molt, illnesses, and failures of all kinds have been attributed to inbreeding.

There really is such a thing as regression of a race through inbreeding. But the problems that the average breeder attributes to inbreeding mostly have other causes. The chief cause is poor selection. One has to know why and with what one is inbreeding.

Scientifically, inbreeding means the mating of two closely related animals. Every Budgie, of course, has two parents, four grandparents, eight great grandparents, and 16, 32, 64, 128, etc. forebears in earlier generations. After 20 generations the group of forebears numbers well over two million. That would take in most of the Budgies in the country. As a result, if we would stop bringing in fresh blood from abroad, this would mean that every Budgie in the country is related to every other in one way or another.

If you pair two birds at random from this "family," however, you can't call it inbreeding, even if you can demonstrate a relation in the so-maniest degree. You can speak of inbreeding only when mating the closest of relatives—parents with young, brothers with sisters, or two cousins together.

Actually, even breeders with a strong dislike for inbreeding resort to this practice at some time. They are striving for a certain goal, and to reach this goal, and to reach it quickly, inbreeding is often the only possible means.

I mentioned earlier that you may only have to buy one new bird of a certain color variation in order to establish that variation in your stock. I mentioned that the way to achieve this is to use inbreeding.

For example, say you want to breed fallows and have only one fallow bird to work with. You begin by crossing this fallow with a "not fallow." The progeny is 100 percent "split for fallow"—birds that carry the fallow as a hidden factor. To get fallows from the next generation, you have to mate the "split for fallows" with their pure fallow parent. That's inbreeding! The result is 50 percent "split for fallows" and 50 percent pure fallows.

Another motive for inbreeding might be that you have a bird of especially beautiful conformation. If you want to keep this conformation in your breeding, you can easily select a mate from the same family. You mate the good bird with one of its own young that exhibits the same superior conformation. The result will be young that maintain this trait. In this way, you can breed a whole race of birds with the trait.

There is a "but" attached to inbreeding, however. Inbreeding transmits not only the good but also the bad traits. As you know, when a sperm cell fertilizes an egg cell, each contributes half of the chromosomes and genes of the parent birds. The new individuals inherit the traits of the male and the female by way of these chromosomes and genes—good ones as well as poor ones. The breeder has to try to maintain and strengthen the favorable traits in the progeny of these birds—and to get rid of the unfavorable ones. With good luck, the male and female have the same good trait, and the young will inherit this trait in augmented form. With bad luck, both parents have a certain unfavorable trait, and the young inherit this bad trait in augmented form.

So you understand why rigorous selection needs to be maintained when you inbreed. Not all inbred young have inherited the good traits of the parents without any of the bad ones. You would preferably breed further with the young that inherited the good traits and not the bad ones. That is called *selective inbreeding.*

Say for example, that you have opalines that stand out for their attractive design but also have a hollow back. Selective breeding can be your means to try to maintain the design while getting rid of the hollow back. You keep looking for related birds that have the desired design at its most attractive and have the least noticeable hollow back.

In theory, this method should make it possible to breed a pure white Budgie—one that is not an albino. Perhaps it is possible to achieve it in reality as well. One would keep selecting the whitest Budgies and inbreed from them. Slowly, you would breed a Budgie without underlying color.

Through inbreeding one can achieve great purity within a family—it reduces the likelihood of variations.

Since selection is essential, inbreeding requires the breeder to work with relatively large numbers of birds. It is recommended to breed in so-called parallel series—for example, brother-sister matings. The selection for further inbreeding is increased in this way and the breeder isn't tempted so easily to use birds with bad traits for further breeding.

However, inbreeding is not recommended as the only way to achieve the goal of well-formed Budgies of an attractive color. You can use non-related birds to breed a line with desirable traits through intelligent selection. Outside help from an unrelated bird can often yield results that are at least as favorable. The decision is yours. To make it, you need more than you can learn from a text. You need experience and, even more important, love for your task.

Dominant and Recessive Faults

I have spoken in depth about dominant ("aggresive") and recessive ("shy") traits—mostly in connection with color selection. The same forces are at work with all inherited traits, including undesirable ones.

A good example in Budgies is black spots on the throat. Birds with the dominant gene for these spots will transmit this factor to their young when mated with other birds having this gene. People like the spots, so this is a desirable trait.

But undesirable traits also can be caused by dominant genes. Matings of two birds with the same undesirable dominant genes can make the throat spots disappear from the race, in whole or in part. If you mate a bird with a dominant gene for a certain fault with another that has the gene in its recessive form, then the fault will appear in part of the descendants. You can then use selection to eliminate the fault in future generations. A breeder who values attractive, large, round throat spots has to concentrate on finding birds with the dominant fault and to eliminate them from further breeding. He would make a few trial selections to rather simply detect the undesirable birds.

Recessive faults are harder to detect. They may suddenly appear in a race that had been considered pure. These are called *throwbacks*. No breeder likes them, but if he has a sufficiently large number of birds, he will be able to eliminate the problem.

Modifications and Mutations

A number of elements can cause changes in color and conformation in Budgies (and other animals and plants). For example, dyes in the food can cause or augment coloration of Budgies. (Some canary breeders use dyed food as the principal method of achieving red coloration!) The changes of color achieved in this way are called *modifications*. They cannot be inherited and disappear as soon as the cause—in this case, dyed food— is removed.

Modifications can develop from special foods, shortage of food, influences of light and air, chemicals, and other artificial agents. They have the trademark of being impermanent; they disappear as soon as normal conditions are reinstituted.

Mutations are different. Suddenly, there appears on the scene a variation in color or form that is indeed heritable. The reason is generally not known or provable.

In some cases, mutations can be induced. I have been fascinated by the trial conducted with flower bulbs by Dr. W.E. de Mol of Oud-Loosdrecht in the Netherlands. He has been able to induce mutations by treating bulbs with X-rays. He changed the composition of chromosomes in ways that generate completely new varieties, the Budgie tulip and the cyclamen tulip, for example.

What Dr. de Mol achieved with radiation can also occur in Nature, for one reason or another. The composition of the chromosomes is changed, leading to the development of a variation in color or form—the *mutation*.

Mutations that are visible to the eye occur extremely rarely, although new evidence suggests that the number of mutations is greater than is ordinarily assumed. Most mutations are either invisible or go unrecognized.

If a breeder notices a desirable mutation in his birds that has some promise, he will, of course, try to establish this trait through further breeding. Most current color variations have been established in this way. The original green Budgie was changed to a blue variant through a mutation. What happened is that the mutant lost the yellow component of the original green, leaving blue. Loss of blue through another mutation produced the yellow Budgie.

Albinos also developed by mutation—one that caused the Budgie to lose all its color. Other types of variations also are attributable to mutations. For example, in 1938 the late Mr. Van Dijk discovered a green male with a small yellow spot in the back of its head. He bred the first pied Budgie from this mutation by crossing the mutant to a lutino female. Further inbreeding developed the "Dutch pied" out of this mutation—where blue Budgies have white spots and green Budgies have yellow spots.

When a breeder notices a mutation that he wants to develop further, the best procedure is to mate the bird with a suitable male or female. (For a color mutation, use a male or female of the mutant color.) You will get young that don't show the mutant variation. They are "split for mutants" that have the trait for the mutation hidden inside them. By breeding them back to the parent that has the mutation, you get a succeeding generation that *does* show the mutation. Rigorous selection can maintain and improve the mutation.

le prijs 225

The breeder's dream is a bird that will win in any company and gain the recognition and admiration of the entire Budgerigar fancy.

Harkema

150

10

Budgerigar Color Varieties

Green Budgerigars

Whenever we speak about green Budgerigars we refer to the varieties that most resemble the original wild Budgie from Australia. Many fanciers consider this the most beautiful color phase of all. Indeed, a good green bird is a particularly beautiful sight.

We distinguish light greens, dark greens, and olive greens. The coloration of the light greens is as follows: The mask is buttercup yellow. The upper part of the back and background of the wings are somewhat lighter yellow. There is a regularly spaced, black, wavy design on the wings, the back of the head, and the upper part of the back. The long tail feathers are blue-black. The rest of the body is a bright, grass green without lighter or darker spots. On the right and left side of the neck there are three bright, round, black spots, the last of which is partially hidden under the purple cheek patch.

The coloration of the dark greens is as follows: the body is darker green, and the tail feathers are darker as well. For the rest, the coloration resembles that of the light green Budgie.

The coloration of the olive green is as follows: The body is deep olive green, and the tail feathers are darker. For the rest, the coloration resembles that of the light green Budgie.

The yellow of the green Budgie may not be too light, and the green should be the true color. Colors should not be mixed. I wouldn't consider a Budgie light green if it looks almost like a dark green bird.

Dark and olive green Budgies have a common fault—the green is mixed with blue, or exhibits lighter spots. The risk of running into this fault is always present when one breeds blue into a green line. The best procedure is to achieve light green by repeat breeding with light greens.

You can achieve dark green best by crossing light green with olive green. That way, you avoid the possibility that the dark green bird gets too much blue, which would make the color too pronounced.

Olive green is achieved by crossing olive yellow or olive green with mauve. From the first of these crossings you are more likely to get birds that show a warmer tint of olive green.

Blue Budgerigars

Blue Budgies also occur in three color variations: skyblue, cobalt, and mauve. Many people consider the blue a very attractive bird, although the color almost never shows the luster that makes greens such marvelously beautiful birds.

Skyblues have the following coloration: The mask is clear white. The upper part of the back and background of the wings are white. There is a regularly spaced, black, wavy design on the upper part of the back and back of the head. The long tail feathers are blue-black. The rest of the body is bright sky blue, without lighter or darker spots. On the right and left side of the neck there are three bright, round, black spots of considerable size, the last of which are partially hidden under the purple cheek patch.

Cobalts have a deep but clear cobalt-blue color. The tail feathers are somewhat darker than those of the light blues. The rest of the coloration is like that of the light blues.

Mauves have a purplish-mauve body, not matte, and evenly colored. The tail feathers are even somewhat darker than those of the cobalts. The rest of the coloration is like that of the light blues.

With the mauve Budgie, especially, it seems to be difficult to have an evenly-distributed color. A lifeless color that shades too far towards gray should be avoided. Generally, it's best to breed birds of the same color with each other time after time and to practice careful selection. That's the way to get blues of a good color. This means to breed skyblues with skyblues, cobalts with cobalts, and mauves with mauves. Over time, you get better color than if you bred skyblue to mauve in order to get cobalt.

The general public usually prefers skyblues, just as it prefers light greens over dark greens and olive greens. The skyblue Budgie is homozygous for the absence of the dark factor, while the mauve Budgie is homozygous for the presence of this factor. Cobalt is heterozygous for the dark factor. A well-bred light blue Budgie has an intense glow on the feathers, just like the luster that makes greens so attractive. The color of mauves can perhaps be described best as a mix of blue, purple, and pearl gray.

152

Yellow Budgerigars

Any mention of yellow Budgies refers only to birds of normal type—not lutinos. The common yellow also is divided into color gradations: light yellow, dark yellow, and olive yellow.

The coloration of the light yellow Budgie is as follows: The mask is buttercup yellow, like the rest of the body. There is no green subcolor. The design on the wings is completely or mostly absent. There are no black throat spots. The purple cheek spot is almost invisible. The pin feathers of the wing and large tail feathers are lighter than the rest of the body.

Dark yellow Budgies have a darker yellow body color than light yellows. For the rest, they are the same as light yellows.

Olive yellow Budgies have a mustard-colored body. For the rest, they are just like the light yellows.

The cinnamon-light yellow Budgie, the cinnamon-dark yellow and the cinnamon-olive yellow have the same color and design as the light yellow, dark yellow and olive yellow. There is no apparent difference to the eye. I will discuss cinnamons in a following chapter.

Breeding good yellow birds (not lutinos) is difficult. It takes considerable patience before the color becomes pure without encountering the infamous green reflection. The color of a good light yellow must look like that of the lutino. The light yellow is preferred above dark and olive yellow. By crossing them with albinos one has been able to breed very light yellow birds that differ only in eye color from true lutinos.

Graywings

Graywings come about through the operation of a dilution factor, which thins or bleaches the color of the striped design. All the previously named blue and green color variants can also occur as graywings. In other words, you can find graywing light green, graywing dark green, graywing olive green, graywing skyblue, graywing cobalt, and graywing mauve. That does not exhaust the graywing repertoire. New graywings will come into the picture as new color variants are developed.

Graywing light yellow, dark yellow and olive yellow variants don't exist, at least not in visible form, because the trademark of the yellow Budgie precisely is that the wavy design of the wings is nearly or completely invisible. In fact, they do exist, of course, but they look just like ordinary light yellow, dark yellow, and olive yellow Budgies.

Graywing light green coloration is as follows: The mask is buttercup yellow. The wavy design on the wings, back of the head, and upper back is gray—between white and black. The long tail feathers are gray with a bluish tint. Body color is pale light green. At both sides of the neck, there are three round, gray spots. The last spot is partially hidden under a pale purple cheek patch.

153

Graywing dark green coloration is like the light green in the design. The body color is darker and more toward blue, although the bird must remain green. The tail feathers are somewhat darker.

Graywing olive green coloration is like that of light green in the design. The body color is light olive green. The tail is darker than with graywing dark green.

Graywing skyblue coloration is as follows: The mask is white. The wavy design on the wings, back of the head and upper back is gray—between white and black. The long tail feathers are grayish blue. The body color is light and clear skyblue. Each side of the neck has three round, gray spots, of which the last one is partially hidden under a light purple cheek patch.

Graywing cobalt has a design like graywing skyblue. The body color is pale cobalt. The long tail feathers are cobalt.

Graywing mauve has a design like graywing skyblue. The body color is pale mauve. The tail is mauve.

The gray color has influenced the color of graywings to the extent that generally the body color of blue and green has become a bit more matte than the colors of the corresponding normal color variants. This is less noticeable with the blue, because it is less influenced by gray than green is.

The gray has to lie precisely between white and black. It may not be too light and not too dark. The body color is the same as that of normal Budgies, but less deep. The gray ought to be clear—not muddy.

Sex-linked Heredity

After all we have said so far about chromosomes and genes, you will not be surprised that the sex also is determined by these factors. In Budgerigars, the egg cell of the female has two sex chromosomes—one X or male chromosome and one Y or female chromosome. The sperm cell of the male also has two chromosomes, which determine gender, but these are both X chromosomes, that is male chromosomes. If a male chromosome of a female (an X chromosome) is linked with a chromosome contributed by the male (always an X chromosome) then a male young results. If the female chromosome of the hen is linked to a male chromosome from the father, then a female young results. In other words, a bird with XX chromosomes is a male, and a bird with XY chromosomes is a female.

The situation is reversed with mammals, in which the male determines the gender of the young. For example, a bull has only one male chromosome, while a cow has two. If at fertilization a male chromosome of the bull encounters a male chromosome of the cow, then the calf will be a bull. If the male chromosome of the cow does not meet a male chromosome from the bull sperm—but a 0, or null chromosome—then the calf will be a cow.

Whenever a linkage exists between a color factor of a Budgerigar and the sex chromosomes, one speaks of sex-linked color inheritance. In such a case the sex is tied to a certain externally visible trait of the bird. One can sometimes use the color to see whether a bird is male or femals. The simple reason is that the sex goes along with a certain color. For example, if you breed a "split for lutino" male with a normal colored (green or wild color) female, you can be sure that all resulting lutinos will be females.

Sex linkage seems rather complex when you first hear how it works, but in practice it won't cause you much trouble. Early on people thought that it would play a role in the heredity of a large number of color variations in Budgies, but it didn't turn out that way. There are sex-linked albinos and lutinos, as well as non-sex-linked birds. In all cases, the factors for opalines, slate blues, and cinnamons are sex-linked.

For example, if you mate a cinnamon Budgie with a non-cinnamon Budgie, all the young that look cinnamon are female. All the males are "split for cinnamon." They don't look cinnamon, but they carry the hidden factor for that color trait. Knowing that all males are "split for cinnamon" can help you in future mating plans.

For the rest, sex linkage is not all that important for the Budgie breeder. With a little patience, he will find out which young from a certain mating are males by noting the color of the ceres.

Sex linkage is more important to a commercial poultry breeder. In that business, it is important to know quickly which chicks are male and which female. The breeder can avoid the regular "sexing" procedure by breeding, say, a Rhode Island Red rooster to a white Wyandotte hen. All the female chicks will be red and all the male chicks, whitish. This method is 100 percent certain.

In a line with so-called "sorter" chicks, it isn't necessary to make crosses to get Nature to do the sexing. For example, Dr. A. L. Hagedoorn of Soesterberg in the Netherlands succeeded in fixing the so-called "cuckoo" factor in a line of chickens. All the males in this line are white at birth, and all females, brown.

The Cinnamon Factor

The cinammon Budgie is differentiated from the normal and graywing Budgie mainly by the wavy design on the wings, which is neither black nor gray, but cinnamon-colored. The cinnamon is born with red eyes. As soon as the young are hatched, you can see their red eyes through the eyelids. The eyes appear to be dark red when the young first open their eyes, but that doesn't last long. Ordinarily, the eye changes color before the young are a week old, and it takes on the normal coloration.

A white cinnamon chick has a bright rose-red skin, and the developing pin feathers are brownish. The legs are rose red, and the beak is orange. The feathering of cinnamons is best compared with that of lutinos and albinos; usually it is silky.

155

A male cinnamon can have the cinnamon gene as a "null," as a "single" or as a "double." Only in the last case does he exhibit the cinnamon color. With a single cinnamon gene, the male is split for cinnamon. And without the gene, a male from a cinnamon line is a normal-colored green Budgie. Because of the sex linkage, a female can only be either normal-colored green or true, visible cinnamon. Split for cinnamon is an impossibility for females.

We have been talking about the cinnamon factor as if it involved an "extra" factor. Actually, a factor is missing, namely one of the genes determining black coloration, the so-called "melanin factor."

There are two variants of cinnamon. The lighter of the two is called cream wing; the other is darker and is called bronze wing. Both variants also are sex-linked.

Five types of crosses are possible with the cinnamon factor.

1. *Cinnamon male x cinnamon female*. If you want to breed cinnamons, this cross is the surest method. Both the females and the males issuing from this cross will be cinnamons.

2. *Cinnamon male x normal female*. The young will be cinnamon females and split for cinnamon males. You will be able to distinguish the female chicks from this cross immediately because they have the outward appearance of cinnamons. The male chicks look like normal Budgies, but we can be sure that they all have the cinnamon factor hidden inside them.

3. *Split for cinnamon male x cinnamon female*. That's a useful cross, too, because we know that all males are either cinnamons or split for cinnamons. This means that all males that don't have the cinnamon trait visible still carry it hidden within them. The females are visibly cinnamon or normal.

4. *Split for cinnamon male x normal female*. I don't recommend this cross in practice. You should consider it only if you can't arrange any other combination because you only have one or more split for cinnamon males.

The result of this mating includes both split for cinnamon males and normal males, which aren't visually distinguishable. You will have to do test matings to establish which males have the cinnamon factor and which don't. The females are either cinnamon or normal.

5. *Normal male x cinnamon female*. I don't recommend this cross either. It results in only split for cinnamon males and normal females.

To see how the young from a certain cross will look, let's take an example from cross #3: A light green/cinnamon blue male and a cinnamon skyblue female.

The designation for these birds would be:

Male Ff On On bb c

Female ff On On bb cc.

The cinnamon factor is designated by c's. Since the male is split for cinnamon, he has the cinnamon factor in single form, designated by the one "c." The female, which can't have the split form, has the cinnamon factor in double dose, designated by "cc."

156

There is a marked consistency of type and overall conformation in these four beautiful Budgies. They offer proof positive of an intelligent, purposeful breeding program in operation. *van Herk*

In a diagram, the cross looks like this:

Male: Light green/cinnamon blue
Ff On On bb c

		F On b	f On b c
Female: cinnamon skyblue ff On On bb cc	f On b c	Ff On On bb c Light green/ cinnamon blue	ff On On bb cc Skyblue cinnamon
	f On b c	Ff On On bb c Light green/ cinnamon blue	ff On On bb cc Skyblue cinnamon

The cross, as the diagram shows, gives us light green/cinnamon blue and skyblue cinnamon. For the normal color variation, we would expect to get both males and females from each of these color combinations. But in this case, things are somewhat different because of the sex linkage. As we already have shown, the female can't be a split for cinnamon. Females have to be cinnamon or normal. Therefore, all the birds with the description light green/cinnamon are males. Skyblue cinnamon can be male or female. The normal females don't have any cinnamon factor, not even a split for cinnamon. The normal females, however, would have been split for cinnamon if they had been males.

The cinnamon factor can be bred into all color variations of the Budgie. It's possible even with albinos and lutinos, even though the factor wouldn't be visible and could be attained only in the split for cinnamon form.

Like the graywing factor the cinnamon color factor softens all the other colors on the rest of the Budgie. The blue and the green of the cinnamon are also less brilliant than the colors of a normal blackwing. And the quills, which are gray in graywings, are brown in cinnamons.

Cinnamon Budgerigars

The coloration of the cinnamon is as follows:

Cinnamon light green. The mask is yellow. The wavy design on the wings, back of the head and neck is cinnamon brown on a yellow background. The rest of the body is pale grass green. The long tail feathers are dark blue with dark quills. There are three large, round cinnamon spots on both sides of the neck, although the last of these is partially hidden under a purple cheek patch.

Cinnamon dark green. The mask is yellow. The wavy design on the wings, back of the head and neck is cinnamon brown on a yellow background. The rest of the body is dark grass green. The long tail feathers are darker than those

158

of the light green cinnamon. There are three large, round cinnamon spots on both sides of the neck. The last of these is partially hidden under a purple cheek patch.

Cinnamon olive green. The mask is yellow. The wavy design on the wings, back of the head and neck is cinnamon brown on a yellow background. The rest of the body is muted olive green. The long tail feathers are darker than the dark green cinnamon. The three large, round spots on both sides of the neck are cinnamon, although the last is partially hidden by a purple cheek patch.

Cinnamon skyblue. The mask is white. The wavy design on the wings, back of the head and neck is cinnamon brown on a white background. The rest of the body is skyblue. The long tail feathers are blue with a brown quill. The three large, round spots on both sides of the neck are brown, although the last is partially hidden by a purple cheek patch.

Cinnamon cobalt. The mask is white. The wavy design on the wings, back of the head and neck is cinnamon brown on a white background. The rest of the body is pale cobalt. The long tail feathers are darker than with the cinnamon skyblue. The quills are dark brown. The three large, round spots on both sides of the neck are brown, although the last spot is partially hidden by the purple cheek patch.

Cinnamon mauve. The mask is white. The wavy design on the wings, back of the head and neck is cinnamon brown on a white background. The rest of the body is pale olive green. The long tail feathers are darker than with the cinnamon cobalt. They have brown quills. The three large, round spots on both sides of the neck are cinnamon brown, although the last one is partially hidden by the purple cheek patch.

The Opaline Factor

Opalines show the wavy design as usual on the wings but not on the rest of the body. The mutation appeared first in 1933, but where it happened is not known. The early green opalines had top feathers on the wings with a border of green on a blue foundation. The opalines that were bred later had blue with a white or black border.

The green with its yellow head became more or less multi-colored: green, yellow, blue, and black. Further breeding developed the graywing opaline, the cinnamon opaline, and the fancy opaline. The last of these was a further new mutation, which reduced the number of rows in the wavy design on the upper part of the wing from five to three.

The opaline factor is sex-linked in the same way as the cinnamon factor. Just as with cinnamon, it seems that the opaline Budgie has more factors than the normal bird, but again, this is not the case. In reality something is missing—the wavy design on the head and neck (although it generally remains vaguely visible). On the upper part of the back, between the wings, the wavy design generally is somewhat more visible. The degree to which the wavy design is visible on head and neck determines the quality of an opaline. The less visible, the better.

The opaline factor goes along with a less bright color, but the sheen and silkiness of the opaline exceeds that of normal birds in most cases.

Ordinarily, opalines have very distinct throat spots, and the black of the wavy design also is more distinct than with normal Budgies. This situation is explained by the theory that the opaline has the normal amount of black coloration (melanin) but that the opaline factor distributes this black coloration over a limited surface. This makes the color more distinct, or deeper.

The inheritance of the opaline factor works as follows:

1. *Opaline male x opaline female.* This combination will produce opaline males and opaline females.

2. *Opaline male x normal female.* This combination will produce split for opaline males and opaline females.

3. *Split for opaline male x opaline female.* From this combination comes opaline males, opaline females, split for opaline males, and normal females.

4. *Split for opaline male x normal female.* This will result in split for opaline males, normal females, normal males, and opaline females.

5. *Normal male x opaline female.* This pairing produces split for opaline males and normal females.

With opalines, also, the first three matings are the most important because they allow us to produce the largest number of opalines and split for opalines. We know that all males are opalines or split for opalines, so that they may or may not look like opalines but always at least have the hidden factor for opaline. The sex linkage determines that the females of these matings are either opalines or normal.

The fourth and fifth matings are less useful. The fourth can produce both split for opaline and normal males, which can't be distinguished visually. The fifth produces only split for opaline males. It could be of use, however, if a breeder only had an opaline female available. The split for opalines that would be produced by this mating would then have to be backcrossed on the opaline female (mating #3). One could develop a line of opalines in this way from a female opaline.

If a breeder only had a split for opaline male on hand, he still could develop a line of opalines. He first would do mating #4, and then he would backcross the opaline females from that mating to the male.

The opaline factor is designated much like the cinnamon factor—by adding letters behind the basic designation: two for the apparent opaline and one for the split for opaline. The designation for light green/opaline blue is: Ff On On bb op. The designation for opaline skyblue is: ff On On bb op op.

The requisites of a good opaline include an even wavy design on the wings and a very vague or totally invisible wavy design on the back and neck.

Continuous selection is essential. The opaline blue has a tendency to have the blue run into the white mask. Selection is needed also to sharply separate the yellow or the white of the head from the rest of the body.

Opaline Budgerigars

The heritage of opaline obeys the following rules:

Opaline light green. Mask is buttercup yellow to the tip of the wings, where it shades into bright grass green. This green should continue between the wings and form a triangle there—with little, or preferably no wavy design. The rest of the body is bright grass green. The wings show a symmetrical design on a grass green reflecting background. The long tail feathers are not lighter in color than the rest of the body. The neck has three large, round spots on both sides, the last of which are hidden under the purple cheek patch.

Opaline dark green. The color distribution is the same as with opaline light green, but the color itself is dark grass green. The long tail feathers are darker than with opaline light green.

Opaline olive green. The color distribution is the same as with opaline light green, but the color itself is bright olive green. The long tail feathers are darker than with opaline dark green.

Opaline skyblue. The color distribution is the same as with opaline light green. The body color is a bright, light skyblue. The mask is white. The long tail feathers are darker blue than the rest of the body.

Opaline cobalt. The color distribution is the same as with opaline skyblue, but the color itself is bright cobalt. The long tail feathers are darker than with opaline skyblue.

Opaline mauve. The color distribution is the same as with opaline skyblue. The body is mauve. The long tail feathers are darker than with opaline cobalt.

Slateblue Budgerigars

Slates, one of the newest color mutants, inherit a sex-linked color trait. The color should not be confused with Australian gray, which was developed from a mutation that occurred in Australia. It also should not be confused with English gray, which is deeper and warmer than Australian gray, and originated in England in 1947.

The slate color of slateblue Budgies can be found in light, medium, and dark variations. It sometimes is difficult to distinguish a dark English gray from a slateblue medium.

Slateblue in general hasn't caught on too well. Most people seem to prefer the gray colors.

The sex linkage of the slateblue trait is similar to that of cinnamon and opaline. The breeder can use the same rules of heredity for slates as for cinnamons or opalines by just substituting the word "slateblue" for cinnamon or opaline. The expected results of the various crosses follows the same pattern, too. Just add the single or double slate factor to the designtion— single for split for slateblue and double for slateblue.

Slateblue has been combined with the basic green, yellow, blue, and graywing colorations, and also with the blue-whitewing and green-yellowwing coloration.

Albinism

The concept of albinism is quite generally known. It can be defined as an abnormal trait caused by loss of pigment in the body. It produces the appearance of colorlessness.

An albino animal is one that has no coloration. It looks white because our eye gets an impression of white from the "structural color" of the hair or feathers brought about by the air trapped within them. Partial albinism exists, but a true albino has no color pigment anywhere. Where it has no hair or feathers, the blood shines through the colorless skin, making those parts appear red or pink. Examples are eyes, legs, and beaks.

Albinism occurs rarely in Nature. It probably is brought about by a disturbance in the sex organs of one of the parents. Everyone knows about white mice with red eyes and rabbits of like description. There are albino ravens (very rare), blackbirds, sparrows, and large mammals. The phenomenon also occurs in humans.

Albinism is a mutation, and therefore a heritable trait. There is no factor for color in any cell, not even sex cells.

It is fairly easy to propagate albinism, even though the phenomenon is rare in Nature. In the wild, an albino stands little chance of reproducing itself because to do so, it would have to find another albino with which to mate. Backcrossing in Nature just doesn't happen; there are far too many other propagative possibilities. Furthermore, albinos don't have much opportunity to breed in the first place, because the variant animal is generally shunned by others of its species. On top of that, albinos are easy prey for their enemies. Their white appearance makes them stand out and they can't take evasive action very well because their sight is impaired. The iris of their eyes lacks color like the rest of the body, and the light entering the eyes is not toned down.

Albino Budgerigars

The first albino of modern breeding developed in Germany in 1932. The owner followed the usual procedure to propagate the mutation. He mated the albino, which was a female, with another Budgie and got some young with coloration that led him to suspect that they should be split for albino. He backcrossed the male young to their mother and indeed got some albino young as a result—true albinos because they received the albino factor from

An ideal bird room is convenient for those who must work in it and comfortable for the birds living in it. For example, if albino Budgies are kept, lighting facilities should allow for the albinos' sensitivity to bright light. *Harkema*

163

both their father and mother. By breeding these birds carefully, with proper selection, he could bring albino birds on the market fairly quickly and they earned him a considerable amount of money!

Albinos are white with a silky sheen. The eyes and legs are light red.

Some people say that albinos are weaker than normally-pigmented Budgies, but that never has been proven. Albinos should be kept in properly shaded cages because their eyes just can't stand sunlight.

Lutino Budgerigars

Lutinos sometimes are called yellow albinos. This is a good name for them because albinos and lutinos are brought about by the same factor, the one that removes melanin, the black pigment. More precisely, the lutino is the "albino" of the green and yellow color series, while the true albino belongs to the blue color series. So, actually albino and lutino are not really separate colors, as odd as this may seem. They are *albinised* green or yellow birds or *albinised* blue birds—except that in the case of the lutino they still retain the basic ground color.

A lutino light green/white, therefore, looks like a usual yellow lutino with red eyes and rose-colored legs. Actually it is a light green split or white Budgie that lost its coloration through albinism and therefore appears to be lutino.

Lutinos can be bred by crossing albinos or split for albinos with Budgies carrying the yellow or green factor. Albinos are bred by mating lutinos with Budgies carrying the blue or white factor.

Not all birds from these matings turn out to be albino or lutino after the first cross. Sex linkage is somehow involved. At first, one thought all lutinos and albinos inherited sex-linked traits. Only later was it discovered that some albinos and lutinos had sex-linked traits but that others didn't. Apparently, a second mutation came about after the original one in Germany, and this second mutation is not sex-linked.

The two types of albinos can't be distinguished visually from one another. Only by breeding can the difference be discovered.

Sex-linked Lutino and Albino Budgerigars

Lutino and albino Budgies with the sex-linked trait follow the same rules of inheritance as sex-linked cinnamons, opalines, and slates. These rules dictate the following:

Lutino or albino male x lutino or albino female produces lutino females and lutino males.

Albino or lutino male x normal female produces albino or lutino females, and split for albino or lutino males.

Split for albino or lutino male x albino or lutino female produces albino or lutino females, albino or lutino males, split for albino or lutino males, and normal females.

164

Split for albino or lutino male x normal female produces split albino or lutino males, normal males and females, and albino or lutino females.

Normal male x albino or lutino female produces split for albino or lutino males and normal females.

In the above rules of inheritance, reference to "normal" males or females means birds of the appropriate color variation. That is, blue and white for albinos and green or yellow for lutinos.

Once again we see that the three first-mentioned rules produce the best results for the breeder. The other two are not recommended. The fourth produces normal males and split males, which are not distinguishable, and the breeder would have to make test matings to determine which birds had the albino or lutino factor. The fifth produces only split males and normal females.

With the sex-linked trait, there are no split females that carry a hidden factor for lutino or albino—as you would expect.

The hidden color factors in albino and lutino birds are passed on to their offspring and act as if albinism or lutinism didn't exist. Consider a cross of an albino/skyblue male with an albino/mauve female. (An albino/mauve female is a real combination because the sex linkage affects only the albino trait. In other words, the female can't carry a hidden factor for albino, but she can very well carry a hidden factor for mauve.) This mating produces 100 percent albinos that all carry the hidden factor for cobalt. The invisible color inheritance continues despite all. If the offspring is crossed with normal males or females, the hidden color would surface.

With this set of facts in mind, it isn't hard to determine the remaining rules of heredity for albinos and lutinos. Just follow the rules for blue and white or yellow and green Budgies. (Refer to the earlier discussion in the section on CROSSBREEDING.) Just add the albino or lutino factor to the various designations, making due allowance for the sex-linked inheritance.

Take, for example, the cross: Male mauve/white x female graywing cobalt. The following colors are possible in the young:

mauve/graywing
cobalt/graywing
graywing mauve/white
graywing cobalt/white.

Now follow heredity rule #3, add the albino factor, and the following outcome becomes possible:

Males: albino/mauve graywing   mauve/albino graywing
albino/cobalt graywing   cobalt/albino graywing
albino/graywing mauve white   graywing mauve/albino white
albino/graywing cobalt white   graywing cobalt/albino white

Females:	albino/mauve graywing	mauve/graywing
	albino/cobalt graywing	cobalt/graywing
	albino/graywing mauve white	graywing mauve/white
	albino/graywing cobalt white	graywing cobalt/white

Notice that some of the offspring are albino and some split for albino. The split for albinos all are males; the albinos can be male or female. The normal green Budgies from this cross all are female; all males that don't look like albinos are split for albinos.

Again, you won't find the entire inventory in one single brood. However, the possibility exists that a number of broods out of this cross will produce all these color varieties in the young.

From this discussion you now understand that if you breed from albinos, you can be sure that they are descended from blues. If you want to know specifically which blue is involved, mate them with blue Budgies and you will find out.

Non-sex-linked Lutino and Albino Budgerigars

Since the eye can't distinguish between lutinos and albinos that are sex-linked and those that are not, the only way to know which factor is involved is to conduct test matings.

The non-sex-linked albino or lutino factor is recessive and follows the same rules as the factor for skyblue. Consider the basic possible matings once again, keeping in mind that albino and lutino birds being discussed here are all non-sex-linked. To make this clear, let's use the abbreviation NSL (for "non-sex-linked") in all cases.

NSL albino or lutino x NSL lutino or albino produces NSL albino or lutino young of both sexes.

NSL lutino or albino x split for NSL albino or lutino produces 50 percent NSL albino or lutino and 50 percent split for NSL albino or lutino.

NSL albino or lutino x normal produces young of both sexes that are split for NSL albino or lutino.

Split for NSL albino or lutino x split for NSL albino or lutino produces 25 percent NSL lutino or albino, 25 percent normal and 50 percent split for NSL albino or lutino.

Split for NSL albino or lutino x normal produces half normal and half split for NSL albino or lutino.

Keep in mind throughout that split for NSL albinos and lutinos all look like normal Budgies. For example, they have black eyes—not red eyes. Breeders say of them that they carry albino or lutino genes. That is because you can breed albinos or lutinos out of them without having to mate them with true, red-eyed albinos or lutinos.

In this list of basic possible matings, the last two crosses once again are

166

not recommended. One can't tell the difference between the normal Budgies and Budgies with the albino gene that comes out of these crosses.

I also don't recommend crossing albinos and lutinos carrying the sex-linked factor with those that have non-sex-linked albinism. The resulting young all would have the typical red eyes. But even with the first generation, you can't tell which of the young inherited the sex-linked trait and which inherited the non-sex-linked trait. The number of black-eyed birds in this case is much greater than one would expect, and it takes a great deal of trouble to purify the line.

Fallow Budgerigars

The first fallow appeared in California in 1931. It was a mutation of a green/blue Budgie that had a dark brown wavy design on a golden yellow background. The rest of the bird was olive yellow, the eyes were dark red and the legs were pink.

This description suggests that there is only a small difference between fallow and cinnamon. Indeed, there are fallows that could be confused with cinnamons at first blush. However, the fallow's brown is darker than the cinnamon's. Fallows have more nearly the brown of bronzes. Fallows, however, have one easily distinguishable feature, namely, their dark red eyes. The red is darker than that of the albino and lutino eye.

The hereditary factor for fallow is recessive to the factors of normal Budgies. That means, you lose the features of the fallow when you cross them with other color variants. To describe the fallow factor, let's compare it with albino and lutino. With the latter, it is a case of an absent melanin factor, the one that produces pigment. The melanin factor is double; it consists of black and dark brown pigment. Switching to fallows, in their case there is a color change in the melanin, where the black is apparently pushed aside by the brown. The recessive fallow factor is not sex-linked.

The rules for the inheritance of fallow are:

Fallow x fallow produces all fallows.

Fallow x split for fallow produces half fallows and half split for fallows.

Fallow x normal produces all split fallows.

Split for fallow x split for fallow produces 25 percent fallows, 25 percent normal Budgies, and 50 percent split for fallows.

Split for fallow x normal produces half split fallows and half normal Budgies.

Once again, the last two crosses are not recommended. However, if you only have split for fallows available for breeding, you might have no other choice. Both of these crosses produce split for fallows and normal Budgies that are not distinguishable by their appearance. The split for fallows have dark eyes. You can sort out the young for the fallow factor only by test matings.

A group of young Budgies following their first molt.

An immaculate group of well-cared-for birds waiting to enter their night shelter.

168

The calculation of the result of a certain mating doesn't involve many difficulties even if we bring in the fallow factor.

As an example, use the following cross:

fallow white cobalt x mauve/white fallow.

Without the fallow factor, we would have the cross of white cobalt x mauve/white, which results in:

mauve/white, cobalt/white, white mauve and white cobalt.

In this case, the fallow factor is involved as fallow x split for fallow, which results in 50 percent fallows and 50 percent split for fallows. So if we add the fallow factor to the calculation, we get:

Half: fallow mauve/white, fallow cobalt/white, fallow white mauve, and fallow white cobalt.

Half: Mauve/white fallow, cobalt/white fallow, white mauve/fallow and white cobalt/fallow.

Soon after the development of the fallows, breeders succeeded in breeding other colors of fallow as well. The complete list contains:

Fallow light green. The mask is yellow. The wavy design on the wings, back of the head and neck is dark brown on a white background. The long tail feathers are dark blue-gray. There are three dark brown spots on both sides of the neck; the last of these is hidden behind the purple cheek patch. The rest of the body is yellowish green. The eyes and legs are red.

Fallow dark green. This variant looks like light green, except that the body is pale grass green.

Fallow olive green. This also resembles the light green fallow. However, the long tail feathers are darker and the body color is a dull olive green with a brownish tint.

Fallow skyblue. The mask is white. The wavy design on the wings, back of the head, and back of the neck is dark brown on a yellow background. On both sides of the neck, there are three round, dark brown spots, the last of which is partially hidden under the purple cheek patch. The long tail feathers are blue-gray. The rest of the body is pale skyblue. The eyes and legs are red.

Fallow cobalt. Similar to the skyblue. However, the tail feathers are darker and the body color is pale cobalt.

Fallow mauve. Similar to the fallow cobalt. However, the long tail feathers are darker and the body color is purplish mauve.

Yellow-Faced Budgerigars

Many casual observers not familiar with Budgies will single out a yellow-face in a cage full of other birds and say it's something special. This is a remarkable reaction, and yet I don't think yellow-faces are all that special. It's more a case of people recognizing the different color of the mask as something noticeably different.

The yellow-face factor causes a change in the color of the mask. Often we can notice the yellow is noticeable on other parts of the body. The yellow is mostly somewhat lighter than the normal yellow of a green parrot, for example.

The factor can appear in all color variants, even in green Budgies, although it is hardly noticeable in that group. The factor can be single or double, but there is no visible difference between birds with the single and the double factor. The difference comes to the fore in crosses where we normally would expect a white mask—crosses using the blue, white, or graywing color variants.

The yellow-face factor is dominant, so there can be no split for yellow-faces in the list of possible combinations resulting from the various crosses. A Budgerigar has the factor for yellow-face single, double or not at all.

The basic combinations are:

Yellow-face (double factor) x yellow-face (double factor) yields all yellow-faces (double factor).

Yellow-face (double factor) x yellow-face (single factor) produces half yellow-face (double factor) and half yellow-face (single factor).

Yellow-face (double factor) x normal produces all yellow-faces (single factor).

Yellow-face (single factor) x yellow-face (single factor) produces 25 percent yellow-face (double factor), 25 percent normal, and 50 percent yellow-face (single factor).

Yellow-face (single factor) x normal produces half yellow-face (single factor) and half normal.

Let's now consider how this would apply to a specific example, say yellow-face (single factor) skyblue/graywing x yellow-face (single factor) mauve/white. As a first step, disregard the yellow-face factor and calculate the results of the cross of skyblue/graywing with mauve/white.

This cross would produce: cobalt/white, cobalt graywing and graywing cobalt/white.

Now add the effects of crossing yellow-face (single factor) with yellow-face (single factor), which produces 25 percent yellow-face (double factor), 25 percent normal and 50 percent yellow-face (single factor).

The overall results would be:

yellow-face (double factor) cobalt
yellow-face (double factor) cobalt/white
yellow-face (double factor) cobalt graywing
yellow-face (double factor) graywing cobalt/white

yellow-face (single factor) cobalt
yellow-face (single factor) cobalt/white
yellow-face (single factor) cobalt graywing
yellow-face (single factor) graywing cobalt/white

plain cobalt
plain cobalt/white
plain cobalt graywing
plain graywing cobalt/white

Remember that the yellow-face factor has an effect not only on the mask but also on other parts of the body in most cases. Blue yellow-face Budgies, for example, have a greenish color to the blue on the breast and neck. It is possible to create the so-called pastel-colored Budgie by continuous breeding with double-factor yellow-faces and white or yellow wings. The basic color of pastels is blue, but the yellow effect is present throughout the body, so that the bird gets the appearance of being yellow-green with a blue reflection. In this case, we are not speaking about a new mutation but the product of selective breeding in which the dominant yellow-face factor has played an important role.

Gray Budgerigars

Once graywinged Budgies appeared on the scene, it was reasonable to also expect the appearance of gray Budgies. The mutation indeed took place—in two locations, no less. As a result, we have recessive gray Budgies and dominant grays, the so-called Australian grays.

Grays belong to the most recent types of Budgie, along with the violets. They appeared even after the Danish pied.

There is very little visible difference between the Australian (or dominant) gray and the English (or recessive) gray. The English variant is closer to pearl gray and the color is a little livelier. Both types have a gray body and a white mask. The wavy design is an intense black, perhaps because the gray intensifies the "color" of the black. Breeders have been successful in breeding grays in which the mask also has taken on the gray color, so that the whole bird is pearl gray. They also have bred the yellow-face factor, graywing, and whitewing into the English grays.

Australian gray inherits in the same manner as the yellow-face factor. This means that the factor for Australian gray can appear as single, double, or nul. "Split for gray" does not exist.

The rules for the inheritance of Australian gray are:

Austr. gray (double factor) x Austr. gray (double factor) produces all Austr. gray (double factor).

Austr. gray (double factor) x Austr. gray (single factor) yields half Austr. gray (double factor) and half Austr. gray (single factor).

Austr. gray (double factor) x normal produces all Austr. gray (single factor).

Aust. gray (single factor) x Austr. gray (single factor) produces 25 percent Austr. gray (double factor), 25 percent normal and 50 percent Austr. gray (single factor).

171

Austr. gray (single factor) x normal produces half Austr. gray (single factor) and half normal.

With this color variant, it also is impossible to use the eye to distinguish between single and double factors. The grays have to be crossed with normal Budgies in order to know which is which. If it is a double factor, the offspring all are gray (single factor); if it is a single factor, the offspring are half grays (single factor) and half normal.

Normal Budgies from any color series can be used for these test matings. The normal color can then be found in split form in the offspring. (The gray, as stated, is *not* possible in split form.)

Australian grays are available in three color gradations, light, medium and dark. Among themselves, these gradations inherit like skyblue, cobalt, and mauve.

The English grays, which are recessive, appear as gray, full gray, white gray, cinnamon gray, fallow gray and gray yellow-face. With English grays, as stated, the factor for gray *can* be carried in split form.

Blue-Whitewing and Green Yellow-Wing Budgerigars

Blue-whitewings and green yellow-wings are among the prettiest color variants to be seen in Budgies. The blue-whitewing, for example, is a regal bird, with its cream-white wings and light blue trunk, set off sharply from the white.

Both color variants depend on a recessive factor, except for the white and yellow Budgies. If you cross a blue-whitewing with a white Budgie, a dominant factor is at work. As a result, you get only blue-whitewing young. Or else, you get half blue-whitewings and half white Budgies.

The difference lies in the factor controlling blue-whitewings, which appears in single and double form. Crossing a blue-whitewing (double factor) with a white Budgie, yields all blue-whitewings that only have one factor. However, crossing a single factor blue-whitewing with white, yields half whites and half blue-whitewings (single factor).

The rules for the inheritance involved are:

Blue-whitewing (double factor) x blue-whitewing (double factor) produces all blue-whitewings (double factor).

Blue-whitewing (double factor) x blue-whitewing (single factor) produces half blue-whitewing (double factor) and half blue-whitewing (single factor).

Blue-whitewing (single factor) x blue-whitewing (single factor) produces 25 percent blue-whitewing (double factor), 25 percent normal (white) and 50 percent blue-whitewing (single factor).

The same rules also apply to green yellow-wings.

If one crosses blue-whitewings x yellow, the result is green or green yellow-wing because yellow dominates white.

172

If you want to introduce the whitewing or yellow-wing factor into other color variants (gray, violet, slate, cinnamon, and opaline), it's best to use birds of the white series.

Only the blue-whitewings and green yellow-wings with a double factor are purely inheriting, that is, homozygous. All blue-whitewings and green yellow-wings consequently are heterozygous, that is, impurely inheriting, if they carry the single factor. This means that these heterozygotes carry a hidden trait for another color in addition to the one that is visible to the eye. This hidden color can be recovered easily if the breeder knows the coloration of the parents.

Violet Budgerigars

Violet is one of the newer color variations in Budgies. It shouldn't be confused with mauve; some breeders do make that mistake. I have seen violets at shows, however, that convinced me that this is truly a new color variant.

The violet is derived from the blue. The mutation had been expected for a long time, because the Budgie has a purple cheek spot that points to the existence of violet pigment.

In actuality, violets are cobalts with one or two extra factors for violet. To appear violet, a bird must have a double blue factor plus a dark factor (D), plus one or two violet factors. Even if skyblues, mauves, or even greens have the violet factor in single or double form, they don't look truly violet. You *can* see differences, slight ones, from the skyblue, mauve, or green Budgie.

The designation for the visible violet is:
ff On On Bb v   *or*   ff On On Bb vv.

If you want to breed violets, you have to be continually careful to make crosses that will produce young having the cobalt factor plus one or two violet factors. In practice, that means crossing a violet Budgie with a cobalt or mauve; the young inherit the dark factor *and* the violet factor in this way.

The factor for violet dominates normal. That means that other color variants can carry the violet factor even if this is hard to see—as I just mentioned. But if you mate, say, a skyblue Budgie with a mauve, you get violets with a visible violet color.

A violet skyblue or mauve is somewhat darker than the normal skyblue or mauve, but in no way can these birds be considered violets. (Still, a violet mauve often does have a few violet feathers on its breast.)

You can introduce the violet factor into other cobalts as long as you are careful not to lose the dark factor of the cobalt. In this way, you get graywing-violet, fallow-violet, opaline-violet, violet-whitewing, and cinnamon-violet.

The violet-whitewing is an especially beautiful Budgie, but it requires careful breeding. Crosses of green with violet or yellow with violet can carry the violet factor, but they give outward signs of it only through a slightly variant color.

Here's a photo to learn from—this head is virtually perfect and provides graphic emphasis of the breeder's goal.   *van Herk*

Young Budgies in this enclosure are kept away from older birds so they may get extra feedings and specialized items such as rearing food and extra oats without competition from aggressive adults.
                                                                                                van Herk

Crested and Frizzy Budgerigars

Crested and frizzy Budgerigars probably are the result of one basic mutation. Breeding them offers many interesting possibilities that often have been neglected. Japanese breeders have concentrated most on these possibilities, and they have developed Budgies with fancy crests and with feathering reminiscent of the frizzy canary.

One of the most recent mutants is the so-called chrysanthemum Budgerigar, which has all its body feathers elongated and curled.

The three standard crests are: (1) Tufted, (2) Half circular and (3) Full circular. The mutation originated in New South Wales, Australia, in the aviaries of A. Mathews in 1935. It is inherited in the same manner as the crests of canaries and Bengalese finches. This means that the crest factor is dominant and that the double crest factor is lethal. There are no living Budgies with a double crest factor.

The lethal aspect of double crested is, of course, quite important in breeding these birds. To produce them, mate a crested bird with a non-crested one. If you breed two crested birds together, you get 25 percent birds without crest and 50 percent crested birds (with a single crested factor). The other 25 percent of the young die because they have the double crested factor.

The preferred cross (crested x not crested) produces progeny, of which half are crested and half not crested. The crested x crested option produces the same percentage of crested birds (50 percent), but the total production of young is diminished by 25 percent.

The crest can be improved by continuous selection of the best individuals. Select uncrested birds with wide skulls for these matings. This will increase the likelihood that you will produce young with heads suited for crests.

Pied Budgerigars

The first pied Budgies were bred in the Netherlands by the late breeder Van Dijk in 1938. He started with a mutant male that had a yellow patch in the back of his neck. This male was crossed with a lutino female, giving rise to the first pied (multi-patched) Budgerigar. Van Dijk continued crossing until he had Budgies that had white patches on a blue background and yellow patches on a green background.

There had been an earlier pied mutation in 1929, the two-colored Budgie, which was blue on its left side and green on its right side. It was a remarkable phenomenon which, unfortunately, could not be maintained.

English breeders continued working with the Van Dijk mutation more than others. They developed two-colored pied Budgies that show a horizontal dividing line between the yellow and the green or the white and the blue. This dividing line splits the body in half at the height of the start of the thighs. These are the preferred pied Budgies.

Many deviant Budgies have been called pied. For example, the erroneous designation includes birds that don't show color separations but have patches that preferably are spread evenly over the body. I saw a Budgie at the exhibition *Aviarum* in Eindhoven, the Netherlands, in 1953, which then already was identified as Danish pied. I would never have accepted it as such. The bird was white, with a few blue patches on the bottom of its body; on the wings, it had a symmetrical design of black patches superimposed on somewhat larger patches. A more proper name for this bird would have been "Delft blue." The description was certainly appropriate.

The heredity of normal pied is recessive, as you will note in the rules of heredity detailed below.

Perhaps it would be useful to use the term "spotted" along with the term "pied" to describe birds that don't exhibit the distinguishing feature of pied, namely the color separation at the level of the thighs. Too many birds now called Danish or Dutch pied lack this important feature.

Below is a description of the various color combinations of pied Budgerigars.

Light green, dark green, and olive green pied are bright yellow above the color separation at thigh level. Below it, they show a somewhat lighter shade of green than the green of the normal light green, dark green, and olive green Budgies. The color runs in a V-shape into the yellow-colored tail.

Skyblue, cobalt, and mauve pied are snow white above the color separation at thigh level. Below it, they show a somewhat lighter shade of blue than the blue of the normal skyblue, cobalt, and mauve Budgies. The color runs in a V-form into a white tail.

Light yellow, dark yellow and olive yellow pied are bright yellow above the color separation at thigh level. Below it, they have a very light green color, which runs in a V-shape into a yellow tail.

White blue, white cobalt, and white mauve pied are snow white above the color separation at thigh level. Below that, they have a very light blue color that runs in a V-shape into a white tail.

The pied factor is inherited as follows:

Pied x pied produces all pied.

Pied x split for pied produces half pied and half split for pied.

Pied x normal produces all split for pied.

Split for pied x split for pied produces 25 percent pied, 25 percent normal, and 50 percent split for pied.

Split for pied x normal produces half split for pied and half normal.

The two last matings are not recommended because there will be normal and split for pied Budgies among the young that can't be distinguished from one another. Test matings would be needed to determine which of the young carried the pied factor.

An example of a pied mating, borrowed from F. S. Elliott and E. W. Brooks, would be:

Pied skyblue/white x pied light green/white.

Without the pied factor, this mating produces:

Light green/blue, light green/white, skyblue, skyblue/white, light yellow/white and white blue.

That, in other words, would be the result of the cross of skyblue/white with light green/white. After adding the pied factor, we get the following results:

Pied light green/blue
Pied light green/white
Pied skyblue
Pied skyblue/white
Pied light yellow/white
Pied white blue

Note that we added "pied" to all the designations. As stated, mating pied with pied produces all pied young.

Danish Pied and Dutch Pied Budgerigars

Danish pied Budgerigars (sometimes called Harlequins) originated during World War II from a mutation among birds owned by the director of the Helsinki Zoo, Mr. C. Enehjelm. The mutant was yellow with a green underside and an asymmetric black patch on the breast, head, and wings. This conforms to the concept of "pied."

The mutation is a very interesting one. It seems to consist of a number of linked recessive factors—factors that only appear together and furnish the proper color and design.

Why the mutant was called Danish pied remains a mystery. Finnish pied would seem more appropriate. The notable feature of the variant is its apparently enlarged eye, compared with birds of other color variations. This is an illusion, caused by the black eye ring, or periophthalmic ring, characteristic of this variant. The black patch, which originally was asymmetric, now also occurs in symmetric form. I suspect that in the future, once the line is purified through lengthy selection, the symmetrical design will be mandatory. The patch normally is deep black—as if the black coloring (melanin) had been concentrated on these few small patches. The legs of Danish pied Budgies are pink.

Danish pied quickly became a favorite the world over. Today, the best Danish pied are bred in Belgium and Switzerland. The line does not yet breed pure, and it will probably take lengthy selection to achieve consistency. As a result, two Danish pied birds can differ considerably from one another. The one basic requirement remains a demarcation in color at thigh level and a design of (preferably a limited number of) spots on the head near the eye and on the wings.

Danish pied, like Dutch pied, is recessive. Dutch pied (or white and yellow clear-flighted) resembles Danish pied to a great extent. Both are recessive to "not pied."

A new and particularly attractive color mutation is the Australian pied. It is modeled in this group by the last bird on right and occurs in both the green and blue series.

Breeders expected one day to develop gray Budgies, like this fine young cock, once the graywing factor appeared and became well-established. *Harkema*

The color demarcation of Dutch pied lies somewhat higher. The eyes of adult Dutch pied are gray. The primary flight feathers are white in blue-colored birds and light yellow in the greens. There is a light patch of varying size at the back of the head (especially noticeable in normal greens). Normals have dark tails with others showing white or yellow. Often one tail feather is dark, the other white.

A cross of Dutch pied with Danish pied results in black-eyed yellow birds without the green reflection.

The rules of heredity for Danish pied follow those for previously discussed pied variants. In the rules, just substitute Danish pied for every mention of pied.

For example, Danish pied light green/blue x skyblue/Danish pied white produces (without the Danish pied factor): Light green/blue, light green/white, skyblue, and skyblue/white. Adding the Danish pied factor, we get Danish pied x split for Danish pied, which yields half Danish white and half split for Danish pied.

The results of the cross turn out to be:

Half light green/Danish pied blue, light green/Danish pied, white, skyblue/Danish pied, and skyblue/Danish pied white.

And half Danish pied light green/blue, Danish pied light green/white, Danish pied skyblue, and Danish pied skyblue/white.

Australian Pied Budgerigars

One of the newest mutations in Budgies is the Australian pied. It originated in Australia and at first viewing seems a mutation of the well-known blue-whitewing and green yellow-wing. The white Australian pied Budgie has a white head with standard markings. The wings are white without markings. The breast and tail have the color of the blue series (light blue, cobalt, mauve, and violet); but under the upper edge of the forewings, a white, finger-wide band runs across the breast.

The green Australian pied has a yellow head with standard markings and the wings are yellow without markings. The breast and tail have the color of the green series (light green, dark green, and olive green). Under the upper edge of the forewings, a yellow, finger-wide band runs across the breast.

Australian pied Budgies often have the same round patch on the back of the head seen in Dutch and Danish pied. Breeding the Australian pied also is as difficult as breeding the Dutch and Danish pied. The color band has to be broad and horizontal and must be set off sharply against the blue or green. A serious breeder will have to exercise rigorous selection. Crossing Australian pied with other pied variants is not recommended.

Australian pied has the usual "pied" heredity:

Austr. pied x Austr. pied produces all Austr. pied.

Austr. pied x split for Austr. pied produces half Austr. pied and half split for Austr. pied.

Austr. pied x normal produces all split for Austr. pied.

Split for Aust. pied x split for Austr. pied produces 25 percent Austr. pied, 25 percent normal, and 50 percent split for Austr. pied.

Split for Austr. pied x normal produces half split for Austr. pied and half normal birds.

The last two crosses are not recommended because they produce both normals and splits that are not visually distinguishable.

Ino Mutations

This rather new mutant has red eyes and feathers of lutino yellow. All white birds also exist. The lutinos belong to the green series; the albino, to the blue. Genetically, both are albinos, animals completely without pigment. In lutinos, only the yellow remains.

Good birds have a deep, warm yellow tint, with white cheek spots, flight feathers and tail. The eyes are surrounded by a whitish iris ring.

Most of the birds are small in appearance and tend to remain so. The pale yellow lutinos, in comparison, are often rather large and plump in conformation.

If birds of these two varieties are mated, a 100 percent lutino of both types will result. Lutino x lutino produces a pure color, but body and fertility diminish rapidly after several generations. Quality can be raised again by breeding with normal females occasionally. Yellows are best; greens are possible.

As I mentioned, all red-eyed Budgies, except fallows, have a sex-linked heredity. Mating a lutino male with a green female produces lutino females. A lutino female mated to a green male produces only split males, plus homozygous (purely inheriting) green females.

The albinos are not as popular. They are pure white with red eyes. They generally are weaker and often have a blue (instead of a green) shine on the rump. Breeding them to gray Budgies results in larger, sturdier birds and the blue shine disappears.

Note, that all ino males have pink-violet ceres, while that of the females are brownish, like that of the greens. Legs and toes in both sexes have the same pink color, except in the darker Budgies of all shades, where they are bluish gray.

All the birds tend to avoid the light because of their unpigmented eyes. They dislike sitting in sunny or brightly-lit areas. They tend to become active at dusk and during the night, if you leave a night light on. It's best, therefore, not to breed them in outside aviaries.

The heredity of ino mutations is analogous to that of cinnamon and opaline factors.

Lacewings were first noticed in England. The birds are yellow or white, with a weak, light brown, interrupted design on the wing feathers and back,

180

reminiscent of lace. They developed from completely bleached Inos. The eyes are red, with a light iris. Legs and toes are pink. There heredity, also, is sex-linked.

Future Possibilities

What surprises will Budgie breeding bring to light, given the operation of Nature and patience of the breeder? That's hard to predict, as with most surprises. Even the most able breeder can't force Nature to produce unnatural results.

This is not meant to infer that no further mutations will occur. Somebody with more patience than I has calculated that Budgies now exist in more than *840 varieties!* That figure can be expanded by the hundreds even if one only works with currently known color variants.

I can give you an example to show that theoretically you can produce 27 colors and color combinations with just one pair of Budgies. For this exercise, we need a white-blue Budgie, which we'll mate to a homozygous olive green. The young are all dark green and heterozygous for white. If in the next round of matings we inbreed brothers and sisters we already have the 27 named possibilities: 1. light green; 2. dark green; 3. olive green; 4. light green/blue; 5. dark green/blue; 6. olive green/blue; 7. light green/yellow; 8. dark green/yellow; 9. olive green/yellow; 10. light green/white; 11. dark green/white; 12. olive green/white; 13. light yellow; 14. dark yellow; 15. olive yellow; 16. light yellow/white; 17. dark yellow/white; 18. olive yellow/white; 19. skyblue; 20. cobalt; 21. mauve; 22. skyblue/white; 23. cobalt/white; 24. mauve/white; 25. white blue; 26. white cobalt; and 27. white mauve.

The dreamers among us breeders visualize a black Budgie, a solid blue or solid green Budgie, or a dark brown Budgie. The color pigments are available. The new variants would come about if one color would disappear and another would dominate.

Could one perhaps breed a red bird out of a true violet? And then on to orange (in combination with yellow), pink (with white), and dark red (with green)? Pied birds with black wings? Or white birds with black wings? Yellow opaline, yellow greenwings, and white bluewings?

Already people have bred rainbow Budgies—or, put more scholarly— yellow-faced opaline clearwings. (A clearwing comes about through a combination of yellow-wing and whitewing.)

Now here's an interesting question: Would we need to attempt a breeding with a related species to finally get red Budgies, or can it be done with existing genetic material? Could we even parallel what's been done with Canaries, which got their red from the Hooded Siskin of South America?

Most breeders seriously doubt the feasibility of bringing in new colors with the help of other parakeet species. They see too much difference in size and type. People have been able to interbreed Budgies with *Agapornis*

That all Budgie colors came originally from wild-colored or light green birds such as this one is an amazing natural phenomenon. The patience of those who worked with spontaneous mutations to develop the beautiful colors seen today led to a wonderful, absorbing and wholesome hobby now enjoyed by millions.

fischeri, but nothing could be accomplished with the resulting crossbreeds because they appeared to be infertile.

Another intriguing question: Could something special be accomplished if artificial insemination ever were applied to Budgies? Could one possibly even generate mutations by inducing a purposeful change in the composition of chromosomes and genes?

Whatever the answer is to these questions, we can assume that we haven't yet reached the end of the road. That realization makes Budgie breeding as a hobby a source of ongoing experimentation and absorbing study.

There was a time when the sight of yellow or blue birds in a Budgie nest came as a great surprise to the breeder. There may come a time when many as yet undreamed-of colors will be developed to extend the fascination and appeal of the world's most popular cage bird.   *Wissink*

183

The Ideal Budgerigar

Courtesy of the Budgerigar Society (England)

ON THE OPPOSITE PAGE is the illustration issued to all members of the Budgerigar Society (England) and below the current Budgerigar Society Ideal Budgerigar Standard and scale of points which emphasizes those features regarded as significant for judging.

Condition is essential. If a bird is not in condition it should never be considered for any award.

Type—Gracefully tapered from nape of neck to tip of tail, with an approximately straight back line, and a rather deep, nicely curved chest.

Length—The ideal length is 8½ inches from crown of the head to the tip of the tail. Wings well braced, carried just above the cushion of the tail and not crossed. The ideal length of the wing is 3¾ inches from the butt to the tip of the longest primary flight, which must contain seven visual primary flight feathers fully grown and not broken. *No bird showing "long-flighted" characteristics shall be eligible to take any award.*

Head—Large, round, wide and symmetrical when viewed from any angle; curvature of skull commencing at cere, to lift outward and upward, continuing over the top and to base of head in one graceful sweep.

Beak—Set well into face.

Eye—To be bold and bright, and positioned well away from front, top and back skull.

Neck—To be short and wide when viewed from either side or front.

Wings—Approximately two-fifths the total length of the bird, well braced, carried just above the cushion of the tail and not crossed.

Tail—To be straight and tight with two long tail feathers.

Position—Steady on perch at an angle of 30 degrees from the vertical, looking fearless and natural.

Mask and Spots—Mask to be clear, deep and wide, and where demanded by the Standard should be ornamented by six evenly spaced large round throat spots, the outer two being partially covered at the base by cheek patches, the size of the spots to be in proportion of the rest of the make-up of the bird as shown in the illustrated Ideal. Spots can be either too large or too small.

Legs and Feet—Legs should be straight and strong, and two front and two rear toes and claws firmly gripping perch.

Markings—Wavy markings on cheek, head, neck, back and wings to stand out clearly.

Color—Clear and level and of an even shade.

Rendering of the Budgerigar Society's ideal bird—the ideal
height is 8½ inches from the crown of the head to the tip of
the tail.

The Budgerigar Society's Scale of Points

REVISED SCALE OF POINTS **Remember: Condition is Supremely Important**	*Size shape bal- ance and de- port- ment*	*Size and shape of head*	*Colour*	*Mask and spots*	*Wing mark- ings*
Green (Light, Dark or Olive)	45	20	15	15	5
Grey Green (Light, Medium or Dark)	45	20	15	15	5
Yellow (incldg. Op. Yell. but excldg. Lutino)	45	20	35	—	—
Olive Yellow (including Cinnamon Olive Yellow)	45	20	35	—	—
Skyblue, Cobalt, Mauve or Violet	45	20	15	15	5
Grey (Light, Medium or Dark)	45	20	15	15	5
White (Light Suffusion including Opaline White but excluding Albino)	45	20	*35	—	—
Whitewing (Skyblue, Cobalt, Mauve, Violet or Grey)	45	20	*35	—	—
Yellow-wing (Light, Dark, Olive or Grey Green)...............................	45	20	*35	—	—
Greywing (Light, Dark, Olive or Grey Green)...............................	45	20	10	10	15
Greywing (Skyblue, Cobalt, Mauve, Violet or Grey)	45	20	10	10	15
Cinnamon (Light, Dark, Olive or Grey Green)...............................	45	20	10	10	15

REVISED SCALE OF POINTS **Remember: Condition is Supremely Important**	*Size shape balance and deportment*	*Size and shape of head*	*Colour*	*Mask and spots*	*Wing markings*
Cinnamon (Skyblue, Cobalt, Mauve, Violet or Grey)	45	20	10	10	15
Fallow (Light, Dark, Olive or Grey Green) ...	45	20	15	15	5
Fallow (Skyblue, Cobalt, Mauve, Violet or Grey)..............................	45	20	15	15	5
Lutino...............................	45	20	35	—	—
Albino...............................	45	20	35	—	—
Opaline (Light, Dark, Olive or Grey Green)............................	40	20	†25	10	5
Opaline (Skyblue, Cobalt, Mauve, Violet or Grey)	40	20	†25	10	5
Opaline Cinnamon (Light, Dark, Olive or Grey Green)	40	20	†25	10	5
Opaline Cinnamon (Skyblue, Cobalt, Mauve, Violet or Grey)......................	40	20	†25	10	5
Opaline Greywing (Light, Dark, Olive or Grey Green)	40	20	†25	10	5
Opaline Greywing (Skyblue, Cobalt, Mauve, Violet or Grey)......................	40	20	†25	10	5
Yellow-faced (All varieties in Blue series except Pieds)	45	20	15	15	5
Pied (Dominant varieties)	45	20	§15	10	‡10
Pied (Clear Flighted varieties)	45	20	10	10	#15
Pied (Recessive varieties)	45	20	‡20	—	‡15
Dark-eyed Clear varieties	45	20	35	—	—
Lacewings	45	20	10	10	15

* Points allocated for depth of colour and clearness of wings.

† Including clear mantle and neck (10 points).

‡ Including contrast in variegation.

\# Including clear flights and tail.

§ Includes band.

Teams of six birds of any one colour or teams of four birds of any one colour.
Points: General quality, 50; Uniformity, 50.

Budgerigar
Color Standards

Courtesy of the American Budgerigar Society

Light Green

Mask, buttercup of an even tone ornamented on each side of throat with three clearly defined black spots, one of which is at the base of the cheek patch. *Cheek patches,* violet. *General body color,* back, rump, breast, flanks and underparts, bright grass-green of a solid and even shade throughout; markings on cheeks, back of head, neck, and wings black and well defined on a buttercup ground. *Tail,* long feathers blue-black.

Dark Green

As above, but of a dark laurel green body color. *Tail,* long feathers darker in proportion.

Olive Green

As above but of a deep olive green body color. *Tail,* long feathers darker in proportion.

Grey Green

This variety conforms to the standard for light green except in the following details: *Cheek patches,* grey, *General body color,* dull mustard green. *Tail,* long feathers black.
NOTE: There are light, medium and dark forms of the grey green.

Light Yellow

Mask, buttercup. *Cheek patches,* light blue. Spots, light grey. Back, rump, breast, flanks, wings and underparts, buttercup and as free from green suffusion as possible. Primaries lighter than body. *Tail,* long feathers, lighter than body color.

Dark Yellow

As above, but deeper body color. *Cheek patches,* light blue.

Olive Yellow

As above, but mustard body color. *Cheek patches,* blue.

Skyblue

Mask, clear white ornamented on each side of throat with three clearly defined black spots, one of which appears at the base of the cheek patch. *Cheek patches,* violet. *General body color,* back, rump, breast, flanks and underparts, pure skyblue; markings on cheeks, back of head, neck, and wings, black and well defined on a white ground. *Tail,* long feathers, blue-black.

Cobalt

As above, but of a rich deep cobalt blue body color. *Tail,* long feathers darker in proportion.

Mauve

As above, but body color purplish mauve, with a tendency to a pinkish tone. *Tail,* long feathers darker in proportion.

Violet

As skyblue but of a deep intense violet body color. *Tail,* long feathers darker in proportion.

Grey

Mask, white, ornamented on each side of throat with three clearly defined black spots, one of which appears at the base of the cheek patch. *Cheek patches,* grey-blue or slate. *General body color,* back, rump, breast, flanks and underparts solid grey. *Markings* on cheeks, back of head, neck and wings, black and well defined on a white ground. *Tail,* long feathers black.
NOTE: There are light, medium and dark forms of the grey.

189

Whites of Light Suffusion

Mask, white. *General body color,* back, rump, breast, flanks and underparts, white; *Wings and Tail,* pure white. *Cheek patches,* silver.

Greywing Light Green

Mask, yellow, ornamented each side of throat with three clearly defined spots of smoky grey, one of which appears at the base of the cheek patch. *Cheek patches,* pale violet. *General body color,* back rump, breast, flanks and underparts, pale grass green. *Markings,* on cheek, back of head, neck and wings should be smoky grey, half-way between black and zero. *Tail,* long feathers smoky grey with pale bluish tinge.

Greywing Dark Green

As above but of a light laurel green body color. *Tail,* long feathers darker still in proportion.

Greywing Olive Green

As above but of a light olive green body color. *Tail,* long feathers darker still in proportion.

Greywing Skyblue

Mask, white, ornamented each side of throat with three clearly defined grey spots, one of which appears at the base of the cheek patch. *Cheek patches,* light violet. *General body color,* back, rump, breast, flanks and underparts, clear pale skyblue. *Markings* on cheeks, back of head, neck and wings, pure grey, half-way between black and zero. *Tail,* long feathers greyish blue.

Greywing Cobalt

As above, but of a pale cobalt body color, with tail of corresponding color.

Greywing Violet

As greywing skyblue, but of a pale violet body color, with tail of corresponding color.

Greywing Mauve

As above, but of a pale mauve body color, with tail of corresponding color.

190

Greywing Grey Green

As greywing light green but with body color of light mustard green. *Cheek patches,* light grey. *Tail,* long tail feathers deep grey.

Greywing Grey

As greywing skyblue but with body color of pale grey. *Cheek patches,* pale grey, *Tail,* feathers deep grey.

Cinnamon Light Green

Mask, yellow, ornamented on each side of throat with three clearly defined cinnamon brown spots, one of which appears at the base of the cheek patch. *Cheek patches,* violet. *General body color,* back, rump, breast, flanks, and underparts, apple-grass green. *Markings,* on cheeks, back of head, neck and wings, cinnamon brown well defined on a yellow ground. *Tail,* long feathers dark blue with brown quill. *Feet,* pink.

Cinnamon Dark Green

As above, but of a light laurel green body color. *Tail,* long feathers darker in proportion.

Cinnamon Olive Green

As above, but with a light olive green body color. *Tail,* long feathers darker in proportion.

Cinnamon Light Yellow

Mask, buttercup. *Cheek patches,* pale violet. Back, rump, breast, flanks, wings and underparts, buttercup and as free from green as possible. *Primaries,* lighter than body. *Tail,* long feathers, lighter than body color. *Feet,* pink.

Cinnamon Skyblue

Mask, white, ornamented on each side of throat with three clearly defined cinnamon brown spots, one of which appears at the base of the cheek patch. *Cheek patches,* violet. *General body color,* back, rump, breast, flanks, and underparts, pale skyblue. *Markings,* on cheeks, back of head, neck and wings cinnamon brown on white ground. *Tail,* long feathers blue with brown quill.

Cinnamon Cobalt

As above, but with general body color pale cobalt. *Tail,* long feathers as above but cobalt.

Cinnamon Mauve

As above, but with general body color pale mauve. *Tail,* long feathers as above, but mauve.

Cinnamon Grey

As cinnamon skyblue but with cheek patches slate and body color of pale grey. *Tail,* long feathers of deep cinnamon shade.

Cinnamon Grey Green

As cinnamon light green but with body color of pale grey green. *Tail,* long tail feathers of deep cinnamon shade.

Cinnamon Violet

As cinnamon skyblue but with general body color of pale violet. *Tail,* long tail feathers of pale cinnamon shade.

NOTE: In all forms of cinnamon the male bird carries a deeper shade than the female.

Cinnamon White of Light Suffusion

Mask, white. *General body color,* back, rump, breast, flanks and underparts, white. *Wings and Tail* pure white. *Feet,* pink.

Fallow Light Green

Mask, yellow, ornamented on each side of throat with three clearly defined brown spots, one of which appears at the base of the cheek patch. *Cheek patches,* violet. *General body color,* back, rump, breast, flanks and underparts, yellowish green. Markings on cheeks, back of head, neck and wings, dark brown on a yellow ground. *Eyes,* clear red with light iris ring. *Tail,* long feathers bluish grey.

Fallow Dark Green

As above but with dark laurel green body color. *Tail,* long feathers darker in proportion.

Fallow Olive Green

As above, but with body color of light mustard olive. *Tail,* long feathers darker in proportion.

Fallow Grey Green

As above but with *Cheek patches* of blue grey. Body color of dull mustard green. *Tail,* long feathers darker in proportion.

Fallow Skyblue

Mask, white, ornamented on each side of throat with three clearly defined brown spots, one of which appears at the base of the cheek patch. *Cheek patches,* violet. General body color, back, rump, breast, flanks and underparts, pale skyblue. *Markings,* on cheek, back of head, neck and wings, dark brown on white ground. Eyes, clear red with light iris ring. *Tail,* long feathers bluish-grey.

Fallow Cobalt

As above, but with a warm cobalt body color. *Tail,* long feathers darker in proportion.

Fallow Mauve

As above, but with a pale mauve body color of a pinkish tone. *Tail,* long feathers darker in proportion.

Fallow Violet

As fallow skyblue but with a pale violet body. *Tail,* long feathers darker in proportion.

Fallow Grey

As fallow skyblue but with pale grey body color. *Cheek patches* of blue grey. *Tail,* long feathers darker in proportion.

Light Forms

The American Budgerigar Society recognizes the existence of a light form of cinnamon and fallow identical to the normal already described, but lighter in body color and markings.

Pure Yellow Red-eyes (Lutinos)

Buttercup throughout. *Cheek patches* silver. *Eyes,* clear red with light iris ring. *Feet,* pink. *Cere,* flesh colored. *Tail,* long feathers and primaries, white.

Pure White Red-eyes (Albinos)

White throughout. *Eyes,* clear red with light iris ring. *Cheek patches,* silver. *Feet,* pink. *Cere,* flesh colored.

Clearwing (Yellow-wing) Light Green

Mask, buttercup, ornamented on each side of throat with three light grey spots. *Cheek patches,* violet. General body color, back, breast, flanks and underparts a bright grass green. *Wings,* buttercup (as free from markings as possible). *Tail,* long feathers light bluish green.

Clearwing (Yellow-wing) Dark Green

As above but with general body color of laurel green; long tail feathers darker in proportion.

Clearwing (Yellow-wing) Olive Green

As above but with general body color of olive green. *Tail,* long feathers darker in proportion.

Clearwing (Yellow-wing) Grey Green

This variety conforms to the standard for Yellow-wing Light Green except: General Body Color, dull mustard green. *Cheek patches* blue grey. *Tail,* long feathers darker in proportion.

Clearwing (Whitewing) Skyblue

Mask, clear white, *Cheek patches,* violet, ornamented on each side of throat with three smoky grey spots, (the paler the better), one of which appears at the base of cheek patch. General body color, back, rump, breast, flanks, and underparts, pure skyblue. *Wings,* pure white. *Tail,* long feathers bluish-white.

Clearwing (Whitewing) Cobalt

As above but of a rich, deep blue cobalt body color.

Clearwing (Whitewing) Mauve

As above, but of a rich deep purplish mauve.

Clearwing (Whitewing) Violet

As above, but body color of an intense violet.

Clearwing (Whitewing) Grey

As above, but body color of grey, *Cheek patches* blue grey. It should be noted that the grey body color may be of any of the three shades, light, medium, or dark grey.

Opaline Light Green

Mask, buttercup yellow, extending over back of head and merging into general body color at a point level with butt of wings, thus leaving a clear "V" effect between top of wings, so desirable in this variety. *Mask* to be ornamented on each side of throat with three clearly defined black spots, one of which is at the base of cheek patch. *General body color,* back, rump, breast, flanks and underparts a bright grass green. *Wings,* to be iridescent and of the same color as body, markings should be normal and symmetrical. Long tail feathers not to be lighter than mantle. *Cheek patch,* violet.

Opaline Dark Green

As above, but of a dark laurel green body color. *Tail,* long feathers darker in proportion.

Opaline Olive Green

As above, but of an olive green body color. *Tail,* long feathers darker in proportion.

Opaline Grey Green

As opaline light green but with body color of dull mustard green. *Tail,* long feathers not to be lighter than mantle. *Cheek patches* of grey.

Opaline Skyblue

As above, but with a skyblue body color and suffusion, and white mask instead of buttercup. *Tail,* long feathers not to be lighter than mantle.

Opaline Cobalt

As skyblue, but of a cobalt body color. *Tail,* long feathers darker in proportion.

Opaline Mauve

As skyblue, but of a mauve body color. *Tail,* long feathers deeper in proportion.

Opaline Violet

As opaline skyblue but of a deep intense violet body color. *Tail,* long feathers darker in proportion.

Opaline Grey

As opaline skyblue but with a body color of solid grey. *Tail,* long tail feathers not to be lighter than mantle, *Cheek patches of grey.*

Opaline Cinnamon Light Green

Mask, buttercup yellow, extending over back of head and merging into general body color at a point level with butt of wings, thus leaving a clear "V" effect between the wings so desirable in this variety. *Mask,* to be ornamented on each side of throat with three clearly defined cinnamon brown spots, one of which is at the base of cheek patch. *Cheek patch,* violet. *General body color,* mantle pale grass green. *Wings,* to be iridescent and of the same color as body. Markings should be normal and symmetrical and cinnamon brown in color. Long tail feathers not to be lighter than mantle.

Opaline Cinnamon Dark Green

As above, but of a light laurel green body color. *Tail,* long tail feathers darker in proportion.

Opaline Cinnamon Olive Green

As above, but with a light olive green body color. *Tail,* long feathers darker in proportion.

Opaline Cinnamon Skyblue

Mask, white ornamented by six clearly defined cinnamon spots, the outer two being partially covered at the base by violet cheek patches. *General body color,* back, rump, breast, flanks, and underparts, pale skyblue. Markings on cheeks, back of head, neck and wings: cinnamon brown on white ground. *Tail,* long feathers not to be lighter than mantle.

Opaline Cinnamon Cobalt

As above, but with general body color of pale cobalt. *Tail,* long feathers darker in proportion.

Opaline Cinnamon Mauve

As skyblue, but of a pale mauve body color. *Tail,* long feathers darker in proportion.

Opaline Cinnamon Violet

As skyblue but with general body color of pale violet. *Tail,* long feathers darker in proportion.

Opaline Cinnamon Grey

As skyblue but with body color of pale grey. *Tail,* long feathers not to be lighter than mantle. *Cheek patches* of grey.

Opaline Cinnamon Grey Green

As opaline cinnamon light green, but with body color of dull mustard green. *Tail,* long feathers not to be lighter than mantle. *Cheek patches* of grey.
NOTE: In all forms of opaline cinnamon, the male bird carries a deeper shade than the female.

SLATE

Light Green

Spots and markings, jet black; *Cheek patches,* violet; *Body,* including back, rump, breast, flanks and underparts, sage green; long tail feathers, blue-black.

Dark Green

Similar to above, body and tail darker.

Olive Green

Body and tail darker.

Skyblue

Body greenish slate; tail, blue-black.

Cobalt

Body and tail darker.

Mauve

Body and tail darker.

Violet

Body color in doubt.

Yellow Face Type (1)

Mask only, yellow, otherwise exactly as corresponding normal variety.
NOTE: Yellow marked feathers in tail permissible.

Yellow Face Type (2)

As above except yellow wash to evenly blend over entire body color.

CLEARFLIGHT—(DUTCH PIEDS)

Clearflight—Light Green

Mask, buttercup yellow of an even color ornamented by six evenly spaced, clearly defined large round black throat spots, the outer two being partially covered at the base by the cheek patches. *Cheek patches*, violet. *General body color*, as the normal light green with the exception of one small patch approximately half an inch by five-eighths of an inch of clear buttercup at the back of the head. Slight collar or extension of the bib, while undesirable, will not penalize. *Wings*, color and markings as the normal light green but with seven visible flight feathers of clear yellow. Dark flights constitute a fault. *Tail*, the two long feathers should be clear yellow, dark tail feathers are a fault. *Cere*, similar to that of a normal light green. *Eyes*, dark with light iris ring. *Beak*, normal horn color.

Clearflight—Dark Green

As above, but with general body color as for normal dark green.

Clearflight—Olive Green

As above, but with general body color as for normal olive green.

Clearflight—Grey Green

As above, but with general body color as for normal grey green. *Cheek patches*, grey blue or slate. (It should be noted that there are light, medium and dark shades of Pied (clearflighted) grey green.)

Clearflight—Skyblue

Mask, white, ornamented by six evenly spaced clearly defined large round black throat spots, the outer two being partially covered at the base by cheek patches. *Cheek patches*, violet. *General body color*, as the normal skyblue with the exception of one small patch approximately one half-inch by five-eighths inch of pure white at the back of the head. Slight collar or extension of bib, while undesirable, will not penalize. *Wings*, as normal skyblue but with seven visible flight feathers of pure white. Dark flights constitute a fault. *Tail*, the two long feathers should be pure white, marked or dark tail feathers are a fault. *Cere*, similar to that of normal skyblue. *Eyes*, dark with light iris ring. *Beak*, normal horn color.

198

Clearflight—Cobalt

As above, but with general body color as for normal cobalt.

Clearflight—Mauve

As above, but with general body color as for normal mauve.

Clearflight—Violet

As above, but with general body color as for normal violet.

Clearflight—Grey

As above, but with general body color as for normal grey. *Cheek patches,* grey-blue to slate. (It should be noted that there are light, medium and dark shades of clearflight grey.) NOTE: Opaline, yellow-face and cinnamon form of clearflight are recognized but these should only be shown in clearflight classes.

Dark-eyed Clear-Yellow

Cheek patches, silvery-white. *General body color,* pure yellow throughout and free from any odd green feathers or green suffusion. *Wings,* pure yellow throughout, free from black or grizzled tickings or green suffusion. All flight feathers paler yellow than rump color. *Tail,* as the flight feathers. *Cere,* fleshy pink in color as in lutinos. *Eyes,* dark without any iris ring. *Beak,* orange colored. *Feet and legs,* fleshy pink.

NOTE: (The actual body color varies in depth according to the genetic make-up, i.e., whether light, dark or olive green, etc.)

Dark-eyed Clear-White

As above, but with white body color and free from any blue suffusion or odd blue feathers. *Flights and tail,* white. *Cere,* fleshy pink in color as in Albinos. A Yellow-faced form of Dark-eyed Clear White is also recognized.

RECESSIVE PIED
(DANISH OR HARLEQUIN)

Recessive Pied-Light Green

Mask, buttercup yellow of an even tone. *Throat spots,* as the normal light green variety, may be present from one to full number. *Cheek patches,* silvery white. *General body color,* irregular patches of clear buttercup yellow and bright grass green with the latter mainly on the lower chest, rump and underparts. Zebra markings on the top of the head and around the eyes cover more than fifteen to twenty per cent of total area. All visible flight feathers should be clear yellow but odd dark flight feathers are not faults. *Cere*, fleshy pink in color as in lutinos. *Eyes*, dark without any iris ring. *Beak*, orange colored. *Feet and legs*, fleshy pink.

Recessive Pied-Dark Green

As above, but with a yellow and dark green body color.

Recessive Pied-Olive Green

As above, but with a yellow and olive green body color.

Recessive Pied-Grey Green

As above, but with a yellow and grey-green body color. *Cheek patches*, grey-blue or slate, or a mixture of both. (It should be noted that there are light, medium and dark shades of recessive pied-grey green.)

Recessive Pied—Skyblue

Mask, white. *Throat spots*, as the normal skyblue variety, may be from one to full number. *Cheek patches*, violet, silvery-white or a mixture of both. *General body color*, irregular patches of white and bright skyblue with the latter mainly on the lower chest, rump, and underparts. Zebra markings on top of head and around the eyes are not faults. *Wings*, black undulations or polka-dot markings should not cover more than fifteen to twenty per cent of total area. All visible flight feathers should be white but odd dark flight feathers are not faults. *Cere*, fleshy pink in color as in albinos. *Eyes*, dark without any light iris ring. *Beak*, orange colored. *Feet, and legs*, fleshy pink.

Recessive Pied—Cobalt

As above, but with a white and cobalt body color.

Recessive Pied—Mauve

As above, but with a white and mauve body color.

Recessive Pied—Violet

As above, but with a white and violet body color.

Recessive Pied—Grey

As above, but with a white and grey body color. *Cheek patches*, grey-blue or slate, or a mixture of both. (It should be noted that there are light, medium and dark forms of recessive pied-grey.) NOTE: An opaline yellow-face and cinnamon form of recessive pied is recognized.

An opaline yellow-face clearwing gray hen and her son. Such birds are excellent additions to a breeding program directed at producing the rainbow mutation.

Top: A clearwing opaline light green cock. Because of its dark brown wing markings, this mutation was once called the "brownwing." *Bottom:* A rainbow violet cock (yellow-face opaline clearwing violet).

A pair of immature lutino cocks. Their color will intensify as they get older.

Above: This albino cock would benefit from having a larger head and broader skull. *Right:* An Australian yellow-face skyblue pied cock.

Right: A recessive normal dark green pied hen whose markings, wings and tail are too dark. However, her excellent, overall type make her valuable in a breeding program. *Below:* An Australian opaline dark blue pied hen of excellent quality.

Left: This Danish recessive gray green pied ("harlequin") hen is an excellent show bird. *Below:* A black-eyed yellow cock of excellent type that would be helped by a stronger head.

Right: This lacewing white cock is an extremely impressive bird of excellent type. *Below:* A "spangle" normal gray green male. In this recent mutation the original ground color becomes the color of the markings while the color of the markings becomes the original ground color. It occurs in all colors but is not visible in whites and yellows.

Above: A normal white blue cock with a semi-circular crest. A very rare mutation, its crest is exceptionally fine. *Left:* This spectacular crested yellow-face Australian pied normal cinnamon gray cock is a very successful show bird. At this writing, birds of comparable quality are few and far between.

AUSTRALIAN PIED

Pied Light Green

Mask, buttercup yellow of an even tone, ornamented by six evenly spaced and clearly defined large round black throat spots, the outer two being partially covered at the base by cheek patches. *Cheek patches,* violet. *General body color,* as the normal light green variety but broken with irregular patches of clear buttercup yellow or with a clear yellow band approximately half an inch wide round its middle just above the thighs. An all-yellow or normal green-colored body should be penalized. Head patch is optional. NOTE: (All other things being equal, preference to be given in accordance with the scale of show points, to birds showing the band.) *Wings,* color and markings as the normal light green but having irregular patches of clear buttercup yellow or with part of the wing edges to shoulder, but clear yellow on an otherwise normal marked wing. Wing markings may be grizzled in appearance. All visible flight feathers should be clear yellow but odd dark flight feathers are not faults. *Tail,* the two long tail feathers may be clear yellow, marked or normal blue-black in color. *Cere,* similar to that of the normal light green or a mixture of normal color and fleshy pink. *Eyes,* dark with light iris ring. *Beak,* normal horn color. *Feet and legs,* blue mottled as the normal light green, fleshy pink or a mixture of both.

Pied Dark Green

As above, but with general body color as for normal dark green.

Pied Olive Green

As above, but with general body colors for normal olive green.

Pied Grey Green

As above, but with general body color as for normal grey green. *Cheek patches,* grey-blue to slate. (It should be noted that there are light, medium and dark shades of pied grey green.)

Pied Skyblue

Mask, white, ornamented by six evenly spaced and clearly defined large round black throat spots, the outer two being partially covered at the base by cheek patches. *Cheek patches,* violet. *General body color,* as the normal skyblue variety but broken with irregular patches of white or with a clear white band approximately half an inch wide around its middle just above the thighs. An all-white or normal blue-colored body should be penalized. Head patch is optional. NOTE: (All other things being equal, preference to be given in accordance with the scale of show points, to birds showing the band.) *Wings,* color and markings as the normal skyblue but having irregular patches of clear white or with part of the wing edges to shoulder but clear white on an otherwise normal marked wing. Wing markings may be grizzled in appearance. All visible flight feathers should be clear white but odd dark feathers are not faults. *Tail,* the two long tail feathers may be clear white, marked or normal blue-black in color. *Cere,* similar to that of normal skyblue. *Eyes,* dark with light iris ring. *Beak,* normal horn color. *Feet and legs,* blue mottled as the normal skyblue, fleshy pink or a mixture of both.

Pied Cobalt

As above, but with general body color as for the normal cobalt.

Pied Mauve

As above, but with general body color as for normal mauve.

Pied Violet

As above, but with general body color as for normal violet.

Pied Grey

As above, but with general body color as for normal grey. *Cheek patches,* grey-blue or slate. (It should be noted that there are light, medium and dark shades of dominant pied grey.) NOTE: An opaline, yellow-face and cinnamon form of dominant pied is recognized but these should only be shown in dominant pied classes.

Crested Light-Green

Head, ornamented with a circular type, a half circular type or a tufted type of crest. *Mask,* buttercup of an even tone ornamented on each side with three well defined round black spots, one of which appears at the base of each cheek patch. *Cheek patches,* violet. *General body color,* back, rump, breast, flanks, and underparts bright grass green of a solid and even shade throughout; markings on cheeks, back of head, neck and wings, black and well defined on a buttercup ground. *Tail,* two long feathers blue-black.

Circular Crest

This should be a flat round crest with the feathers radiating from the center of the head.

Half Circular Crest

This should be a half circle of feathers falling or raised in a fringe above the cere.

Tufted Crest

This should be an upright crest of feathers up to three-eighths of an inch high rising just above the cere.

The above is the Standard for the light green crested form; all other colors will be along similar lines except for the change of color where appropriate.

With varieties not having throat spots and wing markings, the points will be allocated to color.

Shape of Crest

The shape of each type of crest should be well-defined and any untidy feather disturbance(s) a fault.

Laced Clear-Body, Green

Mask, yellow, ornamented on each side of throat with three clearly defined spots of jet black, one of which appears at the base of the cheek patch. *Cheek patches,* silver grey. *General body color,* back, rump, breast, flanks and underparts, and head, pure buttercup yellow. *Wing markings,* should be jet black, well defined on buttercup ground. *Tail,* long feathers jet black.

Laced Clear-Body, Blue

Mask, white, ornamented on each side of throat with three clearly defined spots of jet black, one of which appears at the base of cheek patch. *Cheek patches,* silver grey. *General body color,* rump, breast, flanks and underparts, and head, pure white. *Wing markings,* jet black, well defined on white ground. *Tail,* long feathers jet black.

Red Eye Lacewing, Yellow

Mask, yellow, ornamented by six evenly spaced large round cinnamon throat spots, the outer two being partially covered at the base of the cheek patches. *Cheek patches,* pale violet. *General body color,* back, rump, breast, flanks, and underparts, yellow. *Markings,* on cheeks, back of head, neck, mantle and wings, cinnamon brown on a yellow ground. *Eyes,* clear red with light iris rings. *Tail,* long feathers, cinnamon brown. NOTE: The depth of yellow of the body color, etc., varies according to the normal counterpart being masked by the Lacewing character, i.e., the richest yellow is carried by the Lacewing Olive Green and the lightest by the Lacewing Light Green.

211

Red Eye Lacewing, White

Mask, white, ornamented by six evenly spaced large round cinnamon throat spots, the outer two being partially covered at the base of the cheek patches. *Cheek patches,* pale violet. *General body color,* back, rump, breast, flanks and underparts, white. *Markings,* on cheeks, back of head, neck, mantle and wings, cinnamon brown on a white ground. *Eyes,* clear red with light iris rings. *Tail,* long feathers, cinnamon brown. NOTE: The shade of white of the body color, etc., varies only slightly in tone according to the normal counterpart being masked by the Lacewing character. (A yellow-faced form is recognized.)

American Budgerigar Society Uniform Scale of Points

Size, Shape, Condition and Balance	30
Deportment and Wing Carriage	15
Size and Shape of Head	20
Color	15
Light, dark or olive yellow, whites of light suffusion, albinos, lutinos, clearwings, dark-eyed clear yellow or clear white, recessive pieds (harlequins)	35
Opalines and cinnamon-wing opalines	20
Laced clear-body	25
Greywings, cinnamon-wings, flighted pieds, (clearflights), red-eyed laced wings, crests	10
Mask and Spots	15
Greywings, cinnamons, opalines, dominant pieds, red-eyed lace wings	10
Laced clear-body, crests	5
Wing Markings	5
Clearwings, greywings, cinnamons, clearflighted pieds	15
Australian pieds, red-eyed laced wings	10

NOTE: Budgerigars are NOT judged on the basis of points. The only fully satisfactory method of judging any species is by comparison; by placing the birds side by side and gradually eliminating the poorest, then picking out the best on the basis of straight comparison. That is the method used by all A.B.S. panel judges, and the only one approved by the Executive Committee.

213

Good judges are experienced breeders, and instinctively place the greatest weight on those characteristics most difficult to produce.

When spots are not specified in the Color Standard, the points allotted for mask and spots are transferred to color.

When wing markings are not specified in the Color Standard, the points allotted for wing markings are transferred to color.

Yellow face is judged under the points for mask and spots; yellow factor under color; crest under head.

American Budgerigar Society Revised Scale of Points

	Size, Shape, Condition and Balance	Deportment and Wing Carriage	Size and Shape of Head	Color	Mask and Spots	Wing Markings
Light, Dark & Olive Green	30	15	20	15	15	5
Greygreen, Light, Dark & Medium	30	15	20	15	15	5
Yellow, Light, Dark & Olive	30	15	20	35	—	—
Skyblue, Cobalt, Mauve & Violet	30	15	20	15	15	5
Grey, Light, Medium & Dark	30	15	20	15	15	5
White, Light Suffusion	30	15	20	35	—	—
Yellow-Wing, Lgt., Dark, Olive & Greygreen	30	15	20	35[a]	—	—
Whitewing, Sky, Cobalt, Mauve, Violet, Grey	30	15	20	35[a]	—	—
Greywing, Light, Dark & Olive Green	30	15	20	10	10	15
Greywing, Greygreen, Light, Dark & Med.	30	15	20	10	10	15
Greywing, Sky, Cobalt, Mauve, Violet & Grey	30	15	20	10	10	15
Cinnamon, Light, Dark, Olive & Greygreen	30	15	20	10	10	15

	Size, Shape, Condition and Balance	Deportment and Wing Carriage	Size and Shape of Head	Color	Mask and Spots	Wing Markings
Cinnamon, Sky, Cobalt, Mauve, Violet & Grey	30	15	20	10	10	15
Fallow, Light, Dark, Olive & Greygreen	30	15	20	15	15	5
Fallow, Sky, Cobalt, Mauve, Violet, Grey	30	15	20	15	15	5
Pure Yellow Red Eye (Lutino)	30	15	20	35	—	—
Pure White Red Eye (Albino)	30	15	20	35	—	—
Opaline, Light, Dark, Olive & Greygreen	30	15	20	20[b]	10	5
Opaline, Sky, Cobalt, Mauve, Violet & Grey	30	15	20	20[b]	10	5
Opaline, Cinnamon, Light, Dark, Olive & Greygreen	30	15	20	20[b]	10	5
Opaline, Cinnamon, Sky, Cobalt, Mauve, Violet & Grey	30	15	20	20[b]	10	5
Slate	30	15	20	15	15	5
Yellow Face Type (1)	30	15	20	15	15	5
Yellow Face Type (2)	30	15	20	15	15	5
Flighted Pieds (Clearflight)	30	15	20	10	10	15
Australian Pieds	30	15	20	15[c]	10	10
Recessive Pied (Harlequin)	30	15	20	35[d]	—	—
Laced Clear Body	30	15	20	25	5	5
Red Eyed Sex Linked Lace Wing	30	15	20	15	10	10
Crest	30	15	35[e]	10	5	5
Dark Eyed Clear Yellow	30	15	20	35	—	—
Dark Eyed Clear White	30	15	20	35	—	—

[a] Points Allocated for depth of color and Clearness of wing.
[b] Including Clear Mantle.
[c] Variegation on body and wings.
[d] Including Band.
[e] Including crest size and shape.

216

Budgerigar Color Expectation Tables

THE FOLLOWING 27 tables concern the most familiar and therefore most important colors that can be established by the fancier. For instance: Table 1 gives all the possibilities in order to produce the light green Budgerigar; Table 2 for the dark green phase, etc.

How to Use the Tables

Behind some of the crossings, percentages are presented: 100%, 50%, 25% and 33 1/3%. Other percentages, however, are not given, as in such matters complicated theories must first be explained, such as crossing over type I and II. And because those percentages have no meaning for our tables—the correct results are only given behind the most important crossings—we will not go into these technical and often very complicated matters. In Table 1, for instance, you will find the crossing: dark green/white x light green/white (nr. 40); in other words: a crossing of two birds the first of which is dark green in external appearance (phenotype); the second bird light green; both however are split for the color white (or: carrying white as a recessive color). As all the given crossings in the 27 tables are based on a percentage of 100 birds, it should be understood that this crossing (nr. 40, Table 1) only presents the *possibility* of obtaining a light green Budgie. But, also understandably, not for 100%, as you have a chance of getting young birds of the following colors as well:

1. dark green
2. light green/blue
3. dark green/blue
4. light green/yellow

5. dark green/yellow
6. light green/white
7. dark green/white
8. light yellow
9. dark yellow
10. light yellow/white
11. dark yellow/white
12. skyblue
13. cobalt
14. skyblue/white
15. cobalt/white
16. white blue
17. white cobalt

Hence: together with the light green bird, eighteen (18) possibilities exist altogether.

The following crossing (nr. 41. Table 1) is: dark green/white x dark green/white; this crossing gives no less than 27 possibilities, as, besides the 18 just given results from crossing nr. 40, there are 9 more:

19. olive green
20. olive green/blue
21. olive green/yellow
22. olive green/white
23. olive yellow
24. olive yellow/white
25. mauve
26. mauve/white
27. white/mauve

The crossings with the given percentages present the quickest way to obtain the desired colors. From Table 3, for instance, it becomes obvious that all the young from light green x skyblue are for 100% light green/blue; the same applies when we pair a male skyblue with a light green hen. The second crossing of Table 3 is light green x cobalt; the outcome is 50% light green/blue, and 50% dark green/blue. The crossing dark green x light green/yellow on the other hand presents only 25% dark green/yellow (see Table 6, nr. 12), and further 25% light green, 25% light green/yellow, and 25% dark green/yellow.

Table 4 gives, in nr. 10, the crossing dark green x cobalt. Stated is that 33 1/3% of this crossing will present dark green/blue; the other possibilities are light green/blue, and olive green/blue, each, of course, for 33 1/3%.

YOU CAN USE THESE 27 TABLES IN A DIFFERENT WAY AS WELL!

You have, for example, a pair of Budgerigars, one of which is light green, the other dark yellow. By checking ALL CROSSINGS light green x dark yellow in the 27 tables you are able to find the outcome, as each table deals with only one given color. From the above crossing you may expect: 50% light green/yellow (Table 5, nr. 2), and 50% dark green/yellow (Table 6, nr. 1). A

218

crossing of cobalt x light green/white will present the following possibilities:
1. light green/blue (Table 3, nr. 25), and 2. dark green/blue (Table 4, nr. 37).

Crossing dark yellow x dark yellow/white gives the following possibilities:

1. light yellow (Table 19, nr. 16)
2. dark yellow (Table 20, nr. 19)
3. olive yellow (Table 23, nr. 7)
4. light yellow/white (Table 21, nr. 16) and
5. olive yellow/white (Table 24, nr. 7).

Finding the results this way will not present much of a problem, as all 27 tables are based on a fixed outline of colors. These 27 colors are:

1. light green
2. dark green
3. light green/blue
4. dark green/blue
5. light green/yellow
6. dark green/yellow
7. light green/white
8. dark green/white
9. olive green
10. olive green/blue
11. olive green/white
12. olive green/yellow
13. skyblue
14. skyblue/white
15. cobalt
16. cobalt/white
17. mauve
18. mauve/white
19. light yellow
20. dark yellow
21. light yellow/white
22. dark yellow/white
23. olive yellow
24. olive yellow/white
25. white blue
26. white cobalt
27. white mauve

Table 1. To produce LIGHT GREEN (also called GREEN and NORMAL GREEN) the theoretical expectation is:

1. LIGHT GREEN x LIGHT GREEN (100%)
2. light green x dark green (50%)
3. light green x light green/blue (50%)
4. light green x dark green/blue (25%)
5. light green x light green/yellow (50%)
6. light green x dark green/yellow (25%)
7. light green x light green/white (25%)
8. light green x dark green/white
9. DARK GREEN x LIGHT GREEN (50%)
10. dark green x dark green (33 1/3%)
11. dark green x light green/blue (25%)
12. dark green x dark green/blue
13. dark green x light green/yellow (25%)
14. dark green x dark green/yellow
15. dark green x light green/white
16. dark green x dark green/white
17. LIGHT GREEN/BLUE x LIGHT GREEN/BLUE (33 1/3%)
18. light green/blue x dark green/blue
19. light green/blue x light green/yellow (25%)
20. light green/blue x dark green/yellow
21. light green/blue x light green/white
22. light green/blue x dark green/white
23. DARK GREEN/BLUE x LIGHT GREEN/BLUE
24. dark green/blue x dark green/blue
25. dark green/blue x light green/yellow
26. dark green/blue x dark green/yellow
27. dark green/blue x light green/white
28. dark green/blue x dark green/white
29. LIGHT GREEN/YELLOW x LIGHT GREEN/YELLOW (33 1/3%)
30. light green/yellow x dark green/yellow
31. light green/yello x olive green/yellow
32. light green/yellow x light green/white
33. light green/yellow x dark green/white
34. DARK GREEN/YELLOW x LIGHT GREEN/YELLOW
35. dark green/yellow x dark green/yellow
36. dark green/yellow x light green/white
37. dark green/yellow x dark green/white
38. LIGHT GREEN/WHITE x LIGHT GREEN/WHITE
39. light green/white x dark green/white
40. DARK GREEN/WHITE x LIGHT GREEN/WHITE
41. dark green/white x dark green/white

Table 2. To produce DARK GREEN (also called LAUREL GREEN) the theoretical expectation is:

1. LIGHT GREEN x DARK GREEN (50%)
2. light green x olive green (100%)
3. light green x dark green/blue (25%)
4. light green x olive green/blue (50%)
5. light green x dark green/yellow (25%)
6. light green x olive green/yellow (50%)
7. light green x dark green/white
8. light green x olive green/white (25%)
9. DARK GREEN x LIGHT GREEN (50%)
10. dark green x dark green (33 1/3%)
11. dark green x olive green (50%)
12. dark green x light green/blue (25%)
13. dark green x dark green/blue
14. dark green x olive green/blue (25%)
15. dark green x light green/yellow (25%)
16. dark green x dark green/yellow
17. dark green x olive green/yellow (25%)
18. dark green x light green/white
19. dark green x dark green/white
20. dark green x olive green/white
21. OLIVE GREEN x LIGHT GREEN (100%)
22. olive green x dark green (50%)
23. olive green x light green/blue (50%)
24. olive green x dark green/blue (25%)
25. olive green x light green/yellow (50%)
26. olive green x dark green/yellow (25%)
27. olive green x light green/white (25%)
28. olive green x dark green/white
29. LIGHT GREEN/BLUE x DARK GREEN/BLUE
30. light green/blue x olive green/blue (33 1/3%)
31. light green/blue x dark green/yellow
32. light green/blue x olive green/yellow
33. light green/blue x dark green/white
34. light green/blue x olive green/white
35. DARK GREEN/BLUE x LIGHT GREEN/BLUE
36. dark green/blue x dark green/blue
37. dark green/blue x olive green/blue
38. dark green/blue x light green/yellow
39. dark green/blue x dark green/yellow
40. dark green/blue x olive green/yellow
41. dark green/blue x light green/white
42. dark green/blue x dark green/white
43. dark green/blue x olive green/white
44. OLIVE GREEN/BLUE x LIGHT GREEN/BLUE (33 1/3%)

45. olive green/blue x dark green/blue
46. olive green/blue x light green/yellow (25%)
47. olive green/blue x dark green/yellow
48. olive green/blue x light green/white
49. olive green/blue x dark green/white
50. LIGHT GREEN/YELLOW x DARK GREEN/YELLOW
51. light green/yellow x olive green/yellow (33 1/3%)
52. light green/yellow x dark green/white
53. light green/yellow x olive green/white
54. DARK GREEN/YELLOW x LIGHT GREEN/YELLOW
55. dark green/yellow x dark green/yellow
56. dark green/yellow x olive green/yellow
57. dark green/yellow x light green/white
58. dark green/yellow x dark green/white
59. dark green/yellow x olive green/white
60. OLIVE GREEN/YELLOW x LIGHT GREEN/YELLOW (33 1/3%)
61. olive green/yellow x dark green/yellow
62. olive green/yellow x light green/white
63. olive green/yellow x dark green/white
64. LIGHT GREEN/WHITE x OLIVE GREEN/WHITE
65. DARK GREEN/WHITE x LIGHT GREEN/WHITE
66. dark green/white x dark green/white
67. dark green/white x olive green/white
68. OLIVE GREEN/WHITE x LIGHT GREEN/WHITE
69. olive green/white x dark green/white

Table 3. To produce LIGHT GREEN/BLUE the theoretical expectation is:

1. LIGHT GREEN x SKYBLUE (100%)
2. light green x cobalt (50%)
3. light green x light green/blue (50%)
4. light green x dark green/blue (25%)
5. light green x light green/white (25%)
6. light green x dark green/white
7. light green x skyblue/white (50%)
8. light green x cobalt/white (25%)
9. DARK GREEN x SKYBLUE (50%)
10. dark green x cobalt (33 1/3%)
11. dark green x light green/blue (25%)
12. dark green x dark green/blue
13. dark green x light green/white
14. dark green x dark green/white
15. dark green x skyblue/white (25%)

16. dark green x cobalt/white
17. SKYBLUE x LIGHT GREEN (100%)
18. skyblue x dark green (50%)
19. skyblue x light green/blue (50%)
20. skyblue x dark green/blue (25%)
21. skyblue x light green/yellow (50%)
22. skyblue x dark green/yellow (25%)
23. skyblue x light green/white (25%)
24. skyblue x dark green/white
25. COBALT x LIGHT GREEN (50%)
26. cobalt x dark green (33 1/3%)
27. cobalt x light green/blue (25%)
28. cobalt x dark green/blue
29. cobalt x light green/yellow (25%)
30. cobalt x dark green/yellow
31. cobalt x light green/white
32. cobalt x dark green/white
33. WHITE COBALT x LIGHT GREEN/ BLUE (33 1/3%)
34. white cobalt x dark green/blue
35. LIGHT GREEN/BLUE x LIGHT GREEN/BLUE (33 1/3%)
36. light green/blue x dark green/blue
37. light green/blue x light green/yellow
38. light green/blue x dark green/yellow
39. light green/blue x light green/white
40. light green/blue x dark green/white
41. light green/blue x skyblue/white (25%)
42. light green/blue x cobalt/white
43. DARK GREEN/BLUE x LIGHT GREEN/BLUE
44. dark green/blue x dark green/blue
45. dark green/blue x light green/yellow
46. dark green/blue x dark green/yellow
47. dark green/blue x light green/white
48. dark green/blue x dark green/white
49. dark green/blue x skyblue/white
50. dark green/blue x cobalt/white
51. LIGHT GREEN/YELLOW x LIGHT GREEN/WHITE
52. light green/yellow x dark green/white
53. light green/yellow x skyblue/white (33 1/3%)
54. light green/yellow x cobalt/white
55. DARK GREEN/YELLOW x LIGHT GREEN/WHITE
56. dark green/yellow x dark green/white
57. dark green/yellow x skyblue/white
58. dark green/yellow x cobalt/white
59. LIGHT GREEN/WHITE x LIGHT GREEN/WHITE
60. light green/white x dark green/white

61. light green/white x skyblue/white
62. light green/white x cobalt/white
63. DARK GREEN/WHITE x LIGHT GREEN/WHITE
64. dark green/white x dark green/white
65. dark green/white x skyblue/white
66. dark green/white x cobalt/white

Table 4. To produce DARK GREEN/BLUE the theoretical expectation is:

1. LIGHT GREEN x COBALT (50%)
2. light green x mauve (100%)
3. light green x dark green/blue (25%)
4. light green x olive green/blue (50%)
5. light green x dark green/white
6. light green x olive green/white (25%)
7. light green x cobalt/white (25%)
8. light green x mauve/white (50%)
9. DARK GREEN x SKYBLUE (50%)
10. dark green x cobalt (33 1/3%)
11. dark green x mauve (50%)
12. dark green x light green/blue (25%)
13. dark green x dark green/blue
14. dark green x olive green/blue (25%)
15. dark green x light green/white
16. dark green x dark green/white
17. dark green x olive green/white
18. dark green x skyblue/white (25%)
19. dark green x cobalt/white
20. dark green x mauve/white (25%)
21. OLIVE GREEN x SKYBLUE (100%)
22. olive green x cobalt (50%)
23. olive green x light green/blue (50%)
24. olive green x dark green/blue (25%)
25. olive green x light green/white (25%)
26. olive green x dark green/white
27. olive green x skyblue/white (50%)
28. olive green x cobalt/white (25%)
29. SKYBLUE x DARK GREEN (50%)
30. skyblue x olive green (100%)
31. skyblue x dark green/blue (25%)
32. skyblue x olive green/blue (50%)
33. skyblue x dark green/yellow (25%)
34. skyblue x olive green/yellow (50%)
35. skyblue x dark green/white
36. skyblue x olive green/white (25%)
37. COBALT x LIGHT GREEN (50%)
38. cobalt x dark green (33 1/3%)
39. cobalt x olive green (50%)
40. cobalt x light green/blue (25%)
41. cobalt x dark green/blue

42. cobalt x olive green/blue (25%)
43. cobalt x light green/yellow (25%)
44. cobalt x dark green/yellow
45. cobalt x olive green/yellow (25%)
46. cobalt x light green/white
47. cobalt x dark green/white
48. cobalt x olive green/white
49. MAUVE x LIGHT GREEN (100%)
50. mauve x dark green (50%)
51. mauve x light green/blue (50%)
52. mauve x dark green/blue (25%)
53. mauve x light green/yellow (50%)
54. mauve x dark green/yellow (25%)
55. mauve x light green/white (25%)
56. mauve x dark green/white
57. WHITE COBALT x LIGHT GREEN/ BLUE (25%)
58. white cobalt x dark green/blue
59. white cobalt x olive green/blue (25%)
60. LIGHT GREEN/BLUE x DARK GREEN/BLUE
61. light green/blue x olive green/blue (33 1/3%)
62. light green/blue x dark green/yellow
63. light green/blue x olive green/yellow (25%)
64. light green/blue x dark green/white
65. light green/blue x olive green/white
66. light green/blue x cobalt/white
67. light green/blue x mauve/white (25%)
68. DARK GREEN/BLUE x LIGHT GREEN/BLUE
69. dark green/blue x dark green/blue
70. dark green/blue x olive green/blue
71. dark green/blue x light green/yellow
72. dark green/blue x dark green/yellow
73. dark green/blue x olive green/yellow
74. dark green/blue x light green/white
75. dark green/blue x dark green/white
76. dark green/blue x olive green/white
77. dark green/blue x skyblue/white
78. dark green/blue x cobalt/white
79. dark green/blue x mauve/white
80. OLIVE GREEN/BLUE x LIGHT GREEN/BLUE (33 1/3%)
81. olive green/blue x dark green/blue
82. olive green/blue x light green/yellow (25%)
83. olive green/blue x dark green/yellow
84. olive green/blue x light green/white
85. olive green/blue x dark green/white
86. olive green/blue x skyblue/white (25%)

87. olive green/blue x cobalt/white
88. LIGHT GREEN/YELLOW x DARK GREEN/WHITE
89. light green/yellow x olive green/white
90. light green/yellow x cobalt/white
91. light green/yellow x mauve/white (33 1/3%)
92. DARK GREEN/YELLOW x LIGHT GREEN/WHITE
93. dark green/yellow x dark green/white
94. dark green/yellow x olive green/white
95. dark green/yellow x skyblue/white
96. dark green/yellow x cobalt/white
97. dark green/yellow x mauve/white
98. OLIVE GREEN/YELLOW x LIGHT GREEN/WHITE
99. olive green/yellow x dark green/white
100. olive green/yellow x skyblue/white (33 1/3%)
101. olive green/yellow x cobalt/white
102. LIGHT GREEN/WHITE x DARK GREEN/WHITE
103. light green/white x olive green/white
104. light green/white x cobalt/white
105. light green/white x mauve/white
106. DARK GREEN/WHITE x LIGHT GREEN/WHITE
107. dark green/white x dark green/white
108. dark green/white x olive green/white
109. dark green/white x skyblue/white
110. dark green/white x cobalt/white
111. dark green/white x mauve/white
112. OLIVE GREEN/WHITE x LIGHT GREEN/WHITE
113. olive green/white x dark green/white
114. olive green/white x skyblue/white
115. olive green/white x cobalt/white

Table 5. To produce LIGHT GREEN/YELLOW the theoretical expectation is:

1. LIGHT GREEN x LIGHT YELLOW (100%)
2. light green x dark yellow (50%)
3. light green x light green/yellow (50%)
4. light green x dark green/yellow (25%)
5. light green x light green/white (25%)
6. light green x dark green/white
7. light green x light yellow/white (50%)
8. light green x dark yellow/white (25%)
9. DARK GREEN x LIGHT YELLOW (50%)

226

10. dark green x light green/yellow (25%)
11. dark green x dark green/yellow
12. dark green x light green/white
13. dark green x dark green/white
14. dark green x light yellow/white (25%)
15. dark green x dark yellow/white
16. LIGHT YELLOW x LIGHT GREEN/ BLUE (50%)
17. light yellow x dark green/blue (25%)
18. light yellow x light green/yellow (50%)
19. light yellow x dark green/yellow (25%)
20. light yellow x light green/white (25%)
21. light yellow x dark green/white
22. DARK YELLOW x LIGHT GREEN/ BLUE (25%)
23. dark yellow x dark green/blue
24. dark yellow x light green/yellow (25%)
25. dark yellow x dark green/yellow
26. dark yellow x light green/white
27. dark yellow x dark green/white
28. LIGHT GREEN/BLUE x LIGHT GREEN/YELLOW (25%)
29. light green/blue x dark green/yellow
30. light green/blue x light green/white
31. light green/blue x dark green/white
32. light green/blue x light yellow/white (33 1/3%)
33. light green/blue x dark yellow/white
34. DARK GREEN/BLUE x LIGHT GREEN/YELLOW
35. dark green/blue x dark green/yellow
36. dark green/blue x light green/white
37. dark green/blue x dark green/white
38. dark green/blue x light yellow/white
39. dark green/blue x dark yellow/white
40. LIGHT GREEN/YELLOW x LIGHT GREEN/YELLOW (33 1/3%)
41. light green/yellow x dark green/yellow
42. light green/yellow x light green/white
43. light green/yellow x dark green/white
44. light green/yellow x light yellow/white (25%)
45. light green/yellow x dark yellow/white
46. DARK GREEN/YELLOW x LIGHT GREEN/YELLOW
47. dark green/yellow x dark green/yellow
48. dark green/yellow x light green/white
49. dark green/yellow x dark green/white
50. dark green/yellow x light yellow/white
51. dark green/yellow x dark yellow/white
52. LIGHT GREEN/WHITE x LIGHT GREEN/WHITE

53. light green/white x dark green/white
54. light green/white x light yellow/white
55. light green/white x dark yellow/white
56. DARK GREEN/WHITE x LIGHT GREEN/WHITE
57. dark green/white x dark green/white
58. dark green/white x light yellow/white
59. dark green/white x dark yellow/white

Table 6. To produce DARK GREEN/YELLOW the theoretical expectation is:

1. LIGHT GREEN x DARK YELLOW (50%)
2. light green x olive yellow (100%)
3. light green x dark green/yellow (25%)
4. light green x olive green/yellow (50%)
5. light green x dark green/white
6. light green x olive green/white (25%)
7. light green x dark yellow/white (25%)
8. light green x olive yellow/white (50%)
9. DARK GREEN x LIGHT YELLOW (50%)
10. dark green x dark yellow (33 1/3%)
11. dark green x olive yellow (50%)
12. dark green x light green/yellow (25%)
13. dark green x dark green/yellow
14. dark green x olive green/yellow (25%)
15. dark green x light green/white
16. dark green x dark green/white
17. dark green x olive green/white
18. dark green x light yellow/white (25%)
19. dark green x dark yellow/white
20. dark green x olive yellow/white (25%)
21. OLIVE GREEN x LIGHT YELLOW (100%)
22. olive green x dark yellow (50%)
23. olive green x light green/yellow (50%)
24. olive green x dark green/yellow (25%)
25. olive green x light green/white (25%)
26. olive green x dark green/white
27. olive green x light yellow/white (50%)
28. olive green x dark yellow/white (25%)
29. LIGHT YELLOW x DARK GREEN/ BLUE (25%)
30. light yellow x olive green/blue (50%)
31. light yellow x dark green/yellow (25%)
32. light yellow x olive green/yellow (50%)
33. light yellow x dark green/white
34. light yellow x olive green/white (25%)
35. DARK YELLOW x LIGHT GREEN/ BLUE (25%)

228

36. dark yellow x dark green/blue
37. dark yellow x olive green/blue (25%)
38. dark yellow x light green/yellow (25%)
39. dark yellow x dark green/yellow
40. dark yellow x olive green/yellow (25%)
41. dark yellow x light green/white
42. dark yellow x dark green/white
43. dark yellow x olive green/white
44. OLIVE YELLOW x LIGHT GREEN/
    BLUE (50%)
45. olive yellow x dark green/blue (25%)
46. olive yellow x light green/yellow (50%)
47. olive yellow x dark green/yellow (25%)
48. olive yellow x light green/white (25%)
49. olive yellow x dark green/white
50. LIGHT GREEN/BLUE x DARK
    GREEN/YELLOW
51. light green/blue x olive green/yellow
    (25%)
52. light green/blue x dark green/white
53. light green/blue x olive green/white
54. light green/blue x dark yellow/white
55. DARK GREEN/BLUE x LIGHT
    GREEN/YELLOW
56. dark green/blue x dark green/yellow
57. dark green/blue x olive green/yellow
58. dark green/blue x light green/white
59. dark green/blue x dark green/white
60. dark green/blue x olive green/white
61. dark green/blue x light yellow/white
62. dark green/blue x dark yellow/white
63. dark green/blue x olive yellow/white
64. OLIVE GREEN/BLUE x LIGHT
    GREEN/YELLOW (25%)
65. olive green/blue x dark green/yellow
66. olive green/blue x light green/white
67. olive green/blue x dark green/white
68. olive green/blue x light green/white (33 1/3%)
69. olive green/blue x dark yellow/white
70. LIGHT GREEN/YELLOW x DARK
    GREEN/YELLOW
71. light green/yellow x olive green/yellow
    (33 1/3%)
72. light green/yellow x dark green/white
73. light green/yellow x olive green/white
74. light green/yellow x dark yellow/white
75. light green/yellow x olive yellow/white
    (25%)
76. DARK GREEN/YELLOW x LIGHT
    GREEN/YELLOW
77. dark green/yellow x dark green/yellow

78. dark green/yellow x olive green/yellow
79. dark green/yellow x light green/white
80. dark green/yellow x dark green/white
81. dark green/yellow x olive green/white
82. dark green/yellow x light yellow/white
83. dark green/yellow x dark yellow/white
84. dark green/yellow x olive yellow/white
85. OLIVE GREEN/YELLOW x LIGHT GREEN/YELLOW (33 1/3%)
86. olive green/yellow x dark green/yellow
87. olive green/yellow x light green/white
88. olive green/yellow x dark green/white
89. olive green/yellow x light yellow/white (25%)
90. olive green/yellow x dark yellow/white
91. LIGHT GREEN/WHITE x DARK GREEN/WHITE
92. light green/white x olive green/white
93. light green/white x dark yellow/white
94. light green/white x olive yellow/white
95. DARK GREEN/WHITE x LIGHT GREEN/WHITE
96. dark green/white x dark green/white
97. dark green/white x olive green/white
98. dark green/white x light yellow/white
99. dark green/white x dark yellow/white
100. dark green/white x olive yellow/white
101. OLIVE GREEN/WHITE x LIGHT GREEN/WHITE
102. olive green/white x dark green/white
103. olive green/white x light yellow/white
104. olive green/white x dark yellow/white

Table 7. To produce LIGHT GREEN/WHITE the theoretical expectation is:

1. LIGHT GREEN x WHITE BLUE (100%)
2. light green x white cobalt (50%)
3. light green x light green/white (25%)
4. light green x dark green/white
5. light green x skyblue/white (50%)
6. light green x cobalt/white (25%)
7. light green x light yellow/white (50%)
8. light green x dark yellow/white (25%)
9. DARK GREEN x WHITE BLUE (50%)
10. dark green x white cobalt (33 1/3%)
11. dark green x light green/white
12. dark green x dark green/white
13. dark green x skyblue/white (25%)
14. dark green x cobalt/white
15. dark green x light yellow/white (25%)
16. dark green x dark yellow/white
17. SKYBLUE x LIGHT YELLOW (100%)

18. skyblue x dark yellow (50%)
19. skyblue x light green/yellow (50%)
20. skyblue x dark green/yellow (25%)
21. skyblue x light green/white (25%)
22. skyblue x dark green/white
23. skyblue x light yellow/white (50%)
24. skyblue x dark yellow/white (25%)
25. COBALT x LIGHT YELLOW (50%)
26. cobalt x dark yellow (33 1/3%)
27. cobalt x light green/yellow (25%)
28. cobalt x dark green/yellow
29. cobalt x light green/white
30. cobalt x dark green/white
31. cobalt x light yellow/white (25%)
32. cobalt x dark yellow/white
33. LIGHT YELLOW x LIGHT GREEN/ BLUE (50%)
34. light yellow x dark green/blue (25%)
35. light yellow x light green/white (25%)
36. light yellow x dark green/white
37. light yellow x skyblue/white (50%)
38. light yellow x cobalt/white (25%)
39. DARK YELLOW x LIGHT GREEN/ BLUE (25%)
40. dark yellow x dark green/blue
41. dark yellow x light green/white
42. dark yellow x dark green/white
43. dark yellow x skyblue/white (25%)
44. dark yellow x cobalt/white
45. WHITE BLUE x LIGHT GREEN/BLUE (50%)
46. white blue x dark green/blue (25%)
47. white blue x light green/yellow (50%)
48. white blue x dark green/yellow (25%)
49. white blue x light green/white (25%)
50. white blue x dark green/white
51. WHITE COBALT x LIGHT GREEN/ YELLOW (25%)
52. white cobalt x dark green/yellow
53. white cobalt x light green/white
54. white cobalt x dark green/white
55. LIGHT GREEN/BLUE x LIGHT GREEN/YELLOW (25%)
56. light green/blue x dark green/yellow
57. light green/blue x light green/white
58. light green/blue x dark green/white
59. light green/blue x skyblue/white (25%)
60. light green/blue x cobalt/white
61. light green/blue x light yellow/white (33 1/3%)
62. light green/blue x dark yellow/white
63. DARK GREEN/BLUE x LIGHT GREEN/YELLOW

64. dark green/blue x dark green/yellow
65. dark green/blue x light green/white
66. dark green/blue x dark green/white
67. dark green/blue x skyblue/white
68. dark green/blue x cobalt/white
69. dark green/blue x light yellow/white
70. dark green/blue x dark yellow/white
71. LIGHT GREEN/YELLOW x LIGHT
    GREEN/WHITE
72. light green/yellow x dark green/white
73. light green/yellow x skyblue/white
    (33 1/3%)
74. light green/yellow x cobalt/white
75. light green/yellow x light yellow/white
76. light green/yellow x dark yellow/white
    (25%)
77. DARK GREEN/YELLOW x DARK
    GREEN/WHITE
78. LIGHT GREEN/WHITE x LIGHT
    GREEN/WHITE
79. light green/white x dark green/white
80. light green/white x skyblue/white
81. light green/white x cobalt/white
82. light green/white x light yellow/white
83. light green/white x dark yellow/white
84. DARK GREEN/WHITE x LIGHT
    GREEN/WHITE
85. dark green/white x dark green/white
86. dark green/white x skyblue/white
87. dark green/white x cobalt/white
88. dark green/white x light yellow/white
89. dark green/white x dark yellow/white
90. SKYBLUE/WHITE x LIGHT
    YELLOW/WHITE (25%)
91. skyblue/white x dark yellow/white
92. COBALT/WHITE x LIGHT
    YELLOW/WHITE
93. cobalt/white x dark yellow/white

Table 8. To produce DARK GREEN/WHITE the theoretical expectation is:

1. LIGHT GREEN x WHITE COBALT
   (50%)
2. light green x white mauve (100%)
3. light green x dark green/white
4. light green x olive green/white (25%)
5. light green x cobalt/white (25%)
6. light green x mauve/white (50%)
7. light green x dark yellow/white (25%)
8. light green x olive yellow/white (50%)
9. DARK GREEN x WHITE BLUE (50%)

10. dark green x white cobalt (33 1/3%)
11. dark green x white mauve (50%)
12. dark green x light green/white
13. dark green x dark green/white
14. dark green x olive green/white
15. dark green x skyblue/white (25%)
16. dark green x cobalt/white
17. dark green x mauve/white (25%)
18. dark green x light yellow/white (25%)
19. dark green x dark yellow/white
20. dark green x olive yellow/white (25%)
21. OLIVE GREEN x WHITE BLUE (100%)
22. olive green x white cobalt (50%)
23. olive green x light green/white (25%)
24. olive green x dark green/white
25. olive green x skyblue/white
26. olive green x cobalt/white (25%)
27. olive green x light yellow/white (50%)
28. olive green x dark yellow/white (25%)
29. SKYBLUE x DARK YELLOW (50%)
30. skyblue x olive yellow (100%)
31. skyblue x dark green/yellow (25%)
32. skyblue x dark green/white (25%)
33. skyblue x olive green/white (25%)
34. skyblue x dark yellow/white (25%)
35. skyblue x olive yellow/white (50%)
36. COBALT x LIGHT YELLOW (50%)
37. cobalt x olive yellow (50%)
38. cobalt x light green/yellow (25%)
39. cobalt x dark green/yellow
40. cobalt x light green/white
41. cobalt x dark green/white
42. cobalt x olive green/white
43. cobalt x light yellow/white (25%)
44. cobalt x dark yellow/white
45. cobalt x olive yellow/white (25%)
46. MAUVE x LIGHT YELLOW (100%)
47. mauve x dark yellow (50%)
48. mauve x light green/yellow (50%)
49. mauve x dark green/yellow
50. mauve x light green/white (25%)
51. mauve x dark green/white
52. mauve x light yellow/white (50%)
53. mauve x dark yellow/white (25%)
54. LIGHT YELLOW x DARK GREEN/
    BLUE (25%)
55. light yellow x olive green/blue (50%)
56. light yellow x dark green/white
57. light yellow x olive green/white (50%)
58. light yellow x cobalt/white (25%)
59. light yellow x mauve/white (50%)
60. DARK YELLOW x LIGHT GREEN/
    BLUE (25%)

61. dark yellow x dark green/blue
62. dark yellow x olive green/blue (25%)
63. dark yellow x light green/white
64. dark yellow x dark green/white
65. dark yellow x olive green/white
66. dark yellow x skyblue/white (25%)
67. dark yellow x cobalt/white
68. OLIVE YELLOW x LIGHT GREEN/ BLUE (50%)
69. olive yellow x dark green/blue (25%)
70. olive yellow x light green/white (25%)
71. olive yellow x dark green/white
72. olive yellow x skyblue/white (50%)
73. olive yellow x cobalt/white (25%)
74. WHITE BLUE x DARK GREEN/BLUE (25%)
75. white blue x olive green/blue (50%)
76. white blue x dark green/yellow (25%)
77. white blue x olive green/yellow (50%)
78. white blue x dark green/white
79. white blue x olive green/white (25%)
80. WHITE COBALT x LIGHT GREEN/ YELLOW (25%)
81. white cobalt x dark green/yellow
82. white cobalt x light green/white
83. white cobalt x dark green/white
84. WHITE MAUVE x DARK GREEN/ BLUE (25%)
85. white mauve x light green/yellow (50%)
86. white mauve x dark green/yellow (25%)
87. white mauve x light green/white (25%)
88. white mauve x dark green/white
89. LIGHT GREEN/BLUE x DARK GREEN/YELLOW
90. light green/blue x olive green/yellow (25%)
91. light green/blue x dark green/white
92. light green/blue x olive green/white
93. light green/blue x cobalt/white
94. light green/blue x mauve/white (25%)
95. light green/blue x dark yellow/white
96. light green/blue x olive yellow/white (33 1/3%)
97. DARK GREEN/BLUE x LIGHT GREEN/YELLOW
98. dark green/blue x dark green/yellow
99. dark green/blue x olive green/yellow
100. dark green/blue x light green/white
101. dark green/blue x dark green/white
102. dark green/blue x olive green/white
103. dark green/blue x skyblue/white
104. dark green/blue x cobalt/white

105. dark green/blue x light yellow/white
106. dark green/blue x dark yellow/white
107. OLIVE GREEN/BLUE x LIGHT GREEN/YELLOW (25%)
108. olive green/blue x dark green/yellow
109. olive green/blue x light green/white
110. olive green/blue x dark green/white
111. olive green/blue x skyblue/white
112. olive green/blue x cobalt/white
113. olive green/blue x light yellow/white (33 1/3%)
114. LIGHT GREEN/YELLOW x DARK GREEN/WHITE
115. light green/yellow x olive green/white
116. light green/yellow x cobalt/white
117. light green/yellow x mauve/white (33 1/3%)
118. light green/yellow x dark yellow/white
119. light green/yellow x olive yellow/white (25%)
120. DARK GREEN/YELLOW x LIGHT GREEN/WHITE
121. dark green/yellow x dark green/white
122. dark green/yellow x olive green/white
123. dark green/yellow x skyblue/white
124. dark green/yellow x mauve/white
125. dark green/yellow x light yellow/white
126. dark green/yellow x dark yellow/white
127. dark green/yellow x olive yellow/white
128. OLIVE GREEN/YELLOW x LIGHT GREEN/WHITE
129. olive green/yellow x dark green/white
130. olive green/yellow x skyblue/white (33 1/3%)
131. olive green/yellow x cobalt/white
132. olive green/yellow x light yellow/white (25%)
133. LIGHT GREEN/WHITE x DARK GREEN/WHITE
134. light green/white x olive green/white
135. light green/white x cobalt/white
136. light green/white x mauve/white
137. light green/white x dark yellow/white
138. light green/white x olive yellow/white
139. DARK GREEN/WHITE x LIGHT GREEN/WHITE
140. dark green/white x dark green/white
141. dark green/white x olive green/white
142. dark green/white x skyblue/white
143. dark green/white x cobalt/white
144. dark green/white x mauve/white
145. dark green/white x light yellow/white
146. dark green/white x dark yellow/white

147. dark green/white x olive yellow/white
148. OLIVE GREEN/WHITE x LIGHT GREEN/WHITE
149. olive green/white x dark green/white
150. olive green/white x skyblue/white
151. olive green/white x cobalt/white
152. olive green/white x light yellow/white
153. olive green/white x dark yellow/white
154. SKYBLUE/WHITE x DARK YELLOW/WHITE
155. skyblue/white x olive yellow/white
156. COBALT/WHITE x LIGHT YELLOW/WHITE
157. cobalt/white x dark yellow/white
158. cobalt/white x olive yellow/white
159. MAUVE/WHITE x LIGHT YELLOW/ WHITE
160. mauve/white x dark yellow/white

Table 9. To produce OLIVE GREEN the theoretical expectation is:

1. DARK GREEN x DARK GREEN (33 1/3%)
2. dark green x olive green (50%)
3. dark green x dark green/blue
4. dark green x olive green/blue (25%)
5. dark green x dark green/yellow
6. dark green x olive green/yellow (25%)
7. dark green x dark green/white
8. dark green x olive green/white
9. OLIVE GREEN x DARK GREEN (50%)
10. olive green x olive green (100%)
11. olive green x olive green/blue (50%)
12. olive green x dark green/yellow (25%)
13. olive green x olive green/yellow (50%)
14. olive green x dark green/white
15. olive green x olive green/white
16. DARK GREEN/BLUE x DARK GREEN/BLUE
17. dark green/blue x olive green/blue
18. dark green/blue x dark green/yellow
19. dark green/blue x olive green/yellow
20. dark green/blue x dark green/white
21. dark green/blue x olive green/white
22. OLIVE GREEN/BLUE x DARK GREEN/BLUE
23. olive green/blue x olive green/blue (33 1/3%)
24. olive green/blue x dark green/yellow
25. olive green/blue x olive green/yellow (25%)
26. olive green/blue x dark green/white

27. olive green/blue x olive green/white
28. DARK GREEN/YELLOW x DARK GREEN/YELLOW
29. dark green/yellow x olive green/yellow
30. dark green/yellow x dark green/white
31. OLIVE GREEN/YELLOW x DARK GREEN/YELLOW
32. olive green/yellow x olive green/yellow (33 1/3%)
33. olive green/yellow x dark green/white
34. olive green/yellow x olive green/white
35. DARK GREEN/WHITE x DARK GREEN/WHITE
36. dark green/white x olive green/white
37. OLIVE GREEN/WHITE x DARK GREEN/WHITE
38. olive green/white x olive green/white

Table 10. To produce OLIVE GREEN/BLUE the theoretical expectation is:

1. DARK GREEN x COBALT (25%)
2. dark green x mauve (50%)
3. dark green x dark green/blue
4. dark green x olive green/blue (25%)
5. dark green x dark green/white
6. dark green x olive green/white
7. dark green x cobalt/white
8. dark green x mauve/white (25%)
9. OLIVE GREEN x COBALT (50%)
10. olive green x dark green/blue (25%)
11. olive green x olive green/blue (50%)
12. olive green x dark green/white
13. olive green x olive green/white (25%)
14. olive green x cobalt/white (25%)
15. olive green x mauve/white (50%)
16. COBALT x DARK GREEN (33 1/3%)
17. cobalt x olive green (50%)
18. cobalt x dark green/blue
19. cobalt x olive green/blue
20. cobalt x dark green/yellow
21. cobalt x olive green/yellow (25%)
22. cobalt x dark green/white
23. cobalt x olive green/white
24. MAUVE x DARK GREEN (50%)
25. mauve x dark green/blue (25%)
26. mauve x olive green/blue (50%)
27. mauve x dark green/yellow (25%)
28. mauve x olive green/yellow (50%)
29. mauve x dark green/white
30. mauve x olive green/white (25%)
31. WHITE COBALT x DARK GREEN/BLUE

32. white cobalt x olive green/blue (25%)
33. DARK GREEN/BLUE x DARK
    GREEN/BLUE
34. dark green/blue x olive green/blue
35. dark green/blue x dark green/yellow
36. dark green/blue x olive green/yellow
37. dark green/blue x dark green/white
38. dark green/blue x olive green/white
39. dark green/blue x cobalt/white
40. dark green/blue x mauve/white
41. OLIVE GREEN/BLUE x DARK
    GREEN/BLUE
42. olive green/blue x olive green/blue
    (33 1/3%)
43. olive green/blue x dark green/yellow
44. olive green/blue x olive green/yellow
    (25%)
45. olive green/blue x dark green/white
46. olive green/blue x olive green/white
47. olive green/blue x cobalt/white
48. olive green/blue x mauve/white (25%)
49. DARK GREEN/YELLOW x DARK
    GREEN/WHITE
50. dark green/yellow x olive green/white
51. dark green/yellow x cobalt/white
52. dark green/yellow x mauve/white
53. OLIVE GREEN/YELLOW x DARK
    GREEN/WHITE
54. olive green/yellow x olive green/white
55. olive green/yellow x cobalt/white
56. DARK GREEN/WHITE x DARK
    GREEN/WHITE
57. dark green/white x olive green/white
58. dark green/white x cobalt/white
59. dark green/white x mauve/white
60. OLIVE GREEN/WHITE x DARK
    GREEN/WHITE
61. olive green/white x olive green/white
62. olive green/white x cobalt/white
63. olive green/white x mauve/white

Table 11. To produce OLIVE GREEN/WHITE the theoretical expectation is:

1. DARK GREEN x WHITE COBALT
   (33 1/3%)
2. dark green x white mauve (50%)
3. dark green x dark green/white
4. dark green x olive green/white
5. dark green x cobalt/white
6. dark green x mauve/white (25%)
7. dark green x dark yellow/white
8. dark green x olive yellow/white (25%)

238

9. OLIVE GREEN x WHITE COBALT
   (50%)
10. olive green x white mauve (100%)
11. olive green x dark green/white
12. olive green x olive green/white (25%)
13. olive green x cobalt/white (25%)
14. olive green x mauve/white (50%)
15. olive green x dark yellow/white (25%)
16. olive green x olive yellow/white (50%)
17. COBALT x DARK YELLOW (25%)
18. cobalt x olive yellow (50%)
19. cobalt x dark green/yellow
20. cobalt x olive green/yellow
21. cobalt x dark green/white
22. cobalt x olive green/white
23. cobalt x dark yellow/white
24. cobalt x olive yellow/white (25%)
25. MAUVE x DARK YELLOW (50%)
26. mauve x olive yellow (100%)
27. mauve x dark green/yellow (25%)
28. mauve x olive green/yellow (50%)
29. mauve x dark green/white
30. mauve x olive green/white (25%)
31. mauve x dark yellow/white (25%)
32. mauve x olive yellow/white (50%)
33. DARK YELLOW x DARK
    GREEN/BLUE
34. dark yellow x olive green/blue (25%)
35. dark yellow x dark green/white
36. dark yellow x olive green/white
37. dark yellow x cobalt/white
38. dark yellow x mauve/white (25%)
39. OLIVE YELLOW x DARK
    GREEN/BLUE (25%)
40. olive yellow x olive green/blue (50%)
41. olive yellow x dark green/white
42. olive yellow x olive green/white (25%)
43. olive yellow x cobalt/white (25%)
44. WHITE COBALT x DARK
    GREEN/YELLOW
45. white cobalt x olive green/yellow (25%)
46. white cobalt x dark green/white
47. WHITE MAUVE x DARK
    GREEN/BLUE (25%)
48. white mauve x olive green/blue (50%)
49. white mauve x dark green/yellow (25%)
50. white mauve x olive green/yellow (50%)
51. white mauve x dark green/white
52. white mauve x olive green/white (25%)
53. DARK GREEN/BLUE x DARK
    GREEN/YELLOW
54. dark green/blue x olive green/yellow

55. dark green/blue x dark green/white
56. dark green/blue x olive green/white
57. dark green/blue x cobalt/white
58. dark green/blue x mauve/white
59. dark green/blue x dark yellow/white
60. dark green/blue x olive yellow/white
61. OLIVE GREEN/BLUE x DARK GREEN/YELLOW
62. olive green/blue x olive green/yellow (25%)
63. olive green/blue x dark green/white
64. olive green/blue x olive green/white
65. olive green/blue x cobalt/white
66. olive green/blue x mauve/white (25%)
67. olive green/blue x dark yellow/white
68. olive green/blue x olive yellow/white (33 1/3%)
69. DARK GREEN/YELLOW x DARK GREEN/WHITE
70. dark green/yellow x olive green/white
71. dark green/yellow x cobalt/white
72. dark green/yellow x mauve/white
73. dark green/yellow x dark yellow/white
74. dark green/yellow x olive yellow/white
75. OLIVE GREEN/YELLOW x DARK GREEN/WHITE
76. olive green/yellow x olive green/white
77. olive green/yellow x cobalt/white
78. olive green/yellow x mauve/white (50%)
79. olive green/yellow x dark yellow/white
80. olive green/yellow x olive yellow/white (25%)
81. DARK GREEN/WHITE x DARK GREEN/WHITE
82. dark green/white x olive green/white
83. dark green/white x cobalt/white
84. dark green/white x mauve/white
85. dark green/white x dark yellow/white
86. dark green/white x olive yellow/white
87. OLIVE GREEN/WHITE x DARK GREEN/WHITE
88. olive green/white x olive green/white
89. olive green/white x cobalt/white
90. olive green/white x mauve/white
91. olive green/white x dark yellow/white
92. olive green/white x olive yellow/white
93. COBALT/WHITE x DARK YELLOW/WHITE
94. cobalt/white x olive yellow/white
95. MAUVE/WHITE x DARK YELLOW/WHITE
96. mauve/white x olive yellow/white

Table 12. To produce OLIVE GREEN/YELLOW the theoretical expectation is:

1. DARK GREEN x DARK YELLOW (33 1/3%)
2. dark green x olive green (50%)
3. dark green x dark green/yellow
4. dark green x olive green/yellow
5. dark green x dark green/white
6. dark green x olive green/white
7. dark green x dark yellow/white
8. dark green x olive yellow/white
9. OLIVE GREEN x DARK YELLOW (50%)
10. olive green x olive yellow (100%)
11. olive green x dark green/yellow (25%)
12. olive green x olive green/yellow (50%)
13. olive green x dark green/white
14. olive green x olive green/white (25%)
15. olive green x dark green/white (25%)
16. olive green x olive yellow/white (50%)
17. DARK YELLOW x DARK GREEN/ BLUE
18. dark yellow x olive green/blue (25%)
19. dark yellow x dark green/yellow
20. dark yellow x olive green/yellow (25%)
21. dark yellow x dark green/white
22. dark yellow x olive green/white
23. OLIVE YELLOW x DARK GREEN/ BLUE (25%)
24. olive yellow x olive green/blue (50%)
25. olive yellow x dark green/yellow (25%)
26. olive yellow x olive green/yellow (50%)
27. olive yellow x dark green/white
28. olive yellow x olive green/white (25%)
29. DARK GREEN/BLUE x DARK GREEN/YELLOW
30. dark green/blue x olive green/yellow
31. dark green/blue x dark green/white
32. dark green/blue x olive green/white
33. dark green/blue x dark yellow/white
34. dark green/blue x olive yellow/white
35. OLIVE GREEN/BLUE x DARK GREEN/YELLOW
36. olive green/blue x olive green/yellow (25%)
37. olive green/blue x dark green/white
38. olive green/blue x olive green/white
39. olive green/blue x dark yellow/white
40. olive green/blue x olive yellow/white (33 1/3%)
41. DARK GREEN/YELLOW x DARK GREEN/YELLOW
42. dark green/yellow x olive green/yellow
43. dark green/yellow x dark green/white
44. dark green/yellow x olive green/white

45. dark green/yellow x dark yellow/white
46. dark green/yellow x olive yellow/white
47. OLIVE GREEN/YELLOW x DARK GREEN/YELLOW
48. olive green/yellow x olive green/yellow (33 1/3%)
49. olive green/yellow x dark green/white
50. olive green/yellow x olive green/white
51. olive green/yellow x dark yellow/white
52. olive green/yellow x olive yellow/white (25%)
53. DARK GREEN/WHITE x DARK GREEN/WHITE
54. dark green/white x olive green/white
55. dark green/white x dark yellow/white
56. dark green/white x olive yellow/white
57. OLIVE GREEN/WHITE x DARK GREEN/WHITE
58. olive green/white x olive green/white
59. olive green/white x dark yellow/white
60. olive green/white x olive yellow/white

Table 13. To produce SKYBLUE the theoretical expectation is:

1. SKYBLUE x SKYBLUE (100%)
2. skyblue x light green/blue (50%)
3. skyblue x dark green/blue (25%)
4. skyblue x light green/white (25%)
5. skyblue x dark green/white
6. skyblue x skyblue/white (50%)
7. skyblue x cobalt/white (25%)
8. COBALT x SKYBLUE (50%)
9. cobalt x cobalt (25%)
10. cobalt x light green/blue (25%)
11. cobalt x dark green/blue
12. cobalt x light green/white
13. cobalt x dark green/white
14. cobalt x skyblue/white (25%)
15. cobalt x cobalt/white
16. LIGHT GREEN/BLUE x LIGHT GREEN/BLUE (33 1/3%)
17. light green/blue x dark green/blue
18. light green/blue x light green/white
19. light green/blue x dark green/white
20. light green/blue x skyblue/white (25%)
21. light green/blue x cobalt/white
22. DARK GREEN/BLUE x LIGHT GREEN/BLUE
23. dark green/blue x dark green/blue
24. dark green/blue x light green/white
25. dark green/blue x dark green/white
26. dark green/blue x skyblue/white

242

27. dark green/blue x cobalt/white
28. LIGHT GREEN/WHITE x DARK GREEN/WHITE
29. light green/white x skyblue/white
30. light green/white x cobalt/white
31. DARK GREEN/WHITE x LIGHT GREEN/WHITE
32. dark green/white x dark green/white
33. dark green/white x cobalt/white
34. SKYBLUE/WHITE x SKYBLUE/WHITE (33 1/3%)
35. skyblue/white x cobalt/white
36. COBALT/WHITE x SKYBLUE/WHITE
37. cobalt/white x cobalt/white

Table 14. To produce SKYBLUE/WHITE the theoretical expectation is:

1. SKYBLUE x WHITE BLUE (100%)
2. skyblue x white cobalt (50%)
3. skyblue x light green/white (25%)
4. skyblue x dark green/white
5. skyblue x skyblue/white (50%)
6. skyblue x cobalt/white (25%)
7. skyblue x light yellow/white (50%)
8. skyblue x dark yellow/white (25%)
9. COBALT x WHITE BLUE (50%)
10. cobalt x white cobalt (25%)
11. cobalt x light green/white
12. cobalt x dark green/white
13. cobalt x skyblue/white (25%)
14. cobalt x cobalt/white
15. cobalt x light yellow/white (25%)
16. WHITE BLUE x LIGHT GREEN/BLUE (50%)
17. white blue x dark green/blue (25%)
18. white blue x light green/white (25%)
19. white blue x dark green/white
20. white blue x skyblue/white (50%)
21. white blue x cobalt/white (25%)
22. WHITE COBALT x LIGHT GREEN/BLUE (25%)
23. white cobalt x dark green/blue
24. white cobalt x light green/white
25. white cobalt x dark green/white
26. white cobalt x skyblue/white (25%)
27. white cobalt x cobalt/white
28. LIGHT GREEN/BLUE x LIGHT GREEN/WHITE
29. light green/blue x dark green/white
30. light green/blue x skyblue/white (25%)
31. light green/blue x cobalt/white

243

32. light green/blue x light yellow/white (33 1/3%)
33. light green/blue x dark yellow/white
34. DARK GREEN/BLUE x LIGHT GREEN/WHITE
35. dark green/blue x dark green/white
36. dark green/blue x skyblue/white
37. dark green/blue x cobalt/white
38. dark green/blue x light yellow/white
39. dark green/blue x dark yellow/white
40. LIGHT GREEN/WHITE x DARK GREEN/WHITE
41. light green/white x skyblue/white
42. light green/white x cobalt/white
43. light green/white x light yellow/white
44. light green/white x dark yellow/white
45. DARK GREEN/WHITE x LIGHT GREEN/WHITE
46. dark green/white x dark green/white
47. dark green/white x skyblue/white
48. dark green/white x cobalt/white
49. dark green/white x light yellow/white
50. dark green/white x dark yellow/white
51. SKYBLUE/WHITE x SKYBLUE/WHITE (33 1/3%)
52. skyblue/white x cobalt/white
53. skyblue/white x light yellow/white (25%)
54. skyblue/white x dark yellow/white
55. COBALT/WHITE x SKYBLUE/WHITE
56. cobalt/white x cobalt/white
57. cobalt/white x light yellow/white
58. cobalt/white x dark yellow/white

Table 15. To produce COBALT the theoretical expectation is:

1. SKYBLUE x COBALT (50%)
2. skyblue x mauve (100%)
3. skyblue x dark green/blue (25%)
4. skyblue x olive green/blue (50%)
5. skyblue x dark green/white
6. skyblue x olive green/white (25%)
7. skyblue x cobalt/white (25%)
8. skyblue x mauve/white (50%)
9. COBALT x SKYBLUE (50%)
10. cobalt x cobalt (33 1/3%)
11. cobalt x mauve (50%)
12. cobalt x light green/blue (25%)
13. cobalt x dark green/blue
14. cobalt x olive green/blue (25%)
15. cobalt x light green/white
16. cobalt x dark green/white
17. cobalt x olive green/white

18. cobalt x skyblue/white (25%)
19. cobalt x cobalt/white
20. cobalt x mauve/white (25%)
21. MAUVE x SKYBLUE (50%)
22. mauve x cobalt (50%)
23. mauve x light green/blue (50%)
24. mauve x dark green/blue (25%)
25. mauve x light green/white (25%)
26. mauve x dark green/white
27. mauve x skyblue/white (50%)
28. mauve x cobalt/white (25%)
29. LIGHT GREEN/BLUE x DARK GREEN/BLUE
30. light green/blue x olive green/blue (33 1/3%)
31. light green/blue x dark green/white
32. light green/blue x olive green/white
33. light green/blue x cobalt/white
34. light green/blue x mauve/white (25%)
35. DARK GREEN/BLUE x LIGHT GREEN/BLUE
36. dark green/blue x dark green/blue
37. dark green/blue x olive green/blue
38. dark green/blue x light green/white
39. dark green/blue x dark green/white
40. dark green/blue x olive green/white
41. dark green/blue x skyblue/white
42. dark green/blue x cobalt/white
43. dark green/blue x mauve/white
44. OLIVE GREEN/BLUE x LIGHT GREEN/BLUE
45. olive green/blue x dark green/blue
46. olive green/blue x light green/white
47. olive green/blue x dark green/white
48. olive green/blue x skyblue/white
49. olive green/blue x cobalt/white
50. LIGHT GREEN/WHITE x DARK GREEN/WHITE
51. light green/white x olive green/white
52. light green/white x cobalt/white
53. light green/white x mauve/white
54. DARK GREEN/WHITE x LIGHT GREEN/WHITE
55. dark green/white x dark green/white
56. dark green/white x olive green/white
57. dark green/white x skyblue/white
58. dark green/white x cobalt/white
59. dark green/white x mauve/white
60. OLIVE GREEN/WHITE x LIGHT GREEN/WHITE
61. olive green/white x dark green/white
62. olive green/white x skyblue/white
63. olive green/white x cobalt/white
64. SKYBLUE/WHITE x COBALT/WHITE

65. skyblue/white x light yellow/white (25%)
66. COBALT/WHITE x SKYBLUE/WHITE
67. cobalt/white x cobalt/white
68. cobalt/white x mauve/white
69. MAUVE/WHITE x SKYBLUE/WHITE
(33 1/3%)
70. mauve/white x cobalt/white

Table 16. To produce COBALT/WHITE the theoretical expectation is:

1. SKYBLUE x WHITE COBALT (50%)
2. skyblue x white mauve (100%)
3. skyblue x dark green/white
4. skyblue x olive green/white (25%)
5. skyblue x cobalt/white (25%)
6. skyblue x mauve/white (50%)
7. skyblue x dark yellow/white (25%)
8. skyblue x olive yellow/white (50%)
9. COBALT x WHITE/BLUE (50%)
10. cobalt x white cobalt (33 1/3%)
11. cobalt x white mauve (50%)
12. cobalt x light green/white
13. cobalt x dark green/white
14. cobalt x olive green/white
15. cobalt x skyblue/white (25%)
16. cobalt x mauve/white (25%)
17. cobalt x light yellow/white (25%)
18. cobalt x dark yellow/white
19. cobalt x olive yellow/white
20. MAUVE x WHITE BLUE (100%)
21. mauve x white cobalt (50%)
22. mauve x light green/white (25%)
23. mauve x dark green/white
24. mauve x skyblue/white (50%)
25. mauve x cobalt/white (25%)
26. mauve x mauve/white (50%)
27. mauve x dark yellow/white (25%)
28. WHITE BLUE x DARK
GREEN/BLUE (25%)
29. white blue x olive green/blue (50%)
30. white blue x dark green/white
31. white blue x olive green/white
32. white blue x cobalt/white (25%)
33. white blue x mauve/white (50%)
34. WHITE COBALT x LIGHT
GREEN/BLUE (25%)
35. white cobalt x dark green/blue
36. white cobalt x olive green/blue (25%)
37. white cobalt x light green/white
38. white cobalt x dark green/white
39. white cobalt x olive green/white
40. white cobalt x skyblue/white (25%)

246

41. white cobalt x cobalt/white
42. white cobalt x mauve/white (25%)
43. WHITE MAUVE x LIGHT
    GREEN/BLUE (50%)
44. white mauve x dark green/blue (25%)
45. white mauve x light green/white (25%)
46. white mauve x dark green/white
47. white mauve x skyblue/white (50%)
48. white mauve x cobalt/white (25%)
49. LIGHT GREEN/BLUE x DARK
    GREEN/WHITE
50. light green/blue x olive green/white
51. light green/blue x cobalt/white
52. light green/blue x mauve/white (25%)
53. light green/blue x dark yellow/white
54. light green/blue x olive green/white
    (33 1/3%)
55. DARK GREEN/BLUE x LIGHT
    GREEN/WHITE
56. dark green/blue x dark green/white
57. dark green/blue x olive green/white
58. dark green/blue x skyblue/white
59. dark green/blue x cobalt/white
60. dark green/blue x mauve/white
61. dark green/blue x light yellow/white
62. dark green/blue x dark yellow/white
63. dark green/blue x olive yellow/white
64. OLIVE GREEN/BLUE x LIGHT
    GREEN/WHITE
65. olive green/blue x dark green/white
66. olive green/blue x skyblue/white
67. olive green/blue x cobalt/white
68. olive green/blue x light yellow/white
    (33 1/3%)
69. olive green/blue x dark yellow/white
70. LIGHT GREEN/WHITE x DARK
    GREEN/WHITE
71. light green/white x olive green/white
72. light green/white x cobalt/white
73. light green/white x mauve/white
74. light green/white x dark yellow/white
75. light green/white x olive yellow/white
76. DARK GREEN/WHITE x LIGHT
    GREEN/WHITE
77. dark green/white x dark green/white
78. dark green/white x olive green/white
79. dark green/white x skyblue/white
80. dark green/white x cobalt/white
81. dark green/white x mauve/white
82. dark green/white x light yellow/white
83. dark green/white x dark yellow/white
84. dark green/white x olive yellow/white

85. OLIVE GREEN/WHITE x LIGHT
    GREEN/WHITE
86. olive green/white x dark green/white
87. olive green/white x skyblue/white
88. olive green/white x cobalt/white
89. olive green/white x light yellow/white
90. olive green/white x dark yellow/white
91. SKYBLUE/WHITE x COBALT/
    WHITE
92. skyblue/white x mauve/white (33 1/3%)
93. skyblue/white x dark yellow/white
94. skyblue/white x olive yellow/white
    (25%)
95. COBALT/WHITE x SKYBLUE/
    WHITE
96. cobalt/white x cobalt/white
97. cobalt/white x mauve/white
98. cobalt/white x light yellow/white
99. cobalt/white x dark yellow/white
100. cobalt/white x olive yellow/white
101. cobalt/white x olive yellow/white
102. MAUVE/WHITE x SKYBLUE/
     WHITE (33 1/3%)
103. mauve/white x cobalt/white
104. mauve/white x light yellow/white (25%)
105. mauve/white x dark yellow/white

Table 17. To produce MAUVE the theoretical expectation is:

1. COBALT x COBALT (33 1/3%)
2. cobalt x mauve (50%)
3. cobalt x dark green/blue
4. cobalt x olive green/blue (25%)
5. cobalt x dark green/white
6. cobalt x olive green/white
7. cobalt x cobalt/white (25%)
8. MAUVE x COBALT (50%)
9. mauve x mauve (100%)
10. mauve x dark green/blue (25%)
11. mauve x olive green/blue (50%)
12. mauve x dark green/white
13. mauve x olive green/white (25%)
14. mauve x cobalt/white (25%)
15. mauve x mauve/white (50%)
16. DARK GREEN/BLUE x DARK
    GREEN/BLUE
17. dark green/blue x olive green/blue
18. dark green/blue x dark green/white
19. dark green/blue x olive green/white
20. dark green/blue x cobalt/white
21. dark green/blue x mauve/white
22. OLIVE GREEN/BLUE x DARK
    GREEN/BLUE

248

23. olive green/blue x olive green/blue
24. olive green/blue x dark green/white
25. olive green/blue x olive green/white
26. olive green/blue x cobalt/white
27. olive green/blue x mauve/white (25%)
28. DARK GREEN/WHITE x DARK GREEN/WHITE
29. dark green/white x olive green/white
30. dark green/white x cobalt/white
31. dark green/white x mauve/white
32. OLIVE GREEN/WHITE x DARK GREEN/WHITE
33. olive green/white x olive green/white
34. olive green/white x cobalt/white
35. olive green/white x mauve/white
36. COBALT/WHITE x COBALT/WHITE
37. cobalt/white x mauve/white
38. MAUVE/WHITE x COBALT/WHITE
39. mauve/white x mauve/white (33 1/3%)

Table 18. To produce MAUVE/WHITE the theoretical expectation is:

1. COBALT x WHITE COBALT (33 1/3%)
2. cobalt x white mauve (50%)
3. cobalt x dark green/white
4. cobalt x olive green/white
5. cobalt x cobalt/white
6. cobalt x mauve/white (25%)
7. cobalt x dark yellow/white
8. cobalt x olive yellow/white
9. MAUVE x WHITE COBALT (50%)
10. mauve x white mauve (100%)
11. mauve x dark green/white
12. mauve x olive green/white (25%)
13. mauve x cobalt/white (25%)
14. mauve x mauve/white (50%)
15. mauve x dark yellow/white (25%)
16. mauve x olive yellow/white (50%)
17. WHITE COBALT x DARK GREEN/ BLUE
18. white cobalt x olive green/blue (25%)
19. white cobalt x dark green/white
20. white cobalt x olive green/white
21. white cobalt x cobalt/white
22. white cobalt x cobalt/white
23. white cobalt x mauve/white (25%)
24. WHITE MAUVE x DARK GREEN/ BLUE (25%)
25. white mauve x olive green/blue (50%)
26. white mauve x dark green/white
27. white mauve x olive green/white (25%)
28. white mauve x cobalt/white (25%)
29. white mauve x mauve/white (50%)

30. DARK GREEN/BLUE x DARK GREEN/WHITE
31. dark green/blue x olive green/white
32. dark green/blue x cobalt/white
33. dark green/blue x mauve/white
34. dark green/blue x dark yellow/white
35. dark green/blue x olive green/white
36. OLIVE GREEN/BLUE x DARK GREEN/WHITE
37. olive green/blue x olive green/white
38. olive green/blue x cobalt/white
39. olive green/blue x mauve/white (25%)
40. olive green/blue x dark yellow/white
41. olive green/blue x olive yellow/white (33 1/3%)
42. DARK GREEN/WHITE x DARK GREEN/WHITE
43. dark green/white x olive green/white
44. dark green/white x cobalt/white
45. dark green/white x mauve/white
46. dark green/white x dark yellow/white
47. dark green/white x olive yellow/white
48. OLIVE GREEN/WHITE x DARK GREEN/WHITE
49. olive green/white x olive green/white
50. olive green/white x cobalt/white
51. olive green/white x mauve/white
52. olive green/white x dark yellow/white
53. olive green/white x olive yellow/white
54. COBALT/WHITE x COBALT/WHITE
55. cobalt/white x mauve/white
56. cobalt/white x dark yellow/white
57. cobalt/white x olive yellow/white
58. MAUVE/WHITE x COBALT/WHITE
59. mauve/white x mauve/white (33 1/3%)
60. mauve/white x dark yellow/white
61. mauve/white x olive yellow/white (25%)

Table 19. To produce LIGHT YELLOW the theoretical expectation is:

1. LIGHT YELLOW x LIGHT YELLOW (100%)
2. light yellow x dark yellow (50%)
3. light yellow x light green/yellow (50%)
4. light yellow x dark green/yellow (25%)
5. light yellow x light green/white (25%)
6. light yellow x dark green/white
7. light yellow x light yellow/white (50%)
8. light yellow x dark yellow/white (25%)
9. DARK YELLOW x LIGHT YELLOW (50%)

10. dark yellow x dark yellow (33 1/3%)
11. dark yellow x light green/yellow (25%)
12. dark yellow x dark green/yellow
13. dark yellow x light green/white
14. dark yellow x dark green/white
15. dark yellow x light yellow/white (25%)
16. dark yellow x dark yellow/white
17. LIGHT GREEN/YELLOW x LIGHT GREEN/YELLOW (33 1/3%)
18. light green/yellow x dark green/yellow
19. light green/yellow x light green/white
20. light green/yellow x dark green/white
21. light green/yellow x light green/white (25%)
22. light green/yellow x dark yellow/white
23. DARK GREEN/YELLOW x LIGHT GREEN/YELLOW
24. dark green/yellow x dark green/yellow
25. dark green/yellow x light green/white
26. dark green/yellow x dark green/white
27. dark green/yellow x light yellow/white
28. dark green/yellow x dark yellow/white
29. LIGHT GREEN/WHITE x LIGHT GREEN/WHITE
30. light green/white x dark green/white
31. light green/white x light yellow/white
32. light green/white x dark yellow/white
33. DARK GREEN/WHITE x LIGHT GREEN/WHITE
34. dark green/white x dark green/white
35. dark green/white x light yellow/white
36. dark green/white x dark yellow/white
37. LIGHT YELLOW/WHITE x LIGHT YELLOW/WHITE (33 1/3%)
38. light yellow/white x dark yellow/white
39. DARK YELLOW/WHITE x LIGHT YELLOW/WHITE
40. dark yellow/white x dark yellow/white

Table 20. To produce DARK YELLOW the theoretical expectation is:

1. LIGHT YELLOW x DARK YELLOW (50%)
2. light yellow x olive yellow (100%)
3. light yellow x dark green/yellow (25%)
4. light yellow x olive green/yellow (50%)
5. light yellow x dark green/white
6. light yellow x olive green/white (25%)
7. light yellow x dark yellow/white (25%)
8. light yellow x olive yellow/white (50%)
9. DARK YELLOW x LIGHT YELLOW (50%)
10. dark yellow x dark yellow (33 1/3%)
11. dark yellow x olive yellow (50%)

12. dark yellow x light green/yellow (25%)
13. dark yellow x dark green/yellow
14. dark yellow x olive green/yellow
15. dark yellow x light green/white
16. dark yellow x dark green/white
17. dark yellow x olive green/white
18. dark yellow x light yellow/white (25%)
19. dark yellow x dark yellow/white
20. dark yellow x olive yellow/white (25%)
21. OLIVE YELLOW x LIGHT YELLOW (100%)
22. olive yellow x dark yellow (50%)
23. olive yellow x light green/yellow
24. olive yellow x dark green/yellow
25. olive yellow x light yellow/white (50%)
26. olive yellow x dark yellow/white (25%)
27. LIGHT GREEN/YELLOW x DARK GREEN/YELLOW
28. light green/yellow x olive green/yellow (33 1/3%)
29. light green/yellow x dark green/white
30. light green/yellow x olive green/white
31. light green/yellow x dark yellow/white
32. light green/yellow x olive yellow/white (25%)
33. DARK GREEN/YELLOW x LIGHT GREEN/YELLOW
34. dark green/yellow x dark green/yellow
35. dark green/yellow x olive green/yellow
36. dark green/yellow x light green/white
37. dark green/yellow x dark green/white
38. dark green/yellow x olive green/white
39. dark green/yellow x light yellow/white
40. dark green/yellow x dark yellow/white
41. dark green/yellow x olive yellow/white
42. OLIVE GREEN/YELLOW x LIGHT GREEN/YELLOW (33 1/3%)
43. olive green/yellow x dark green/yellow
44. olive green/yellow x light green/white
45. olive green/yellow x dark green/white
46. olive green/yellow x light yellow/white (25%)
47. olive green/yellow x dark yellow/white
48. LIGHT GREEN/WHITE x DARK GREEN/WHITE
49. light green/white x olive green/white
50. light green/white x dark yellow/white
51. light green/white x olive yellow/white
52. DARK GREEN/WHITE x LIGHT GREEN/WHITE
53. dark green/white x dark green/white
54. dark green/white x olive green/white
55. dark green/white x light yellow/white

252

56. dark green/white x dark yellow/white
57. dark green/white x olive yellow/white
58. OLIVE GREEN/WHITE x LIGHT GREEN/WHITE
59. olive green/white x dark green/white
60. olive green/white x light yellow/white
61. olive green/white x dark yellow/white
62. olive green/white x light yellow/white
63. olive green/white x dark yellow/white
64. LIGHT YELLOW/WHITE x DARK YELLOW/WHITE
65. light yellow/white x olive yellow/white (33 1/3%)
66. DARK YELLOW/WHITE x LIGHT YELLOW/WHITE
67. dark yellow/white x dark yellow/white
68. dark yellow/white x olive yellow/white
69. OLIVE YELLOW/WHITE x LIGHT YELLOW/WHITE (33 1/3%)
70. olive yellow/white x dark yellow/white

Table 21. To produce LIGHT YELLOW/WHITE the theoretical expectation is:

1. LIGHT YELLOW x WHITE BLUE (100%)
2. light yellow x white cobalt (50%)
3. light yellow x light green/white (25%)
4. light yellow x dark green/white
5. light yellow x skyblue/white (50%)
6. light yellow x cobalt/white (25%)
7. light yellow x light yellow/white (50%)
8. light yellow x dark yellow/white (25%)
9. DARK YELLOW x WHITE BLUE (50%)
10. dark yellow x white cobalt (33 1/3%)
11. dark yellow x light green/white
12. dark yellow x dark green/white
13. dark yellow x skyblue/white (25%)
14. dark yellow x cobalt/white
15. dark yellow x light yellow/white (25%)
16. dark yellow x dark yellow/white
17. WHITE BLUE x LIGHT GREEN/YELLOW (50%)
18. white blue x dark green/yellow (25%)
19. white blue x light green/white (25%)
20. white blue x dark green/white
21. white blue x light yellow/white (50%)
22. white blue x dark yellow/white (25%)
23. WHITE COBALT x LIGHT GREEN/YELLOW (25%)
24. white cobalt x dark green/yellow
25. white cobalt x light green/white
26. white cobalt x dark green/white
27. white cobalt x light yellow/white (25%)

28. white cobalt x dark yellow/white
29. LIGHT GREEN/YELLOW x LIGHT GREEN/WHITE
30. light green/yellow x dark green/white
31. light green/yellow x skyblue/white (33 1/3%)
32. light green/yellow x cobalt/white
33. light green/yellow x light yellow/white
34. light green/yellow x dark yellow/white
35. DARK GREEN/YELLOW x LIGHT GREEN/WHITE
36. dark green/yellow x dark green/white
37. dark green/yellow x skyblue/white
38. dark green/yellow x cobalt/white
39. dark green/yellow x light yellow/white
40. dark green/yellow x dark yellow/white
41. LIGHT GREEN/WHITE x LIGHT GREEN/WHITE
42. light green/white x dark green/white
43. light green/white x cobalt/white
44. light green/white x light yellow/white
45. light green/white x dark yellow/white
46. DARK GREEN/WHITE x LIGHT GREEN/WHITE
47. dark green/white x dark green/white
48. dark green/white x skyblue/white
49. dark green/white x cobalt/white
50. dark green/white x light yellow/white
51. dark green/white x dark yellow/white
52. SKYBLUE/WHITE x LIGHT YELLOW/WHITE (25%)
53. skyblue/white x dark yellow/white
54. COBALT/WHITE x DARK YELLOW/ WHITE
55. LIGHT YELLOW/WHITE x LIGHT YELLOW/WHITE (33 1/3%)
56. light yellow/white x dark yellow/white
57. DARK YELLOW/WHITE x LIGHT YELLOW/WHITE
58. dark yellow/white x dark yellow/white

Table 22. To produce DARK YELLOW/WHITE the theoretical expectation is:

1. LIGHT YELLOW x WHITE COBALT (50%)
2. light yellow x white mauve (100%)
3. light yellow x dark green/yellow (25%)
4. light yellow x dark green/white
5. light yellow x olive green/white (25%)
6. light yellow x cobalt/white (25%)
7. light yellow x mauve/white (50%)
8. light yellow x dark yellow/white (25%)

9. light yellow x olive yellow/white (50%)
10. DARK YELLOW x WHITE BLUE (50%)
11. dark yellow x white cobalt (33 1/3%)
12. dark yellow x white mauve (50%)
13. dark yellow x light green/white
14. dark yellow x dark green/white
15. dark yellow x olive green/white
16. dark yellow x skyblue/white (25%)
17. dark yellow x cobalt/white
18. dark yellow x mauve/white (25%)
19. OLIVE YELLOW x WHITE BLUE
    (100%)
20. olive yellow x white cobalt (50%)
21. olive yellow x light green/white (25%)
22. olive yellow x dark green/white
23. olive yellow x skyblue/white (50%)
24. olive yellow x cobalt/white (25%)
25. olive yellow x light yellow/white (50%)
26. olive yellow x dark yellow/white (25%)
27. WHITE BLUE x OLIVE GREEN/
    YELLOW (50%)
28. white blue x dark green/white
29. white blue x dark yellow/white (25%)
30. white blue x olive yellow/white (50%)
31. WHITE COBALT x LIGHT GREEN/
    YELLOW (25%)
32. white cobalt x dark green/yellow
33. white cobalt x olive green/yellow
34. white cobalt x light green/white
35. white cobalt x dark green/white
36. white cobalt x olive green/white
37. white cobalt x light yellow/white (25%)
38. white cobalt x dark yellow/white
39. white cobalt x olive yellow/white (25%)
40. WHITE MAUVE x LIGHT GREEN/
    YELLOW (50%)
41. white mauve x dark green/yellow (25%)
42. white mauve x light green/white (25%)
43. white mauve x dark green/white
44. white mauve x light yellow/white (50%)
45. white mauve x dark yellow/white (25%)
46. LIGHT GREEN/YELLOW x DARK
    GREEN/WHITE
47. light green/yellow x olive green/white
48. light green/yellow x cobalt/white
49. light green/yellow x mauve/white
    (33 1/3%)
50. light green/yellow x dark green/white
51. light green/yellow x olive green/white
    (25%)
52. DARK GREEN/YELLOW x LIGHT
    GREEN/WHITE
53. dark green/yellow x dark green/white

54. dark green/yellow x skyblue/white
55. dark green/yellow x cobalt/white
56. dark green/yellow x mauve/white
57. dark green/yellow x light yellow/white
58. dark green/yellow x dark yellow/white
59. OLIVE GREEN/YELLOW x LIGHT GREEN/WHITE
60. olive green/yellow x dark green/white
61. olive green/yellow x skyblue/white (25%)
62. olive green/yellow x cobalt/white
63. olive green/yellow x light green/white
64. olive green/yellow x dark yellow/white
65. LIGHT GREEN/WHITE x DARK GREEN/WHITE
66. light green/white x olive green/white
67. light green/white x cobalt/white
68. light green/white x mauve/white
69. light green/white x dark yellow/white
70. light green/white x olive yellow/white
71. DARK GREEN/WHITE x LIGHT GREEN/WHITE
72. dark green/white x dark green/white
73. dark green/white x olive green/white
74. dark green/white x skyblue/white
75. dark green/white x cobalt/white
76. dark green/white x mauve/white
77. dark green/white x light yellow/white
78. dark green/white x dark yellow/white
79. dark green/white x olive yellow/white
80. OLIVE GREEN/WHITE x DARK GREEN/WHITE
81. olive green/white x skyblue/white
82. olive green/white x cobalt/white
83. olive green/white x light yellow/white
84. olive green/white x dark yellow/white
85. SKYBLUE/WHITE x DARK YELLOW/WHITE
86. skyblue/white x olive yellow/white (25%)
87. COBALT/WHITE x LIGHT YELLOW/WHITE
88. cobalt/white x dark yellow/white
89. MAUVE/WHITE x LIGHT YELLOW/ WHITE
90. mauve/white x dark yellow/white
91. LIGHT YELLOW/WHITE x DARK YELLOW/WHITE
92. light yellow/white x olive yellow/white (33 1/3%)
93. DARK YELLOW/WHITE x LIGHT YELLOW/WHITE
94. dark yellow/white x dark yellow/white
95. dark yellow/white x olive yellow/white

96. OLIVE YELLOW/WHITE x LIGHT
    YELLOW/WHITE (33 1/3%)
97. olive yellow/white x dark yellow/white

Table 23. To produce OLIVE YELLOW the theoretical expectation is:

1. DARK YELLOW x DARK YELLOW
   (33 1/3%)
2. dark yellow x olive yellow (50%)
3. dark yellow x dark green/yellow
4. dark yellow x olive green/yellow (25%)
5. dark yellow x dark green/white
6. dark yellow x olive green/white
7. dark yellow x dark yellow/white
8. dark yellow x olive yellow/white (25%)
9. OLIVE YELLOW x DARK YELLOW (50%)
10. olive yellow x olive yellow (100%)
11. olive yellow x dark green/yellow (25%)
12. olive yellow x olive green/yellow (50%)
13. olive yellow x dark green/white
14. olive yellow x olive green/white (25%)
15. olive yellow x dark yellow/white (25%)
16. olive yellow x olive yellow/white (50%)
17. DARK GREEN/YELLOW x DARK
    GREEN/YELLOW
18. dark green/yellow x olive green/yellow
19. dark green/yellow x dark green/white
20. dark green/yellow x olive green/white
21. dark green/yellow x dark yellow/white
22. dark green/yellow x olive yellow/white
23. OLIVE GREEN/YELLOW x DARK
    GREEN/YELLOW
24. olive green/yellow x olive green/yellow
    (33 1/3%)
25. olive green/yellow x dark green/white
26. olive green/yellow x olive green/white
27. olive green/yellow x dark yellow/white
28. olive green/yellow x olive green/white (25%)
29. DARK GREEN/WHITE x DARK
    GREEN/WHITE
30. dark green/white x olive green/white
31. dark green/white x dark yellow/white
32. dark green/white x olive yellow/white
33. OLIVE GREEN/WHITE x DARK
    GREEN/WHITE
34. olive green/white x olive yellow/white
35. olive green/white x dark yellow/white
36. DARK YELLOW/WHITE x DARK
    YELLOW/WHITE
37. dark yellow/white x olive yellow/white
38. OLIVE YELLOW/WHITE x DARK
    YELLOW/WHITE
39. olive yellow/white x olive yellow/white
    (33 1/3%)

257

Table 24. To produce OLIVE YELLOW/WHITE the theoretical expectation is:

1. DARK YELLOW x WHITE COBALT (33 1/3%)
2. dark yellow x white mauve (50%)
3. dark yellow x dark green/white
4. dark yellow x olive green/white
5. dark yellow x cobalt/white
6. dark yellow x mauve/white (25%)
7. dark yellow x dark yellow/white
8. dark yellow x olive yellow/white (25%)
9. OLIVE YELLOW x WHITE COBALT (50%)
10. olive yellow x white mauve (100%)
11. olive yellow x dark green/white
12. olive yellow x olive green/white
13. olive yellow x cobalt/white (25%)
14. olive yellow x mauve/white (50%)
15. olive yellow x dark yellow/white (25%)
16. olive yellow x olive yellow/white (50%)
17. WHITE COBALT x DARK GREEN/YELLOW
18. white cobalt x olive green/yellow (25%)
19. white cobalt x dark green/white
20. white cobalt x olive green/white
21. white cobalt x dark yellow/white
22. white cobalt x olive yellow/white (25%)
23. WHITE MAUVE x DARK GREEN/YELLOW (25%)
24. white mauve x olive green/yellow (50%)
25. white mauve x dark green/white
26. white mauve x olive green/white (25%)
27. white mauve x dark yellow/white (25%)
28. white mauve x olive yellow/white (50%)
29. DARK GREEN/YELLOW x DARK YELLOW/WHITE
30. dark green/yellow x olive green/white
31. dark green/yellow x cobalt/white
32. dark green/yellow x mauve/white
33. dark green/yellow x dark yellow/white
34. dark green/yellow x olive yellow/white
35. OLIVE GREEN/YELLOW x DARK GREEN/WHITE
36. olive green/yellow x olive green/white
37. olive green/yellow x cobalt/white
38. olive green/yellow x mauve/white (50%)
39. olive green/yellow x dark yellow/white
40. olive green/yellow x olive yellow/white (25%)
41. DARK GREEN/WHITE x DARK GREEN/WHITE
42. dark green/white x olive green/white
43. dark green/white x cobalt/white

44. dark green/white x mauve/white
45. dark green/white x dark yellow/white
46. dark green/white x olive yellow/white
47. OLIVE GREEN/WHITE x DARK GREEN/WHITE
48. olive green/white x olive green/white
49. olive green/white x cobalt/white
50. olive green/white x mauve/white
51. olive green/white x dark yellow/white
52. olive green/white x olive yellow/white
53. COBALT/WHITE x DARK YELLOW/WHITE
54. cobalt/white x olive yellow/white
55. MAUVE/WHITE x DARK YELLOW/WHITE
56. mauve/white x olive yellow/white (25%)
57. DARK YELLOW/WHITE x DARK YELLOW/WHITE
58. dark yellow/white x olive yellow/white
59. OLIVE YELLOW/WHITE x DARK YELLOW/WHITE
60. olive yellow/white x olive yellow/white (33 1/3%)

Table 25. To produce WHITE BLUE the theoretical expectation is:

1. WHITE BLUE x WHITE BLUE (100%)
2. white blue x white cobalt (50%)
3. white blue x light green/white (25%)
4. white blue x dark green/white
5. white blue x skyblue/white (50%)
6. white blue x cobalt/white (25%)
7. white blue x light yellow/white (50%)
8. white blue x dark yellow/white
9. WHITE COBALT x WHITE BLUE (50%)
10. white cobalt x white cobalt (33 1/3%)
11. white cobalt x light green/white
12. white cobalt x dark green/white
13. white cobalt x skyblue/white (25%)
14. white cobalt x cobalt/white
15. white cobalt x light yellow/white
16. white cobalt x dark yellow/white
17. LIGHT GREEN/WHITE x LIGHT GREEN/WHITE
18. light green/white x dark green/white
19. light green/white x skyblue/white
20. light green/white x cobalt/white
21. light green/white x light yellow/white
22. light green/white x dark yellow/white
23. DARK GREEN/WHITE x LIGHT GREEN/WHITE

24. dark green/white x dark green/white
25. dark green/white x skyblue/white
26. dark green/white x cobalt/white
27. dark green/white x light yellow/white
28. dark green/white x dark yellow/white
29. SKYBLUE/WHITE x SKYBLUE/WHITE (33 1/3%)
30. skyblue/white x cobalt/white
31. skyblue/white x light yellow/white (25%)
32. COBALT/WHITE x SKYBLUE/WHITE
33. cobalt/white x cobalt/white
34. cobalt/white x light yellow/white
35. cobalt/white x dark yellow/white
36. LIGHT YELLOW/WHITE x LIGHT YELLOW/WHITE (33 1/3%)
37. light yellow/white x dark yellow/white
38. DARK YELLOW/WHITE x LIGHT YELLOW/WHITE
39. dark yellow/white x dark yellow/white

Table 26. To produce WHITE COBALT the theoretical expectation is:

1. WHITE BLUE x WHITE BLUE (50%)
2. white blue x white mauve (100%)
3. white blue x dark green/white
4. white blue x olive green/white (25%)
5. white blue x cobalt/white (25%)
6. white blue x mauve/white (50%)
7. white blue x dark yellow/white (25%)
8. white blue x olive yellow/white (50%)
9. WHITE COBALT x WHITE BLUE (50%)
10. white cobalt x white cobalt (33 1/3%)
11. white cobalt x white mauve (50%)
12. white cobalt x light green/white
13. white cobalt x dark green/white
14. white cobalt x olive green/white
15. white cobalt x skyblue/white (25%)
16. white cobalt x cobalt/white
17. white cobalt x mauve/white (25%)
18. white cobalt x light yellow/white (25%)
19. white cobalt x dark yellow/white
20. white cobalt x olive yellow/white
21. WHITE MAUVE x WHITE BLUE (100%)
22. white mauve x white cobalt (50%)
23. white mauve x light green/white (25%)
24. white mauve x dark green/white
25. white mauve x skyblue/white (50%)
26. white mauve x cobalt/white (25%)
27. white mauve x light yellow/white (50%)
28. white mauve x dark yellow/white (25%)

29. LIGHT GREEN/WHITE x DARK GREEN/WHITE
30. light green/white x olive green/white
31. light green/white x cobalt/white
32. light green/white x mauve/white
33. light green/white x dark yellow/white
34. light green/white x olive yellow/white
35. DARK GREEN/WHITE x LIGHT GREEN/WHITE
36. dark green/white x dark green/white
37. dark green/white x olive green/white
38. dark green/white x skyblue/white
39. dark green/white x cobalt/white
40. dark green/white x mauve/white
41. dark green/white x light yellow/white
42. dark green/white x dark yellow/white
43. dark green/white x olive yellow/white
44. OLIVE GREEN/WHITE x LIGHT GREEN/WHITE
45. olive green/white x dark green/white
46. olive green/white x skyblue/white
47. olive green/white x cobalt/white
48. olive green/white x light yellow/white
49. olive green/white x dark yellow/white
50. SKYBLUE/WHITE x COBALT/WHITE
51. skyblue/white x cobalt/white
52. skyblue/white x mauve/white (33 1/3%)
53. skyblue/white x dark yellow/white
54. skyblue/white x olive yellow/white (25%)
55. COBALT/WHITE x SKYBLUE/WHITE
56. cobalt/white x cobalt/white
57. cobalt/white x mauve/white
58. cobalt/white x light yellow/white
59. cobalt/white x dark yellow/white
60. cobalt/white x olive yellow/white
61. MAUVE/WHITE x SKYBLUE/WHITE (33 1/3%)
62. mauve/white x cobalt/white
63. mauve/white x light yellow/white (25%)
64. mauve/white x dark yellow/white
65. LIGHT YELLOW/WHITE x DARK YELLOW/WHITE
66. light yellow/white x olive yellow/white (33 1/3%)
67. DARK YELLOW/WHITE x LIGHT YELLOW/WHITE
68. dark yellow/white x dark yellow/white
69. dark yellow/white x olive yellow/white
70. OLIVE YELLOW/WHITE x LIGHT YELLOW/WHITE (33 1/3%)
71. olive yellow/white x dark yellow/white

Table 27. To produce WHITE MAUVE the theoretical expectation is:

1. WHITE COBALT x WHITE COBALT (33 1/3%)
2. white cobalt x white mauve (50%)
3. white cobalt x dark green/white
4. white cobalt x olive green/white
5. white cobalt x cobalt/white
6. white cobalt x mauve/white (25%)
7. white cobalt x dark yellow/white
8. white cobalt x olive yellow/white (25%)
9. WHITE MAUVE x WHITE MAUVE (100%)
10. white mauve x white cobalt (50%)
11. white mauve x dark green/white
12. white mauve x olive green/white (25%)
13. white mauve x cobalt/white (25%)
14. white mauve x mauve/white (50%)
15. white mauve x dark yellow/white (25%)
16. white mauve x olive yellow/white (50%)
17. DARK GREEN/WHITE x DARK GREEN/WHITE
18. dark green/white x olive green/white
19. dark green/white x cobalt/white
20. dark green/white x mauve/white
21. dark green/white x dark yellow/white
22. dark green/white x olive yellow/white
23. OLIVE GREEN/WHITE x DARK GREEN/WHITE
24. olive green/white x olive green/white
25. olive green/white x cobalt/white
26. olive green/white x mauve/white
27. olive green/white x dark yellow/white
28. olive green/white x olive yellow/white
29. COBALT/WHITE x COBALT/WHITE
30. cobalt/white x mauve/white
31. cobalt/white x dark yellow/white
32. cobalt/white x olive yellow/white
33. MAUVE/WHITE x COBALT/WHITE
34. mauve/white x mauve/white (33 1/3%)
35. mauve/white x dark yellow/white
36. mauve/white x olive yellow/white (25%)
37. DARK YELLOW/WHITE x DARK YELLOW/WHITE
38. dark yellow/white x olive yellow/white
39. OLIVE YELLOW/WHITE x DARK YELLOW/WHITE
40. olive yellow/white x olive yellow/white (33 1/3%)

Glossary of Terms

Albino: A bird that lacks dark or color pigments through the effect of a mutation. Birds can be yellow albinos, called lutinos in Budgies. Furthermore, there are cream-colored albinos, which have a double yellow-head factor that turns white into cream.

Apple green: Equivalent to light graywing green. Should not be confused with gray green (See glossary entry).

B: The fourth element of the FOB theory. It stands for degree of pigmentation. For example, olive green is BB; dark green is Bb; and light green is bb. If the pigmentation factor is absent, this is recorded as b.

Cell: The building block out of which plants, animals and humans are composed. Inside the cell, we find the carriers of heredity. Growth takes place by means of cell division (below).

Cell division: Takes place when a cell pinches itself together in the center and splits, forming two cells (true for animals). The nucleus of the cell is partially dissolved for this process. This frees the chromosomes to be pulled apart to two opposite poles of the cell. (One chromosome consists of two chromatids.) A new nucleus forms at the two poles from the two chromatids, each of which develops into a complete chromosome. Each daughter cell, therefore, comes to contain as many chromosomes as the mother cell. When fully developed, the daughter cell can divide anew, resulting in successively 2, 4, 8, 16, 32, 64 cells and so on. The number of chromosomes stays the same.

Cell wall: The wall of the cell. In animals, it is formed from hardened protoplasm (See glossary entry).

Chromosomes: Threadlike bodies found in the nucleus. They consist of two chromatids merged together. Chromosomes contain the hereditary factors that bring about form and color. Derived from the Greek *chroma*—color.

Cinnamon: Sex-linked factor. Causes wings and neck patches to change from

263

black to brown. Young birds start out with red eyes; after several days, they turn black. For the rest, cinnamon is the same as isabel.

Cobalt: The middle of the three shades of blue. Cobalt is very attractive. A cobalt Budgie receives the pigmentation factor from one of the parents (See glossary entry B).

Colony breeding: Breeding several pairs of birds in an aviary or breeding cage. With colony breeding, parentage is impossible to establish since each male can select his own mate.

Crossing over: A situation that occurs during reduction division (See glossary entry). The chromosomes get crossed in the process, causing the actual ratio of various young to vary from the predicted ratio. The various *types* of young don't change. It is indicated by Type I and Type II Budgies.

Dark green: The middle color in the green color series. This green must be deep. It results when only one of the parents contributes a pigmentation factor to the young (See glossary entry B).

Dark yellow: The middle color in the yellow color series. This yellow must be bright and deep, without a green haze. It results when only one of the parents contributes a pigmentation factor to the young (See glossary entry B). The birds have black eyes.

Degeneration: A situation in which the quality of a line becomes worse through an undesirable breeding program. It can occur when poor quality males are bred to poor quality females or through inbreeding (See glossary entry). Conformation, color, type, fertility, and other factors can be affected.

Dominant: A situation in which one hereditary factor overpowers others. It can be noticed once the young are born. When one sees that a green male crossed with a blue female produces green young, one knows that green is dominant over blue.

Egg cell: The female reproductive cell, or gamete.

F: The first element of the FOB theory. It stands for the "fat" factor. If absent, the condition is recorded f. Green and yellow Budgerigars carry the fat factor. Blue and white ones do not.

F1: First generation from a series of matings. For example, the direct offspring of a blue x green mating is the F1 generation. The young of these birds would be F2, and so on. From Latin *filius,* meaning son, or child.

Factor, or hereditary factor: The physical agent behind a trait or condition.

Fancy opaline: A sex-linked factor that produces, in addition to the design changes due to normal opaline, a uniform V-shaped pattern above the wings, near the shoulder.

G: The fifth element of the FOB theory. It stands for "gray" and is used in discussing the wing pattern. The normal black design is indicated with N (Latin *niger,* meaning black). The "G" is combined with "O" (See glossary entry). Homozygous (purebred) graywings are designated Og Og; heterozygous graywings are On Og.

Gamete: Reproductive cell. Both the egg cell of the female and the sperm cell of the male are called gametes.

Gene: Carrier of hereditary elements in the chromosomes. Genes determine color and tendency toward certain developments, such as illnesses, fertility, character, etc.

Gray green: A green Budgie with the factor for Australian gray, which is dominant over blue and white. It is *not* dominant over green. We could say that a gray green Budgie is a bird that is green in color with one or two factors for gray.

Heterozygous: Not breeding pure for a certain factor. A heterozygous Budgie (also called *heterozygote*) does not exhibit external evidence of the genetic factor which it is carrying, but it *can* inherit other visible characteristics.

Homozygous: Breeding pure for a certain characteristic. A homozygous Budgie (also called *homozygote*) does not carry any invisible hereditary trait.

Hybrid: The result of crossing animals from two different species (like horse x donkey, yielding mule).

Inbreeding: Producing young within a family by breeding mother x son, father x daughter, brother x sister or other closely related individuals. Continued inbreeding leads to degeneration (See glossary entry). Two years of inbreeding, however, is not necessarily bad. It is sometimes necessary—for example, to maintain certain colors.

Isabel: A type of cinnamon (See glossary entry).

Jade: Another name for olive green graywing (See APPLE GREEN).

Light green: Lightest of the three shades of green. Under no condition is the color allowed to be pale green or flat green; it has to be nice and bright.

Light yellow: Lightest of the three shades of yellow. It should not be white-yellow. A light yellow Budgie inherits no pigmentation factor from either parent (See B). The birds have black eyes.

Line breeding: Breeding two lines from one family. Experienced breeders call it one of the better breeding methods. One selects two pairs of birds from the descendants of an original set of parents. Further breeding is between the descendants of the two couples. For example, in the third breeding year, one takes a male of the one "line" and mates it with a female of the other line.

Mauve: The darkest shade of blue. A good shade is grayish purple. The color is not very popular, but it is essential for breeding violet. A mauve inherits the pigmentation factor from both parents.

Melanin: Material containing black and/or brown pigment.

Modification: A nonheritable change in a bird, mostly attributable to a specific external change. The modification disappears when the external change disappears.

Mutation: Sudden appearance of a hereditary trait, generally without attributable cause. Breeders profit from mutations because they can be bred into other birds. New color variations generally appear through mutations. A mutation is heritable; a modification isn't.

N: The third element of the FOB theory. It stands for *niger,* Latin for black and is used in discussing the wing pattern. The n is used as a lower case letter combined with "O" (See glossary entry). A green Budgie with the basic pattern on the wings is designated FF On On. As stated earlier, the graywing factor is designated by g, so that full-blooded graywings are designated Og Og; heterozygous graywings are On Og.

O: Second element of the FOB theory. It stands for oxidation—a color factor. If absent, the condition is designated o. Green and blue Budgies are O; yellow and white ones are null for the factor and are designated o.

Olive green: The darkest shade of the three greens. Often birds tend to look rather dirty green, and so they are not very popular. The olive green Budgie inherits the pigmentation factor from both parents (See B). Olive green is very important for breeding dark green.

Olive yellow: The darkest shade of the three yellows. Often birds tend to look rather dirty yellow, augmented by a green haze that is often present—even more than in light yellow. The olive yellow Budgie inherits the pigmentation factor from both parents (See B). The birds have black eyes.

Opaline: A sex-linked factor. It suppresses the design on the shoulder and head and induces an opal sheen on the feathers. Opaline is bred into many color variations, especially in England.

Open class: A competition class offered at bird shows. The open class is for all birds that didn't get their own bands during the last breeding year or those that were banded before the last breeding year. All unbanded birds and purchased stock are also placed in the open class to prevent unethical competition with birds entered as "own breeding."

Own breeding: An expression used at bird shows. Included are young bred by the exhibitor during the last breeding year. They have their own band, available from the bird club to which the exhibitor belongs. (See OPEN CLASS.)

Protoplasm: Liquid contents of a cell in which the nucleus is suspended.

Rainbow: A blue Budgie with clearly visible opaline, yellow head and graywing factor. Whitewings are also included, although rarely seen. All rainbow Budgies are purebred for the named factors. Sharp and dark colors should be avoided as much as possible. Only experienced breeders can produce a bird with soft pastel coloration.

Recessive: Opposite of dominant (See glossary entry). A "shy," or receding trait. Crossbreds don't show a recessive trait.

Reduction division: Cell division producing reproductive cells. In the process, the chromosomes in the cell are halved, so that each reproductive cell (egg or sperm) has half the number of chromosomes of a normal cell.

During reproduction, two reproductive cells meld, reconstituting the normal number of chromosomes.

Sex-linked: A factor tied to the sex chromosome (See X). Opaline, isabel, albino, and lutino are sex-linked factors. Non-sex-linked factors inherit independently of sex and follow the normal pattern of heredity.

Silverwing: Expression occasionally used for skyblue graywings. The name appears to signify more than it does and its use should generally be avoided.

Skyblue: The lightest of the three shades of blue. It should be clear, light blue. A skyblue Budgie has no pigmentation factor—neither from its father's nor from its mother's side (See B).

Sperm cell: Male reproductive cell, or sex cell.

Split: Inheriting but not exhibiting a recessive trait, indicated by separating the invisible, recessive trait with a split in the designation. A blue Budgie that is split for white (blue/white) is blue in appearance but can pass on white genes to its offspring.

White blue: White Budgie with black eyes. It does not have a pigmentation factor—from either parent. Preferably should not show a blue haze.

White cobalt: White Budgie with black eyes. It inherited a pigmentation factor from one of its parents, but doesn't show it. (Therefore, it can pass this factor on to its offspring.) Preferably should not show a blue haze.

White mauve: White Budgie with black eyes. It inherited a pigmentation factor from both its parents, but doesn't show it. (Therefore, it can pass this factor on to its offspring.) Preferably should not show a blue haze.

X: Designation for the male sex chromosome. A male has two sex chromosomes, indicated by XX. The female has only one, indicated by XY (Y stands for an *absent* chromosome). Cinnamon, albino, lutino and opaline are linked to the X chromosome; that's why these traits are sex-linked (See glossary entry).

Y: Designation indicating an absent sex chromosome (See X).

Xygote: Fertilized egg cell.

Appendices

Major Societies

Australia

Avicultural Society of Australia
P.O. Box 48
Bentleigh East
Victoria

Canada:

Canadian Avicultural Society, Inc.
c/o Mr. E. Jones
32 Dromore Crescent
Willowdale 450
Ontario, M2R 2H5

Canadian Institute of Bird Breeders
c/o Mr. C. Snazel
4422 Chauvin Street
Pierrefonds, Quebec

Great Britain:

The Avicultural Society
c/o Mr. H.J. Horsewell
20 Bourbon Street
London W.1.

The Budgerigar Society
57, Stephyn's Chambers
Bank Court
Marlowes, Hemel Hempstead, Herts
(England)

New Zealand:

The New Zealand Federation of Cage Bird Societies
c/o Mr. M.D. Neale
31 Harker Street
Christchurch 2

United States of America:

American Budgerigar Society, Inc.
2 Farnum Road
Warwick, RI 02888

American Federation of Aviculture, Inc.
(See The A.F.A. Watchbird, Pg. 270)

Avicultural Society of America
(See Avicultural Bulletin, below)

Periodicals

American Cage-Bird Magazine (monthly)
1 Glamore Court
Smithtown, NY 11787
(Features a bi-monthly directory of bird societies.)

Avicultural Bulletin (monthly)
Avicultural Society of America, Inc.
734 North Highland Avenue
Hollywood, CA 90038 (USA)

Bird Talk (monthly)
P.O. Box 3940
San Clemente, CA 92672 (USA)

Bird World (bi-monthly)
P.O. Box 70
No. Hollywood, CA 91601 (USA)

Cage and Aviary Birds (weekly)
Surrey House
1, Throwley Way
Sutton, Surrey, SM1 4QQ (England)
(Young birdkeepers under sixteen may like to join the *Junior Bird League.*
Full details can be obtained from the J.B.L., c/o *Cage and Aviary Birds.*)

The A.F.A. Watchbird - American Federation of Aviculture, Inc. (bi-monthly)
P.O. Box 1125
Garden Grove, CA 92642 (USA)

Magazine of the Parrot Society (monthly)
24, Rowallan Drive
Bedford (England)

Bibliography

Alderton, David: *Looking After Cage Birds,* Arco, New York, N.Y.
Armour, Dr. M.D.S.: *Exhibition Budgerigars,* Cage Birds, London.
Binks, Gerald S.: *Best in Show, Breeding and Exhibiting Budgerigars,* Elburry Press, London.
Feyerabend, Cessa and Dr. Matthew M. Vriends: *Breeding Budgerigars,* TFH Publications, Inc., Neptune, N.J.
Idem: *Taming and Training Budgerigars,* TFH Publications, Inc., Neptune, N.J.
Freud, Arthur: *All About the Parrots,* Howell Book House Inc., New York, N.Y.
Rogers, Cyril H.: *Budgerigars,* A Foyles Handbook, London.
Idem: *Budgerigars,* John Gifford, London.
Rutgers, A. and K.A. Norris: *Encyclopedia of Aviculture,* Blandford Press, London.
Scoble, John: *The Complete Book of Budgerigars,* Lansdowne Press, Sydney & New York.
Sutherland, Patricia: *The Pet Bird Handbook,* Arco, New York, N.Y.
Vriends, Dr. Matthew M.: *Popular Parrots,* Howell Book House Inc., New York, N.Y.
Watmough, W.: *The Cult of the Budgerigar,* Cage Birds, London.
Idem: *Budgerigars,* Cassell, London.
Wolter, A.: *Parakeets,* Barron, Woodbury, N.Y.

Books on Bird Diseases

Arnall, L. and J.F. Keymer: *Bird Diseases,* TFH Publications, Inc., Neptune, N.J.
Gallerstein, Gary A., D.V.M.: *Bird Owner's Home Health and Care Handbook,* Howell Book House Inc., New York, N.Y.

Kronberger, Harry: *Haltung von Vogeln - Krankheiten der Vogel* (German -Bird Keeping - Bird Diseases). Gustav Fischer Verlag, Jena. 4th Edition.

Petrak, M.L. et al.: *Diseases of Cage and Aviary Birds.* Bailliere Tindall (London) and Lea & Febiger (Philadelphia). 2nd Edition.